𝕿𝖍𝖊 𝕬𝖒𝖍𝖊𝖗𝖘𝖙 𝕭𝖔𝖔𝖐𝖘

RELIGION IN THE PHILOSOPHY
OF WILLIAM JAMES

RELIGION IN THE PHILOSOPHY OF WILLIAM JAMES

BY

JULIUS SEELYE BIXLER

ASSOCIATE PROFESSOR OF BIBLICAL LITERATURE
IN SMITH COLLEGE

BOSTON
MARSHALL JONES COMPANY
1926

COPYRIGHT · 1926 · BY
MARSHALL JONES COMPANY

Printed May, 1926

FEB 2 0 1941

170062

THE PLIMPTON PRESS · NORWOOD · MASSACHUSETTS
PRINTED IN THE UNITED STATES OF AMERICA

To
M. T. B.
in whom are combined the two qualities
which James found essential for religious
belief — insight and vigor

PREFACE

THIS study of the religious philosophy of William James is a revision of a dissertation presented for the degree of Doctor of Philosophy in Yale University. It attempts to bring together the various strands of James's religious thought, — isolating them on the one hand from those parts of his work which are not related to the study of religion, and co-ordinating them on the other with the larger outlines and main emphases of his world-view. Religion was a topic to which James's mind was constantly turning. References to it crop up in discussions where they would be least expected and are found widely scattered throughout his works. The present study in bringing the most significant of them within the compass of a single volume endeavors to reveal the unity which underlies all James's utterances on the subject.

Some such attempt at synthesis appears to be pertinent especially in view of the publication of James's letters. James has frequently been called to account for inconsistency. But many apparent discrepancies disappear when one catches a glimpse, through these revealing personal documents, of the alternating moods to which James was subject and of the intense human interest which underlay these moods in equal measure, different as they were from each other. As is well known, James often expressed the belief that philosophy is a personal concern, " more a matter of passionate vision than of logic " and especially susceptible to the personal touch when it enters the field of religion. The better we know James's personality, therefore, the more clearly can we understand the significance of his religious ideas. To see something of what went on in his inner experience as we are able to see it in these letters is to gain fresh insight into the unifying purpose of his thought. Large use is made in this study of James's published letters and in some cases reference is had to letters which have not been published.

The study of religion has made progress since James's death in 1910 but it has followed in general the lines which he pointed out. Particularly is this true of the philosophy as contrasted with the psychology of religion. In the latter field James was a pioneer, and the development of the subject since his time is due in large measure to the momentum which his efforts created. But his hypotheses as to the part played in religious experience by the subconscious self are out of date as a result of the great amount of attention which subconscious activity has received from investigators. In the field of the philosophy of religion, however, the situation is different. The issues which James raises here must form an integral part of any discussion of the subject, and the emphases he makes are of permanent importance.

The older rationalistic method of attacking religious problems is less in vogue today than formerly partly because of James's trenchant attacks upon it. In its place two main tendencies can be discerned in the religious thought of our time, each taking its cue from a special part of James's work. The first of these is the empirical, the method employed by James so successfully in his book on *The Varieties of Religious Experience*. The other is a modification of the empirical method and is usually called pragmatic. It follows the lines suggested in James's *The Will to Believe*, making postulates on the basis of experienced need, and it has much to say of human values and their possible identification with cosmic truth.

Two other less clearly formulated features of modern religious thinking which also point to James's influence deserve notice as well. The first of these, running parallel to a similar tendency in modern art, is toward realism. More is known about the universe today than ever before, and with this increase of knowledge has come an increase in sensitiveness to the tragedy of human suffering as well as a heightened sense of the futility of much human activity. As a result religion is looking the facts of life in the face with a gaze which in its unflinching and critical quality is new. In place of the older religious world-view with its rounded outlines and ultimate syntheses, with its conviction as to the beneficence of nature and the final triumphant destiny of man, modern religious thought envisages a universe with ragged and jagged edges, full of yawning abysses, calculated to fill man with a sense of the precariousness rather than the stability of his own position. With such an outlook James's pluralistic philosophy has much in common. The phrase " problem of evil " rarely appears on James's pages, but the idea is ever hovering in the background of his thought. To a generation which is still feeling the effects of the greatest calamity in history, and which regards much of the religious optimism of the past as based on illusion, James's awareness of the tragic element in life and refusal to eliminate it from his religious view of the world comes with a refreshing sense of reality.

But while our religious thinking is realistic in one respect in another it is romantic. This tendency can be seen in the attempt of some of the most recent writers to arrive at religious truth through an imaginative treatment of the *nuances* and subtleties which are involved in any venture at describing man's relation to his cosmic environment. The lure of the ultimate mystery, the fascination of the transcendent, and the possibility of socializing this fascination and turning it to practical account — such subjects as these are being brought to our attention in new and arresting fashion by some of the latest books on religion.

This way of approach dates back to James also, although it has developed a technique and consciousness of its own purposes which he did not have. He paved the way for it, however, in his empiricism, and especially in his implicit suggestion that the most satisfactory statement of man's place in the cosmos will be found in the most inclusive view of what human life really is. Experience is a many-sided thing and can be described from many points of vantage. The most complete truth about human life and its religious relationships will be

found in that description of it which reaches out the farthest
and at the same time penetrates the deepest. The meaning of
the whole human struggle for existence and for value will be
revealed most fully to that interpreter who with sympathy and
insight sees the process as a many-sided whole and refuses to
be content with any single formula or with a description which
is made from any single point of view.

James was well qualified to be such an interpreter. Few
have enjoyed the acute sensitiveness to value which was his
and not many have been able as was he to envisage the larger
relationships by which human life is encompassed. The fact
may be worth dwelling on that James was particularly keenly
aware of the importance and significance of human volitional
activity. It is desirable to make this emphasis at a time like
the present when certain scientific disciplines, claiming direct
descent from James, are pressing the mechanistic view of
human life. It is true that James has given us a scientific
description of experience with the individual consciousness left
out. But it is well to remember that no one has sketched more
boldly than he the possibilities which can only be made actual
through individual personal choice.

The present study of James is thus interested in treating him
as the discoverer of meaning and significance in the affective
and volitional life of human beings. It begins by quoting from
his works to show that he was subject to alternating moods
which directly influenced his philosophical and religious views.
The second chapter, again adducing quotations, traces the implications of one of his moods as they concern his attitude
toward that object of philosophical and religious interest, the
absolute. The third chapter, again with a free use of quotations, endeavors to discover the basis of James's interest in
pluralism. The next three chapters do little more than to
restate James's ideas on the subject of human will and purpose
and to relate these ideas to his general philosophical position.
Chapter VII shows the development of his conception of God,
Chapter VIII makes suggestions as to his views on immortality, Chapter IX points out the connections which mysticism

makes with his philosophy. The concluding chapter points out the indebtedness to James of the religious thought of our day.

A word may be said as to the frequent use of quotations from James's writings. All writers on James draw from him freely because he is so very quotable an author. His style is inimitable. Furthermore the cogency of his argument frequently lies in the suggestiveness of his vocabulary. Especially when he deals with a subject which like religion is a thing of shadings and gradations, of fringes and indefinite margins, does James's power with the written word show itself. The vivid flash of his inspiration can be communicated only by the means he himself uses for expressing it. Another reason for frequent quotations may be offered in the fact that some such method is necessary to avoid the criticism which so many have incurred of reading their own ideas into him. The isolated reference from James is always unreliable. Assurance that one has a main emphasis in James is possible only when evidence is drawn from more than one part of his work.

My obligations in the preparation of this study have been many. In the following list of acknowledgments I wish it to be understood, however, that the mention of a name does not mean that the person referred to indorses the view of James here taken. Indeed only three of those mentioned have read the manuscript. With this understanding, then, I wish first of all to express to the members of the James family my appreciation of their willingness to allow me to use unpublished material, and especially to Mr. William James of Cambridge my gratitude for his kind encouragement and counsel. I am very grateful also to Professor Ralph Barton Perry of Harvard University and to Mr. Walter B. Briggs of the Widener Library for giving me access to the collection of books from James's private collection which is there housed.

For unpublished material I am indebted to Mrs. Ethel Puffer Howes of Scarsdale, N. Y., and to Professor Mary Whiton Calkins of Wellesley College, who have allowed me to quote from letters from James in their possession. I am also indebted to Professor Charles M. Bakewell of Yale for permission to use his collection of letters from James to Thomas Davidson. Another set of letters of which I have made extensive use is a group recently discovered written by James to a cousin, Mrs. William H. Prince, when she was living at the home of President Julius H. Seelye of Amherst College.

A part of Chapter VIII of the present volume was used in an article in *The Journal of Religion*. The word "unpublished" as applied to some of the letters quoted in this chapter must be taken with this reservation. Some new unpublished material appears in this chapter, however, which was not included in the article. A part of Chapter IX combined with a part of Chapter I made up an article published in the *International Journal of Ethics*. I am grateful to the editors of these periodicals for permission to use the material of these articles in the present study.

I wish also to express my indebtedness to my friend, Professor John M. Warbeke of Mt. Holyoke College for criticisms and suggestions, and to Professor Douglas C. Macintosh of Yale University to whom my obligation is of the kind a pupil can owe only to a great teacher.

J. S. B.

NORTHAMPTON, MASS.
April, 1926

CONTENTS

RELIGION IN THE PHILOSOPHY
OF WILLIAM JAMES

"The absolute things, the last things, the overlapping things, are the truly philosophic concerns; all superior minds feel seriously about them, and the mind with the shortest views is simply the mind of the more shallow man."

Pragmatism, p. 108

"In a word, 'Son of Man, *stand upon thy feet* and I will speak unto thee!' is the only revelation of truth to which the solving epochs have helped the disciple. But that has been enough to satisfy the greater part of his rational need."

The Will to Believe and Other Essays, p. 88

RELIGION IN THE PHILOSOPHY OF WILLIAM JAMES

I

THE CONFLICT

AMONG the many commentaries which the work of William James has called forth, few can be found which accord his religious philosophy a place of equal importance with his psychology, ethics, and theory of knowledge. The tendency of those commentators who have devoted any attention to his religious view has been in general to separate it from the context of his thought as a whole, regarding it either as an apologetic, and so as hardly capable of withstanding scientific investigation, or else looking on it as a sort of temporary aberration, the vagary of an otherwise brilliant mind. *The Varieties of Religious Experience,* appearing at about the same time as Ernest Thompson Seton's book of animal stories, was soon nicknamed " Wild Religions I Have Known." *The Will to Believe* was parodied as " Will to Deceive " and " Will to Make-Believe." And James's attempt to find in the phenomena of religious experience evidence for extra-human activity is called, in one of the standard works on the psychology of religion, a " fiasco."

A more moderate opinion, though still an unfavorable one, has been expressed by a pupil of James in an article sympathetic to his work as a whole yet containing the observation that " the union of religious mysticism with biological and psychological empiricism is characteristic of James's work from the beginning." Explaining this comment in conversation with the present writer, the author of this article vigorously asserted his opinion that James's religious philosophy was the least important part of his work, that the " union " mentioned in the article was rather a " conflict " between James's mysticism and his scientific training, and that, as the article goes on to state, James had had to be "weaned " from the mystical Swedenborgian piety of his father by the empiricism of friends like Chauncey Wright and Charles Renouvier.

This comment makes an appropriate starting-place for our discussion. Its appropriateness for clearing the field of preliminary difficulties lies, however, in its almost complete inaccuracy. It seems, in fact, to state the exact opposite of the truth. Evidence which we now have in James's letters bears his own witness to the fact that he was never inclined to be a mystic and that the most that can be asserted is the presence in him of what he called a mystical " germ," or vicarious interest in the mystical experiences of others and willingness to treat them as on a par with other data in their truth-revealing capacity. Furthermore, whatever religious belief James had, mystically germinal or otherwise, was very different from anything that could be called Swedenborgian. Swedenborg's method of looking to divine revelation for light on problems of astronomy and physics is at a far remove from James's method of looking for light on any problem. And the records we have of the religious belief of his father, who considered himself a follower of Swedenborg, show only a very superficial resemblance to James's personal views. Furthermore, James's sympathy with his father, intellectually, became greater rather than less as he grew older. James himself bears testimony to this fact in decisive fashion.

As to the conflict in James's thought — there was indeed a conflict, but it was not between his religious proclivities and his scientific training. The conflict which this discussion will endeavor to disclose was a conflict between two divergent religious interests. It seems not to have been mentioned by writers on James, yet the evidence for it becomes more convincing and its importance grows more clear the more one reads and reflects on James's work as a whole. It throws light on the *pervasiveness* of James's religious interest in all his philosophy, and on some of the motives which prompted that interest. Like the conflict described in the article mentioned, between the rival claims of science and religion, the one which we shall point out has had its analogue in the experience of the race and has been discussed, in that aspect, by Professor Höffding in his *Philosophy of Religion*.[1] Its significance for the individual, also, has been described by Professor Hocking in his chapter on " The Principle of Alternation " in *The Meaning of God in Human Experience*. For, like the apostle Paul, James seems to have found two souls within his breast. Yet, unlike the apostle, James found a decision difficult because the aims of both were so high. Not a choice between good and evil, but a decision as to the better of two good things confronted him. On the one hand he felt the press of the active impulses, their aggressive demands for power, their challenge to the environment and their eager desire to remake it. No one knew more keenly than he the insistent assertiveness of the will to survive, to believe, and to achieve. But on the other hand he was not insensitive to the more passive desire for assurance, stability, and comfort. In the one mood James is ready to scale the highest heaven in his quest for value or to penetrate the deepest abyss in his insistence on the triumphantly conquering and creative ability of the human spirit. In the other his whole being longs for peace, whether of ecstasy or rationality. But in both cases James is religious with the completeness which the intensity of his nature required of any mood.

Our first concern in this study will be with this religious conflict. Our next interest will be to examine James's religious thought in more detail, and to observe how the strands of his religious belief interweave with the main tendencies of his philosophy. We shall see, for example, that what was for

[1] Pp. 88, 157 ff.

James an interesting philosophical antithesis, with the weight of the appeal resting on one side, became a real dilemma and a live issue when the values at stake were religious values. Going on to trace James's active search for the good things of life and his struggle to will values into being, we shall discover that a problem which is central in James's thought is found by him to be insoluble except on moral and religious grounds. We shall then see that the threads of his philosophy converge at one point into a defense of religious faith, and that his ethics and his purposive view of human life lead him to belief in a Deity. Stopping next to examine the results of James's quest we shall notice the kind of God which he found and observe that the development of his conception of God kept pace with the development of his conception of truth. We shall further find, in opposition to the view of some commentators, that James was the possessor of an active religious interest and faith in immortality. Then turning to the more passive side of his experience and thought we shall take up James's study of the possibility of God's intervention in the affairs of men, his conclusions regarding mysticism, and their significance for his philosophy. Finally, we shall comment on the way in which James's philosophy is adapted to be the setting for a religious world-view. And the result of our study will suggest that James's religious philosophy can hardly be called the least important part of his thought, but that, as integrally related to the rest of his thinking, and in places the consummation of it, his religious philosophy deserves a place in the front rank of his work.

Plunging at once *in medias res,* let us now consider some of the evidence for the existence of the religious conflict in James's mind to which allusion has been made. This chapter will not endeavor to trace the conflict in all its detail, but rather to suggest some of the ways in which its presence is shown. A complete account of it will be possible only as our study progresses. In the first place, James himself draws, in objective fashion, a contrast between two conflicting philosophies of life. The clearest account of this contrast is to be

found in his introduction to his father's posthumously published work *The Literary Remains of Henry James*. In this
introduction, especially pp. 115 ff., James talks of pluralism as
" a view to which we all practically incline when in the full
and successful exercise of our moral energy." For " the life we
then feel tingling through us vouches sufficiently for itself, and
nothing tempts us to refer it to a higher source." But then, as
he goes on to explain, " healthy-mindedness is not the whole
of life; and the *morbid* view, as one may by contrast call it,
asks for a philosophy very different from that of absolute
moralism." It asks, that is to say, for a monism, since " to suggest personal will and effort to one ' all sicklied o'er ' with the
sense of weakness, of helpless failure, and of fear, is to suggest
the most horrible of things to him. What he craves is to be
consoled in his very impotence, to feel that the Powers of the
Universe recognize and secure him, all passive and failing as
he is." And the description becomes more than an objective
statement as James continues: " Well, we are all *potentially*
such sick men. The sanest and best of us are of one clay with
lunatics and prison-inmates." The demand for assurance which
springs from the sense of our own helplessness is, as we
shall see in detail, in James's view a demand for a monistic
philosophy.

The whole passage from which these excerpts are taken is a
very illuminating one, and its careful study is recommended to
anyone who wishes to watch the development of James's
thought. Among the items of especial interest, we may note in
the first place that while James wrote it as early as the summer
of 1884, it contains clear references to the pragmatic criterion
of truth, although the name " pragmatism " does not appear
in James's writings until fourteen years later, in the address
delivered at Berkeley on " Philosophical Conceptions and Practical Results." In the second place, the distinction between
monism and pluralism is already " the deepest of all philosophic differences," and pluralism is already championed with
a fair degree of enthusiasm. But the pluralism here described,
contrary to the expectation of those writers who relate plural-

ism primarily to his theory of knowledge, finds its excuse for being in the nature of the moral struggle; it is a pluralism, that is to say, which is moral rather than epistemological. Third, the moral basis of what later came to be known as " radical empiricism " is also present here. The moralist wishes, as James says, to feel his goods and evils "to be *real* goods and evils, with their distinction absolutely preserved." There must be no defining of one in terms of the other; the relations between the two must be external, not constitutive. This, as we shall see later, is one of the cardinal requirements of radical empiricism. Fourth, and most important for our present purposes, James here dwells at length on the struggle which he calls one between " religion " and " moralism," and hints at the possibility that his own sympathies may be divided. The claims of active pluralism are set forth with evident enthusiasm, yet passive monism is not neglected, for " we are all *potentially* such sick men." The question at once arises: Is there evidence that James with all his enthusiasm for pluralism, ever tired of the struggle and felt the need of resting upon the everlasting arms? Did religion ever appeal to him as a means to solace rather than as a means to conquest?

It seems so to have appealed to him in certain moods, even at a comparatively early age. From the objective description of the dualism let us turn now to evidences of an actual struggle in James's own mind. An interesting letter, written when he was twenty-six, to Thomas W. Ward, suggests that the active life may be but a substitute for the deeper yearnings of the spirit. " We long for sympathy," James here says, " for a purely *personal* communication, first with the soul of the world, and then with the soul of our fellows." [2] During this same period, while he was in the late twenties, James went through the mental suffering which thirty years afterward in *The Varieties of Religious Experience* he was able to describe so graphically. The account in the *Varieties* is given on pages 160 and 161 and is there attributed to " a French correspondent," but was later

---

[2] *The Letters of William James,* 1: 130 ff.

known to be from James himself.[3] Of his own experience, then, James writes:

" . . . there fell upon me without any warning, just as if it came out of the darkness, a horrible fear of my own existence. Simultaneously there arose in my mind the image of an epileptic patient whom I had seen in the asylum. . . . *That shape am I*, I felt, potentially. Nothing that I possess can defend me against that fate, if the hour for it should strike for me as it struck for him. . . . After this the universe was changed for me altogether. . . . I have always thought that this experience of mine had a religious bearing. . . . I mean that the fear was so invasive and powerful that if I had not clung to scripture-texts like ' The eternal God is my refuge,' etc., ' Come unto me, all ye that labor and are heavy-laden,' etc., ' I am the resurrection and the life,' etc., I think I should have grown really insane."

Here is as striking evidence as we could wish for the influence of the melancholy mood upon James at an early period. But this mood, though powerful, fortunately was transient. At other times the active impulses were in the ascendancy. Contrast with the last passage this buoyant quotation from a letter written in 1878 to Mrs. James:

" I have often thought that the best way to define a man's character would be to seek out the particular mental or moral attitude in which, when it came upon him, he felt himself most deeply and intensely active and alive. At such moments there is a voice inside which speaks and says ' *This* is the real me.' . . . This characteristic attitude in me always involves an element of active tension, of holding my own, as it were, and trusting outward things to perform their part so as to make it a full harmony, but without any *guaranty* that they will. Make it a guaranty — and the attitude immediately becomes to my consciousness stagnant and stingless. Take away the guaranty, and I feel (provided I am *überhaupt* in vigorous condition) a sort of deep enthusiastic bliss, of bitter willingness to do and suffer anything, which translates itself physically by a

[3] Cf. *Letters*, 1: 145.

kind of stinging pain inside my breast-bone (don't smile at this — it is to me an essential element of the whole thing!) and which, although it is a mere mood or emotion to which I can give no form in words, authenticates itself to me as the deepest principle of all active and theoretic determination which I possess." [4]

James gives us, then, first a description of the conflict between two views of life, and second a suggestion of a reflection of this conflict in the alternating moods of his own experience. Let us now observe one or two evidences of the way in which this conflict was making itself felt in his philosophical thought. An indication of the manner in which it affected his attempt to formulate a theory of knowledge is found in his review of Lewes' *Problems of Life and Mind* written for the *Atlantic Monthly* in 1875 and now reprinted in *Collected Essays and Reviews*.[5] This review also contains a most interesting anticipation of the famous treatment in *The Will to Believe* of the problem of religious assurance. Speaking of the conception of Substance, as an attempt to meet the demand for security, James says:

" Common sense craves for a stable conception of things. We desire to know what to *expect*. . . . Even in regard to the mass of accidents which must be expected to occur in some shape but cannot be accurately prophesied in detail, we set our minds at rest, by saying that the world with all its events has a substantial cause; and when we call this cause God, Love, or Perfection, we feel secure that whatever the future may harbor, it cannot at bottom be inconsistent with the character of this term."

But a few paragraphs further on we come upon the interesting assertion that " skepticism or unrest . . . can always have the last word." So that " . . . at a certain point most of us get tired of the play, resolve to stop, and assuming something for true, pass on to a life of action based on that." There is a volitional element, then, which asserts itself toward the solution of problems of knowledge as well as of conduct, for:

---

[4] *Letters*, 1: 199–200.   [5] Pp. 4 ff.

" In practical life we despise a man who will risk nothing, even more than one who will heed nothing. May it not be that in the theoretic life the man whose scruples about flawless accuracy of demonstration keep him forever shivering on the brink of Belief is as great an imbecile as the man at the opposite pole, who simply consults his prophetic soul for the answer to everything? What is this but saying that our opinions about the nature of things belong to our moral life? " And may we not query, as aptly, whether they do not belong to our religious life, when we are forced to postulate a " God, Love, or Perfection " to make the future secure? Active effort and assurance of safety, — our nature demands them both; and the religious and moral demand is paralleled by that which is implied in the knowing process.

The twofold demand, in its relation to the problem of knowledge, is further dealt with in the first of the two essays which have been printed under the title " The Sentiment of Rationality," this first one having appeared in *Mind,* for 1879, and as a reprint in *Collected Essays and Reviews.*[6] The most important contrast in the field of knowledge is here represented as that between simplicity and clearness, the one implying monism, the other pluralism. Hegel is cited as having shown the most glaring example of " hypertrophy of the unifying passion," while Renouvier is called " the greatest living insister on the principle that unity in our account of things shall not overwhelm clearness." Both demands, for unity and for distinctness, are fundamental, we are told; and no system of philosophy which violates either can hope to gain universal acceptance. If our need for unity could be satisfied, we might realize the sense of restfulness which a monism like that of the *Upanishads* offers. But James thinks it cannot be realized in the knowing process. Even Hegel's " heroic effort " is doomed to failure. " The bottom of Being " is left logically opaque to us," and the volitional element must be brought into play when we realize that it is " something which we simply come upon and find, and about which (if we wish to

6 Pp. 83 ff.

act) we should pause and wonder as little as possible." Here it is that pluralism issues its challenge and dares us to advance into the unknown, for " in this confession lies the lasting truth of Empiricism, and in it Empiricism and imaginative Faith join hands. The logical attitude of both is identical, they both say there is a *plus ultra* beyond all we know, a womb of unimagined other possibility." [7]

Yet the desire for the restfulness of unity is insistent, and, as James goes on to show, men will endeavor to find satisfaction in the attainment of an " uttermost datum " even though it be in itself inexplicable and point to a further mystery beyond. " Such is the attitude of ordinary men in their theism, God's fiat being in physics and morals such an uttermost datum." And the close relation of the demand for unity made in the knowing process with that of religious experience appears when the mystic's endeavor after unity is considered. For, as James says, " The peace of rationality may be sought through ecstasy when logic fails. To religious persons of every shade of doctrine moments come when the world as it is seems so divinely orderly, and the acceptance of it by the heart so rapturously complete, that intellectual questions vanish, nay, the intellect itself is hushed to sleep — as Wordsworth says, ' Thought is not, in enjoyment it expires.' Ontological emotion so fills the soul that ontological speculation can no longer overlap it and put her girdle of interrogation-marks around existence." [8]

In the second essay published under the title of " The Sentiment of Rationality," we find this dualism appearing again. For James here goes on to point out that " rationality " implies a practical as well as theoretic kind of satisfaction. An idea or a system of philosophy will be judged " rational " according as it satisfies the particular practical need of the person who is judging. And the practical needs which a system of philosophy is equipped to satisfy fall into two classes: it can satisfy the need for intimacy, as does idealism in placing a universe of

[7] *Collected Essays and Reviews*, p. 128.
[8] *Collected Essays and Reviews*, p. 133.

thought at the command of the thinker; or it can satisfy the need for activity, as is accomplished by empiricism, with its postulation of new worlds to conquer. " The strife of these two kinds of mental temper," says James, " will, I think, always be seen in philosophy. Some men will keep insisting on the reason, the atonement, that lies in the heart of things, and that we can act *with;* others, on the opacity of brute fact that we must react *against.*" [9]

So much for the reflection in James's early attacks on the problem of knowledge of the conflicting ideas which we have described as warring within him. The next passage to consider comes from his psychological description of the ego. James's *Principles of Psychology,* published in 1890, is not only still a standard text-book in that subject but is one of the most convincing scientific descriptions ever written of the essentially creative function of the human organism. But while the idea of the creative activity of consciousness is dominant in this work, one also finds suggestions as to human dependence in James's description of the fundamental human desire for recognition from the " Absolute Mind," the " Great Companion." " We hear, in these days of scientific enlightenment," says James, " a great deal of discussion about the efficacy of prayer; and many reasons are given us why we should not pray, whilst others are given us why we should. But in all this very little is said of the reason why we *do* pray, which is simply that we cannot *help* praying. It seems probable that, in spite of all that ' science' may do to the contrary, men will continue to pray to the end of time. . . . The impulse to pray is a necessary consequence of the fact that whilst the innermost of the empirical selves of a man is a Self of the *social* sort, it yet can find its only adequate *Socius* in an ideal world." [10]

We have thus found James both describing the conflicting demands of the active and passive moods and giving evidence of the alternation of these moods in himself. We have also found a reflection of this conflict in James's description of the

[9] *The Will to Believe, etc.,* p. 90.   [10] 1: 316.

two needs which are implied in the knowing process, the need for self-assertion and the need for security, and in his suggestion of the alternation between creation and dependence in the experience of the self. The religious bearing of the conflict will be made more clear by following up some of the comments James makes on the religious implications of pluralism compared with those of monism. The contrast is sharply drawn in James's great book on religion, *The Varieties of Religious Experience,* but indications of it appear earlier as well. A letter to Professor G. H. Howison in 1885 is interesting for its suggestion that pluralism was at that time becoming, in James's view, not merely a " moralistic " philosophy, as he had called it in his introduction to his father's book, but a means to truly *religious* value. " Make the world a Pluralism," James exclaims in his letter, " and you forthwith have an object to worship. Make it a Unit, on the other hand, and worship and abhorrence are equally one-sided and equally legitimate reactions. *Indifferentism* is the true condition of such a world." And since this is so, " I prefer to stick to the wooden finitude of an ultimate pluralism, because that at least gives me something definite to worship and fight for." [11]

The religious bearing of a " moralistic " and therefore pluralistic philosophy is further brought out in the essay on " The Moral Philosopher and the Moral Life," first published in the *International Journal of Ethics* in 1891 and now reprinted in *The Will to Believe and Other Essays.* Here James maintains that " in a merely human world without a God, the appeal to our moral energy falls short of its maximal stimulating power." For only when we believe in a God do " the more imperative ideals " utter their " penetrating, shattering, tragically challenging note of appeal." " The capacity of the strenuous mood," James tells us, " lies so deep down among our natural human possibilities that even if there were no metaphysical or traditional grounds for believing in a God, men would postulate one simply as a pretext for living hard,

[11] *Letters,* 1: 238.

and getting out of the game of existence its keenest possibilities of zest." [12]

Obviously it is not the Comforter but the God of battles who is the object of devotion of the moral man in a pluralistic world. The essays published with *The Will to Believe* present this view on the whole fairly consistently. In *The Varieties of Religious Experience* the contrasting attitude receives more attention. Indeed this book describes both points of view so persuasively that it is difficult at times to see with which side James's allegiance lies. Never, it is safe to say, has the gospel of healthy-mindedness been more eloquently set forth. But in like manner never has the "sick soul" been described with such evident sensitiveness to its needs. Which is the deeper mood — the active or the contemplative? Through which do we attain a truer insight into the heart of things? Is religion more consonant with the demands of our nature and more representative of whatever universal reality there may be when it gives us comfort, or when it encourages us to a more aggressive activity? Shall we rest on the everlasting arms or put on the whole armor of God? This is the question which speaks through every page of the *Varieties,* and in it we hear an echo of the conflict which, as we claim, was so pervasive of James's thought.

It is a little surprising at first to find that " healthy-mindedness " as James views it in the *Varieties* is aligned with pluralism. One might have supposed that the insistence that life is worth while would involve the assertion that all is good. But it is significant that James does not look at the matter in this way. Healthy-mindedness, in his opinion, admits the fact of evil as an obstruction to be removed. It refuses to gloss over its existence, but it refuses also to magnify its importance. So James tells us that " the gospel of healthy-mindedness . . . casts its vote distinctly for this pluralistic view. Whereas the monistic philosopher finds himself more or less bound to say, as Hegel said, that everything actual is rational, and that evil, as an element dialectically required, must be pinned in and

[12] *The Will to Believe, etc.,* pp. 212–3.

kept consecrated and have a function awarded to it in the final system of truth, healthy-mindedness refuses to say anything of the sort. Evil, it says, is emphatically irrational, and *not* to be pinned in, or preserved, or consecrated in any final system of truth." [13]

So healthy-mindedness, or at least the kind in which James believes, is deliberately and aggressively optimistic. But, as James goes on to remind us, optimism may be very shallow and very blind. " How *can* things so insecure as the successful experiences of this world afford a stable anchorage? " " In the healthiest and most prosperous existence, how many links of illness, danger and disaster are always interposed? " " The healthy-minded consciousness is left with an irremediable sense of precariousness." " Failure, then, failure! so the world stamps us at every turn." And then in a strain reminiscent of the passage quoted above from the *Principles of Psychology,* we read " The God of many men is little more than their court of appeal against the damnatory judgment passed on their failures by the opinion of this world. . . . We turn to the All-Knower who knows our bad, but knows this good in us also, and who is just. We cast ourselves with repentance on his mercy: only by an All-Knower can we finally be judged. So the need of a God very definitely emerges from this sort of experience in life." [14]

These experiences of failure and futility, these glimpses into the horror of insanity with their first-hand intimations of the awful abyss of agony into which so many have fallen, point to a deeper stratum of reality than that in which healthy-mindedness has its roots. "How irrelevantly remote seem all our usual refined optimisms and intellectual and moral consolations in the presence of a need like this. Here is the real core of the religious problem: Help! Help! No prophet can claim to bring a final message unless he says things that will have a sound of reality in the ears of victims such as these. But the deliverance must come in as strong a form as the complaint, if it is to take effect; and that seems a reason why

---

[13] *Varieties,* p. 132.   [14] Pp. 136 ff.

the coarser religions, revivalistic, orgiastic, with blood and miracles and supernatural operations, may possibly never be displaced. Some constitutions need them too much." [15]

Passages like this bring out an inner dilemma in each member of the conflict. The "sick soul" through its own agony sees that the universe is not wholly good and understands the shallowness of monism. But by the same token it cries out for the relief which only monism can give, for the "peace of rationality" which passeth rationalizing. Its dilemma is: A God who saves is impossible, yet a God who saves is necessary. The negation and the demand are twin elements in its cry. And less poignantly but similarly, the dilemma is present in healthy-mindedness. Salvation must not be assured, "there must be no guaranty," or the tang and the zest which are the heart of healthy-mindedness are gone. But salvation must be achieved; I, the individual, must assert my reality in a way that will endure. For, as James once said, a "nameless '*unheimlichkeit*' comes over us at the thought of there being nothing eternal in our final purposes." [16] I must achieve, yet, as the apostle Paul would have put it, not I, but One who worketh in me!

These passages have all been drawn from James's works published before 1903, the latest from which quotation has been made being the *Varieties* which appeared in 1902. They reflect something of the relation of what we have called the varying active and passive moods in James's experience to the philosophic antithesis which appears so frequently in his works. As the question of monism or pluralism James often refers to it as the most pregnant question in philosophy, and he alludes nearly as often to its variants, the strife between rationalism and empiricism, or between absolutism and individualism. The antithesis, and the personal dilemma it made for James is worth examining. It is of interest in the first place for the student of James, since it suggests a way in which at least some of the contradictions in his works may be explained in terms of this struggle of two conflicting loyalties. A remark which one fre-

[15] P. 162. [16] *Will to Believe, etc.*, p. 83.

quently hears today is that whatever James has asserted on
one page he has denied on another. Like Emerson with whom
he has often been compared (and just as often been contrasted) James is commonly believed to have regarded consistency as an overrated fetish, the hobgoblin of small minds.
Yet much of the inconsistency which the critics have proclaimed is only apparent. The " center of the author's vision "
which he has told us it is so important to catch can be found
in James himself if we can get a glimpse of the intimate and
personal opinion. As he so often insisted, philosophy was for
him more a matter of passionate vision than of logic. If the
vision alternated in intensity and range yet alternated in two
clearly defined directions the center with its controlling unity
should be easier for us to grasp. And in the second place the
conflict is of interest on its own account. To borrow a phrase
from Professor Hocking's classroom (a phrase which, however, so far as the writer knows, Professor Hocking has not
applied to James), the conflict may be described as that between two contrasting types of religious thought — " auto-so-
teric " and " hetero-soteric." The former is humanistic, seeking salvation through its own effort, represented in James by
the belief in the purposive nature of the human organism and
its creative power. The latter is more mystical, reaching out
for help from a higher Power, and represented in James, as
we have seen, in his desire for stability and in his belief in
the actual occurrence and in the value when they do occur of
what he calls " saving experiences " in the religious life.

The most important point to notice here is that this longing
for religious assurance was actually at times translated in
James's mind into sympathy for the monistic point of view in
metaphysics. Apparently monism appealed to him, however,
almost entirely for its religious value. There were times when
James felt the need of the kind of religious support which only
a monistic view could bring. That this doughty champion of
pluralism, should at any time in his life have been inclined to
see the good in monism is interesting enough. But that monism should have appealed to him especially because of its re-

ligious value is particularly interesting for our purposes. It suggests that religious values made a remarkably direct appeal to James and that in their light he was able to see virtue where none had existed before. And if the intimately personal desire for reconciliation and atonement was able at any time to incline him toward monism, we may expect to find his religious vision influencing him in other ways. This indeed is wholly in line with James's own view of what philosophy really is. " A philosophy is the expression of a man's intimate character," he has told us, it cannot be a mere " technical matter " but must embody " the sense of what life honestly and deeply means."

But now, it may be asked, if James really felt the force of this kind of religious appeal, why do we not find a more clearly formulated expression of it in his work? James considers himself a pluralist and indeed has always been regarded as pluralism's most active defender. How is this possible if he really sympathized at times with the other side? The answer is simply that the conflict, while a real one, was not toward the end of his life an indecisive one. James chose pluralism, as we shall see, because the values it brought in its train seemed to him on the whole to be more important than those of monism. And the fact is, of course, as we shall also see, that we do find traces of the monistic inclination even in those works where pluralism is most vigorously defended. May we not also discern a possible trace of bitterness in James's onslaughts on monism? At times he gives the impression of making the more savage attack because he would so willingly have defended it, since its benefits, if they could have come untrammeled, would have been so acceptable.

A word should be said here as to the use of the term " sick soul " which we have come upon in this discussion. Its use, together with the expression " morbid-mindedness," appears to imply a negative evaluation of the passive mood from the outset. But before we discount the ability of the " sick soul " to point the way to truth we must remember, first, that these terms did not connote for James any unfitness for vision or insight. The pathological is to be evaluated not by its roots but by its fruits. Is the insight of the " sick soul " more clear than that of the healthy mind, and does it lead us to more fruitful relations with reality? These are the significant questions for the point at issue. When his sympathies are on the side of monism James indicates that its insight is both more clear and more comprehensive. " It seems to me," he writes in the *Varieties,* " that we are bound to say that morbid-mindedness ranges over the wider scale of experience, and that its survey is the one that overlaps." For, "even though one be quite free from melancholy one's self, there is no doubt that healthy-mindedness is inadequate as a philosophic doctrine, because the evil facts which it refuses positively to account for are a genuine portion of reality; and they may after all be the best key to life's significance, and possibly the only openers of our eyes to the deepest levels of truth." [17]

Then again we must not take the adjectives " sick " and " morbid" too literally. A " morbid " state of mind in this sense is one which recognizes the fact and the force of evil with a peculiar vividness, but not necessarily in an abnormal way. Indeed James was himself often enough a " sick soul " and " morbid-minded " in the sense in which these expressions are used. The terms are used simply to emphasize the extremes to which passivity goes. There are moods when the facts of evil will not be glossed over but insist on making their presence felt and in impressing on us our own helplessness before them. " Unsuspectedly from the bottom of every fountain of pleasure, as the old poet said, something bitter rises up: a touch of nausea . . . a whiff of melancholy, things that sound a knell, for fugitive as they may be, they . . . often have an appalling convincingness."

These quotations have given us not merely evidence of the existence of the conflict itself, but some suggestions as to the standards which James could be expected to employ in coming to a decision. Obviously clearness and comprehensiveness of insight furnish one criterion. Blindness to the facts of life

[17] P. 163.

is an insuperable objection to any philosophy. But another criterion is fully as important. The pragmatic test as applied by James deserves a moment of our attention here, for a part of our study will attempt to bring out the close relation of James's pragmatism to his religious philosophy and in so doing will point to the facility with which pragmatism is brought to bear upon religious problems.

Pragmatism, as we noticed before, is clearly suggested in James's introduction to his father's work. " By their fruits," James here asserts, " ye shall know them." We must appeal to the " umpire of practice." Pragmatic temporalism also is implied in the phrase *" Solvitur ambulando."* In these and in the later passages, James is faithful to the pragmatic view that the truth of a theory is not knowable apart from its effects for life. There is no theoretic difference without a practical difference, and the practical differences in our experience are the best clues we have to differences of theory in all life, but particularly in the religious life. The decisive question is: Which kind of difference is practically more important and so functions as more satisfactory evidence of a difference in ultimate reality? In the matter of this conflict which has a more desirable effect in practical life, assurance and comfort or renewed energy and strengthened will? Which is the greater good? For, since truth is a species of good, the greater good will be the more true. To be sure, " greater good " must here be carefully defined, and logical consistency as well as conformity to the rest of the data of experience must not be overlooked. But consistency and conformity are only two out of many demands. And when we are confronted by questions of religious import we frequently find that there are few data or " facts," so that there may be no question of conformity, and we further find that logic is sometimes irrelevant, while our emotional and volitional demands are always relevant and always insistent. Pragmatism recognizes both the force and the pertinency of these demands and so is especially well qualified to act as arbiter in religious questions.

In his later works James does not merely suggest, but definitely brings into play the pragmatic criterion. In *Pragma-tism* [18] and in *A Pluralistic Universe* [19] he devotes more time and space than ever before to a discussion of the monistic-pluralistic antithesis, but the conflict now rages not so much over " monism " as over " the absolute." The final decision is definitely in favor of the pluralistic, melioristic, empirical view of life and the universe. But the decision does not come without a struggle. The absolute asserts its claim to be heard, and makes its appeal, especially in its religious capacity.

To suggest, however, that James was in any way sensitive to the appeal of the absolute is to make a statement which, in view of his well-known attacks upon that entity, will require further examination. To a study of James's relations with the absolute, accordingly, we must now turn our attention.

[18] Published in 1907.   [19] Published in 1909.

II

THE ABSOLUTE

TO JAMES, in his vigorous moods, the absolute was anathema. At such times, when "the pulse of life tingling through him vouched for itself," the hypothesis of an all-knower or an all-doer or an all-sustainer was absolute only in its absurdity. "Damn the absolute!" he exclaimed to Royce, one morning at Chocorua, and some years later his Oxford audience was scandalized to hear him ejaculate, in the course of his public lecture, "Let the absolute bury its absolute!" "A metaphysical monster" was his name for Bradley's edition of this Being; a "will o' the wisp," one of the "lights that do mislead the morn" and the "mad absolute" he calls it in other connections. "Why does the Absolute Unity make its votaries so much more conceited at having attained it?" he asks, in a letter to Renouvier; and to Hodgson, in a phrase reminiscent of Ritschl, he observes: "There is no superstition like the idolatry of the Whole!"

It is not difficult, even in this age of "power, speed and utility," to understand the fascination which the absolute has exercised over minds philosophically inclined. Absolutism has been defined by Professor J. B. Baillie as "a method of interpreting reality which starts from the point of view of, and constructs a system by direct reference to, the complete unity of the whole."[1] In spite of the formalism of this or any other definition of the attempt to frame a notion of total reality, it must be evident that such an attempt springs from needs which are fundamental in human nature. In the first place, there is

---

[1] Art. "Absolutism" in Hastings' *Encyclopaedia of Religion and Ethics.*

the intellectual need. As thinking beings, we must classify. In order to understand we must relate. We make intellectual progress by bringing apparently diverse particulars under a single heading. Why then should we not reach out for the all-inclusive category, the principle by which all particulars are made knowable, knowable to a great Someone at least, if not to us? So to do is, indeed, merely to assert the triumphantly conquering ability of the human reason. It is to follow the fruitful example of the early Milesians, precursors of the greatest humanistic movement that the world has known, for whom the cosmos itself presented no insuperable difficulties, but who proceeded in the belief that the world was one and that this oneness was expressed in a formula which the human intellect was equipped to discover. This implicit faith in the invincibility of the human spirit as to its intellectual function might be expected to find in James an enthusiastic response.

And absolutism brings, along with its conviction that the world is rational, the promise that it is good. There is no deeper question than that attributed to F. W. H. Myers, "Is the universe friendly?" Absolutists are sure that it is. The rational, after all, is the good. How could it be otherwise? As to whether this means that the words "absolute" and "God" are interchangeable, absolutists differ among themselves. The view that they are is finely expressed by Professor Pringle-Pattison in his Gifford lectures on *The Idea of God,* where mankind is pictured as endeavoring, from the earliest days to our own, to probe the riddle of existence. Man, says this absolutist, "asks the meaning of it all, and he names the name of God." One answer suffices for the final question raised by metaphysics, by the problems of knowledge, by religion. It is absolutism's ability to make man feel at home in the universe, its assurance of cosmic support for spiritual ideals, its apparent capacity to offer a final and satisfactory answer to man's most insistent questionings that James has in mind when he talks of the assurance and sense of stability which belief in the absolute brings.

But while the attempt to reach and know an all-encompass-

ing Reality has, especially since the days of Anselm, had a
religious as well as an intellectual meaning, the attempt itself
has been made, James seems to think, along too exclusively
logical, that is, formal and abstract lines. As one reads the
work of apologists for the absolute, the impression comes that
this criticism of James's has much to back it up. The argument proceeds by analysis and counter-analysis. Ultimate reality is One and all, for it cannot be anything else. If it were
many, we should have a meaningless chaos without an underlying unity. If it were less than all, it would imply the existence of that by which it is less than all. And so the argument
goes, working always for consistency in the propositions with
which it deals. But it is necessary, as others have pointed out,
not only to be consistent, but to have all the facts to be consistent with. Logic is of the highest importance, but logic itself draws its data from the world of human experience. This
seems to be the starting-point of James's objection. And
coupled with this is what might almost, in the vernacular of the
day, be described as a " complex " against the absolute's rigid-
ness and completeness. The conception of an " All-Knower "
satisfies certain religious moods, but the determinism and lack
of scope for individual activity which it implies are incompatible with the moral demands we make upon the cosmos. Any
all-inclusive philosophy, any belief which emphasizes the oneness of reality, any monistic idealism, absolutism, or imper-
sonal mechanistic scheme arouses James's ire. In the essay on
" Is Life Worth Living? " in a manner worthy of J. S. Mill
himself he calls the world of nature a "harlot," to whom " we
owe no allegiance," and this antipathy to a world so unre-
lieved by any sign of responsivness to human and moral concerns is reflected and magnified in his attitude to any ultimate
reality which failed to allow for the possibility of human creative achievement. In spite of the efforts of his absolutistic
friends, Royce, for example, and Miss Mary W. Calkins, to
whom in an unpublished letter he acknowledges his indebtedness, James to the end affirmed his belief that the absolute
failed to meet vital human needs. In his own inimitable manner

he wrote,[2] " The through-and-through universe seems to suffocate me with its infallible, impeccable all-pervasiveness. Its necessity, with no possibilities; its relations, with no subjects, make me feel . . . as if I had to live in a large seaside boarding-house with no private bedroom in which I might take refuge from the society of the place. . . .   Certainly, to my personal knowledge, all Hegelians are not prigs, but I somehow feel as if all prigs ought to end, if developed, by becoming Hegelians. . . . It [the ' through-and-through ' philosophy] seems too buttoned-up and white-chokered and clean-shaven a thing to speak for the vast slow-breathing unconscious Kosmos with its dread abysses and its unknown tides. The ' freedom ' *we* want to see there is not the freedom, with a string tied to its leg and warranted not to fly away, of that philosophy. ' Let it fly away,' we say, ' from *us!* What then? ' "

With the possible exception of F. C. S. Schiller, the " exuberance " of whose " polemic wit " in this regard James himself eyed a little askance, no other writer has given more trenchant expression to his anti-absolutistic feeling. And surely no other writer has presented his opinions so colorfully or in a form so likely to make a lasting impression on the reader. So well are James's attacks on the absolute remembered and so widespread is the opinion of him as the absolute's chief antagonist, that it comes as something of a surprise to find that his opposition was not manifest all through his life, and that there were times, as we have hinted, when he assumed an attitude of receptiveness to the monistic appeal.

Some of the evidence of this alternation we have traced in the previous chapter, observing that a real conflict went on in James's mind which shows in early works and as late as the *Varieties* published in 1902. James continued, until his death in 1910, to state clearly and forcefully the issues of the great antithesis of which the conflict we have described formed one aspect. But in *Pragmatism* and *A Pluralistic Universe*, his last two books which contain a continuous dicussion and sustained argument on the subject, James throws the weight of

[2] *Essays in Radical Empiricism*, pp. 276 ff.

his influence on one side. Not that he fails to come out clearly for pluralism before this final period. The standpoint of *The Will to Believe and Other Essays* is avowedly pluralistic. But in these last books an unusually large amount of attention is given to the antithesis, and the reasons for deciding in favor of one member are given in some detail. In *Pragmatism* the opposition between rationalism and empiricism is made the background for a study of the effectiveness of the pragmatic method for settling metaphysical disputes, and the verdict is rendered for empiricism. And in *A Pluralistic Universe* the quarrel of the absolute with pluralism is settled in favor of the latter. Yet in these works where the decision is so definitely adverse, the absolute is given its due and its claims on men's imagination and sympathy are heard.

Neither in its relation to the problem of knowledge nor in its rôle as a metaphysical and religious Being did the absolute finally make any coercive demand on James, though there were periods in his life when each aspect made its own appeal to him. The absolute as all-knower early engaged James's attention, and for a time his allegiance. In a review of Royce's *The Religious Aspect of Philosophy* printed in the *Atlantic Monthly* for 1885 and now reprinted in *Collected Essays and Reviews* [3] he says, apropos of Royce's idealistic reasoning: " The more one thinks, the more one feels that there is a real puzzle here. Turn and twist as we will, we are caught in a tight trap. . . . An ' Over-Soul ' of whose enveloping thought our thought and the things we think of are alike fractions, — such is the only hypothesis that can form a basis for the reality of truth and of error in the world. . . . To the lay reader this absolute Idealism doubtless seems insubstantial and unreal enough. But it is astonishing to learn how many paths lead up to it. . . . Taken altogether, they end by making about as formidable a convergence of testimony as the history of opinion affords."

One difficulty which the absolute as all-knower enabled James to counter was that of showing how an idea can point

[3] Pp. 276 ff.

to its object. But after nine years of bondage to this use of the absolute, he asserted his independence, saying that Professor Dickinson S. Miller had showed him that " any definite experienceable workings will serve as intermediary between idea and object as well as the absolute mind's intentions." [4] Other tributes to the absolute as having value for the problem of knowledge are paid even in the book where the attack is most bitter. In *Pragmatism* [5] he calls it the " sublimest achievement of intellectualist philosophy," saying that it has supplanted the conception of Substance, Scholasticism's great contribution to the history of thought. And in *A Pluralistic Universe* [6] he admits that absolutists have a " healthy faith " that the world must be rational and self-consistent.

But the chief value of the absolute lies in its religious function. Reference has already been made to the passage in the *Principles of Psychology* where James speaks of the absolute as a " Great Companion." Of similar content is a passage in *A Pluralistic Universe* where he says: " From a pragmatic point of view the difference between living against a background of foreignness and one of intimacy means the difference between a general habit of wariness and one of trust. One might call it a social difference, for after all, the common *socius* of us all is the great universe whose children we are." [7] Absolutism may thus respond to what is the deepest religious need, for as James remarks elsewhere, " the chief call for a God on modern men's part is for a being who will inwardly recognize them and judge them sympathetically." [8]

Working on the supposition that the intimacy which absolute pantheism brings must be retained in any satisfactory religious scheme, James in *A Pluralistic Universe* develops his famous conception of a " confluent consciousness " which has many points in common with the absolute. " May not we ourselves form the margin of some more really central self in things which is co-conscious with the whole of us? " James asks. " May not you and I be confluent in a higher conscious-

[4] Cf. *The Meaning of Truth*, p. 22.   [6] P. 72.   [7] P. 31.
[5] P. 145.   [8] *The Meaning of Truth*, p. 189n.

ness, and confluently active there, though we know it not? " [9]
This great central consciousness seems to be similar to if not
identical with the world-consciousness or cosmic consciousness to which James often alludes elsewhere. In an article
written in reply to W. C. Gore's criticism of Schiller, James
himself suggests the resemblance of the world-consciousness to
an absolute. "The absolute," he says, " is surely one of the
great hypotheses of philosophy; it must be thoroughly discussed. Its advocates have usually treated it only as a logical
necessity; and very bad logic, as it seems to me, have they in-
variably used. It is high time that the hypothesis of a world-
consciousness should be discussed seriously." And he goes on
to say that " So far, Fechner is the only thinker who has
done any elaborate work of this kind on the world-soul question." [10] Similarly, in his discussion of a great "mother-sea"
or "fountain-head" of consciousness in the Ingersoll Lecture
on *Human Immortality,* James comes remarkably near to
professing himself an absolutist. Indeed the chief criticism
made of the lecture, as James shows in the preface to the
second edition, was that it defended a form of absolute pantheism. And the lecture does give some ground for the criticism.
For example, discussing the advantages or disadvantages of
individual immortality as compared with a merging of all individuals in a great "cosmic reservoir" of memories, James
observes: " If all determination is negation, as the philosophers
say, it might well prove that the loss of some of the particular
determinations which the brain imposes would not appear a
matter for such absolute regret." [11] And in a note he feels
constrained to add that "it is not necessary to identify the
consciousness postulated in the lecture, as pre-existing behind
the scenes, with the Absolute Mind of transcendental Idealism, although, indeed, the notion of it might lead in that direction" [12] and apparently did so lead in the minds of many of
his hearers and readers. There are indications, as well, that
the absolutistic aspects of the conception were not absent from

[9] P. 290.
[10] *Journal of Philosophy, etc.,* 1906, 3: 657.
[11] P. 30.
[12] P. 58.

his own mind. Speaking of the possibility of revelation **he** says: " Gleams, however finite and unsatisfying," [because they come through human media] " of the absolute life of the universe, are from time to time vouchsafed." [13] The figure and the phrasing here both suggest the attitude of the worshipper.

But it is not necessary to point to a possible community of consciousness in order to suggest that a peculiar religious intimacy exists between us and the absolute. The monistic ideal itself makes its own appeal and suggests its worshipfulness. Beside it pluralism is a " turbid, muddled, gothic sort of an affair, without a sweeping outline and with little pictorial nobility." [14] Monism is much more " illustrious," it has a kind of " majesty " and " nobility." " A certain emotional response to the character of oneness " might almost be called " a part of philosophic common sense," [15] or more accurately, of philosophic mysticism, for " we may fairly suppose that the authority which absolute monism undoubtedly possesses, and probably always will possess over some persons, draws its strength far less from intellectual than from mystical grounds." " To interpret absolute monism worthily, be a mystic." [16] Elsewhere James speaks of this mystic attitude as though its accomplishments were wholly commendable. " This overcoming of all the usual barriers between the individual and the absolute is the great mystic achievement. In mystic states we both become one with the absolute and we become aware of our oneness. This is the everlasting and triumphant mystical tradition, hardly altered by differences of clime or creed." [17] And the mystic tradition is a catholic tradition. To some degree we all share it. " We all have some ear for this monistic music: it elevates and reassures. We all have at least the germ of mysticism in us." [18]

But while we all respond to this mystical appeal of the absolute, the " sick soul " is especially susceptible to it. James

[13] P. 16.

[14] *A Pluralistic Universe*, p. 45.

[15] *Pragmatism*, p. 131.

[16] *Pragmatism*, p. 151.

[17] *Varieties*, p. 419.

[18] *Pragmatism*, p. 154.

as one who at times was himself a " sick soul " knew whereof
he wrote. " This forms one permanent inferiority of pluralism," he says, " from the pragmatic point of view. It has no
saving message for incurably sick souls. Absolutism, among
its other messages, has that message, and is the only scheme
that has it necessarily. That constitutes its chief superiority,
and is the source of its religious power." [19] And we can all
sympathize with the " sick soul," James thinks, for " There
are moments of discouragement in us all, when we are sick
of self and tired of vainly striving. Our own life breaks down,
and we fall into the attitude of the prodigal son. We mistrust
the chances of things. We want a universe where we can just
give up, fall on our father's neck, and be absorbed into the
absolute life as a drop of water melts into the river or sea."
Then " religious monism comes with its consoling words: ' All
is needed and essential — even you with your sick soul and
heart. All are one with God, and with God all is well. The
everlasting arms are beneath, whether in the world of finite
appearance you seem to fail or to succeed.' " [20] And while
it meets the needs of the sick soul especially capably, the absolute can render a service to the healthy-minded as well,
chiefly in the way of preventing him from getting sick. It gives
him a moral holiday, [21] and enables him to put into practice
the gospel of relaxation. This suggested function of the absolute did not, however, meet with the favor of its defenders, so
in the preface to *The Meaning of Truth* James jocosely took it
back, saying: " The absolute is true in *no* way then, and least
of all, by the verdict of the critics, in the way which I as-
signed."

But whether its gifts of moral holidays be accepted or not,
history shows that the absolute has functioned, and functioned religiously. " The use of the absolute is proved by the
whole course of men's religious history. The eternal arms are
then beneath." [22] Not satisfied with the imposing dignity of
its position as an object apart, possessed of majesty, nobility,

[19] *The Meaning of Truth*, p. 228.   [21] *Pragmatism*, p. 74.
[20] *Pragmatism*, pp. 292–3.   [22] *Pragmatism*, p. 273.

and aesthetic charm, the absolute has reached down to men in their mystical moods and responded to their appeals for aid. It has given security and peace; it has offered encouragement to the failure, companionship to the lonely, comfort to the sick, and to the healthy-minded it has given the chance of a moral holiday. " As a good pragmatist," says James, " I myself ought to call the absolute true ' in so far forth,' then," (as it satisfies these human demands) " and I unhesitatingly now do so." [23]

But unfortunately, to declare the absolute true " so far forth " leaves room for declaring it untrue so far and further. The absolute meets some demands, but it violates others. These we must now consider. In the first place, it is " noble " in a bad, as well as in a good sense. James says: " In this real world of sweat and dirt, it seems to me that when a view of things is ' noble,' that ought to count as a presumption against its truth, and as a philosophic disqualification. The prince of darkness may be a gentleman, as we are told he is, but whatever the God of earth and heaven is, he surely can be no gentleman. His menial services are needed in the dust of our human trials, even more than his dignity is needed in the empyrean." [24]

The absolute is a " dapper " conception. It has a " formal grandeur," but only formal, as it " furnishes a pallid outline for the real world's richness." It is " remote " and it is " sterile." This sterility is for both knowledge and religion, since " the absolute is useless for deductive purposes. It gives us absolute safety, if you will, but it is compatible with every relative danger. . . . It is an hypothesis that functions retrospectively only not prospectively." And, " apart from the cold comfort of assuring us that with it all is well . . . it yields us no relief whatever." [25]

And this is not all. The absolute is not only useless, it is absurd. Idealists represent the absolute as the all-knower.

[23] *Pragmatism*, p. 73.
[24] *Pragmatism*, p. 72.
[25] *A Pluralistic Universe*, pp. 126 ff. cf. *Pragmatism*, pp. 70–71.

But " thinking this view consistently out leads one to frame an almost ridiculous conception of the absolute mind, owing to the enormous mass of unprofitable information which it would then seem obliged to carry." The absolute must know what everything is *not*. This at once suggests an overpowering burden of " explicitly negative " information. And if there be silly ideas, the absolute must carry them to establish their silliness. " One would expect it fairly to burst with such an obesity, plethora, and superfoetation of useless information." [26]

From the ridiculousness of the absolute we pass naturally to its inner inconsistency. And this, for reasons that will appear, requires a somewhat detailed examination.

James begins his attack on the absolute in *A Pluralistic Universe* [27] by showing how difficult it is, logically, to conceive many different minds as forming in themselves one inclusive mind. The difficulty is paralleled by the problem psychology has confronted of showing how many mental elements, ideas or sensations, can themselves constitute one knower, one conscious process. The old atomistic psychology of the sensationist school called the knower the sum of the elements. The knowing process was the psychical elements *feeling themselves*.[28] Rationalists, not content with this, have invoked the aid of a unifying principle, whose function is to relate and whose agent is the Ego, or self. James's own position in the *Principles* involved, he tells us, the rejection alike of the hypothesis that the elements had no unifying agency, and of the counter-hypothesis that this agency was the self. The unifying element was there, he held, as a part of the process, but as a distinct yet immanent entity. The knower consisted of the elements plus something formal and unifying. The twenty-six letters of the alphabet taken together form a twenty-seventh thing. So, although James would not admit the presence of a soul, or self, he did claim that a new element was present. The elements unified are the same as the elements separate only in an

[26] *A Pluralistic Universe,* pp. 127–8.
[27] Chapter V.
[28] Cf. James's article " On Some Omissions of Introspective Psychology." *Mind,* 1884, p. 7.

objective way. They do know the same thing. But aside from this kind of sameness they are different; a new entity is there. Yet the new element is nothing "transcendental," nothing which like a *deus ex machina* has come in from outside to perform unifying process. The unity, when it is there at all, is there as the form of the psychosis, feeling, or state of mind itself. A thought of the alphabet is not a manifold of twenty-six coexisting elements. It is a unity just as every pulse of consciousness is a unity. A mental state whose object is complex is not *composed* of simple mental states. It merely *follows* the simpler states and supersedes them in function.[29]

Now the absolute presents a similar problem. According to the theories of its proponents, the absolute is the sum of our finite selves. It is the whole and we are the parts; it is the sentence and we the words; or it is the word while we are the letters. But by the aid of this, the transcendentalists' own metaphor, we at once see difficulties in the conception of the absolute. First, why is the absolute's experience of us, in one grand Whole, so different from our own experience of ourselves as divided, limited, imperfect, and so full of pain and sin? Second, how can we, ideas in the mind of the Knower, become so active on our own account like characters in search of an author? Third, in the physical world there really are no wholes, but only parts; there is and can be no compounding. In the mental world there are real wholes, the meaning of the sentence is as real as the meaning of each word, but the whole is more than the sum of its parts. A new element has entered. We confront, then, the following dilemma. Accepting, as absolutists do, the idealistic theory that reality is mental, that what is real is what is experienced, we must either agree that pain and evil and division are real, since we experience them, and in this case we deny the absolutistic notion that reality is perfect; or we must admit a distinct agent to do the work of the all-knower, in which case, says James with an almost audible chuckle, we no longer have a monism. It will

[29] Cf. *Principles of Psychology,* 1: 278, *et passim,* and cf. also the modification of this view recorded in *Collected Essays and Reviews,* pp. 397 ff.

not help to claim that the experiences are one thing *quā finite* and another *quā infinite*. A world which is open to such a dualistic interpretation is itself a dualism. The whole difficulty arises over the question as to how any collective experience can ever be logically identical with a lot of distributive experiences. Can we logically accept a belief in a knower, finite or infinite, unless we are willing to admit that he must be a distinct unifying agent? James confesses to an unwillingness to bring in any transcendental agency in either case. The individual soul has served its purpose, and until some pragmatic justification for it is found, it must be relegated to the limbo of obsolete hypotheses. And as for the absolute soul — well, a theistic God would seem a more natural object of belief than an absolute who couldn't be absolute since he must be one member of a dualism.

The absolute is thus impossible logically. But the problem was not allowed to rest there. Apparently the mystic or pragmatic appeal of the absolute was sufficiently strong to keep James's mind working on the problem. Reading Hegel, and disliking Hegel's account of the matter, he was yet attracted by Hegel's idea that the absolute, having no environment, has " attained to being its own other " and transcended the logic of identity. If this be true of the absolute, why not of finite experience, James seems to have reasoned, and he challenged Hegel's denial that this transcending of its own identity was achievable by any finite entity.

He received aid, in his rôle of challenger, from the works of Henri Bergson. With Bergson's aid, he tells us (probably over-modestly, since one of James's important articles in *Mind* for 1884 is cited by Bergson himself in 1889 — *Time and Free Will*, p. 29) James came to see that the conceptual treatment of the flow of reality had a practical rather than a speculative value. Concepts are discrete and disparate, cutting reality up into small bits which bear but little resemblance to the original flux, and valuable only because they afford a basis for a return to the sensible flow of experience. In this stream of feeling consciousness, if anywhere, reality is to be found. And in this flux of reality, we see clearly, the logic of identity cannot apply. Reality overflows our logic. All the Zenos in the world cannot keep Achilles from catching the tortoise. Here any moment of experience is "its own other." The pulses of consciousness interpenetrate. "The rush of our thought forward through its fringes is the everlasting peculiarity of its life."

Here then is the solution of our problem as to how the many can be one. Every smallest pulse of experience is a manifold which is at the same time a unity. The absolute may, as Hegel says, take its other up into itself. But this is just what happens when every individual morsel of the sensational stream takes up its adjacent morsels by coalescing with them. "Here inside the minimal pulses of experience is realized that very inner complexity which the transcendentalists say only the absolute can genuinely possess. . . . Something ever goes indissolubly with something else." [30] So we can no longer have any objection to the hypothesis that states of consciousness can be compounded. Every smallest state of consciousness overflows its own definition. And since in the *Principles* James had advocated the theory that the self was nothing but successive states he now passed easily from the admission that these states are capable of compounding themselves to the admission that finite selves are also capable of such compounding.[31]

The reason for this lengthy digression to examine James's analysis of the logic of the absolute will now become apparent when we observe that while James seems to have cleared away his difficulties as to the logic of the situation, he does not come forward with a glad espousal of the absolute. Instead he brings out a conception wholly as fantastic and much more unusual, Fechner's theory of an over-soul. Why does he choose this rather than the absolute?

Professor Arthur O. Lovejoy writing in the *International Journal of Ethics* for January 1911 makes James's motive for

[30] *A Pluralistic Universe*, p. 284.

[31] An admission in which Royce, for one, took great delight. Cf., e.g., *The Problem of Christianity*, vol. 2, pp. 31 ff.

refusing to accept the claims of idealistic monism wholly logical. James's philosophy, he maintains, was not arbitrarily put together to include all the propositions it would be congenial to believe. " Unlike the English Hegelians, religiously inclined, who try to eat their cake and have it too " James showed a " logical scrupulosity " which forbade his fashioning a theory of being to justify all his religious demands. James indeed claims to be " resentful because my absolutist friends seemed to me to be stealing the privilege of blowing both hot and cold. To establish their absolute they used an intellectualist type of logic which they disregarded when employed against it. It seemed to me that they ought at least to have mentioned the objections that had stopped me so completely. I had yielded to them against my ' will to believe ' out of pure logical scrupulosity." [32]

But need this logical scrupulosity have deterred James any longer after the elaborate argument we have just considered had broken down all logical barriers? James makes a definite break with logic, he tells us, having been shown by Bergson that logic is unable to cope with reality as it is found in the continuum of the sensible flux. Turning from concepts to percepts James solves the problem which had stood between him and the absolute. Many consciousnesses can compound themselves to form one consciousness. Whether, then, we say that he has solved his problem logically or that he has cast logic to the four winds, is it possible longer to maintain that it is " logical scrupulosity " which keeps him from becoming a loyal absolutist?

But if not logic, what did keep him? Our answer is: A sense for religious values both mystically and pragmatically appraised. Logic entered the situation at all only as pragmatic logic. The absolute simply did not satisfy demands which James could not ignore. And these were not primarily the demands of logical consistency. We have seen that James was susceptible to the charms of the absolute. He was at times a " sick soul." He felt keenly the need for security. He never

[32] *A Pluralistic Universe,* p. 197.

tires of repeating the statement that the need for a realm in which our ideals are eventually brought to fruition is one of the deepest needs of the human breast.[33] And in his healthy-minded periods he knew the value of a moral holiday. But with all its virtues, certain qualities of the absolute could not be forgiven or ignored. It was more " intimate " than theism's " exalted monarch," yet not intimate enough. It was noble, yet that very nobility was a disqualification. The God of heaven and earth could not be a gentleman. God is the only being who cannot be remote.

The problem of evil, that ancient stumbling-block, was for James with his human sympathies and interests much too real and too pressing to be passed over lightly. It was not a problem susceptible of a so-called " logical " solution, such as calling it the " privation of good," the dark side of the picture, or the antithesis of the synthesis. As James himself observed, where the problem of evil for absolutism is the speculative one of how evil arose, for pragmatism it is the practical one of how to get rid of it.

James does, it is true, refer in the *Varieties*[34] to the speculative difficulty of finding the origin of evil in a God who is wholly good. And in a certain very limited sense it may be said to be the logic of the situation which drives him to postulate a finite God. But surely the logical sense is most limited. The problem was logical only as every problem can be expressed in logical terms. The issues as they presented themselves in James's mind were living issues first and logically arranged afterward. His interest, emphatically, was not in deciding how evil can come from good. Rather was it the " melioristic " interest in what can be done about it. In so far as the question of origin presented itself at all it was in the reaction: how fearful is the evil of this world and how intolerable is any Deity who does not get rid of it when he has the power to do so! As he expresses it in *Pragmatism*, " The scale of evil defies all human tolerance, and transcendental idealism in Bradley or Royce carries us no further than the book of

[33] Cf. *The Will to Believe, etc.,* p. 83; *Pragmatism,* p. 106.   [34] P. 131.

Job. . . . A God who can relish such superfluities of horror is no God for human beings to appeal to." [35] Here again we see that the insight of the "sick soul" is not to be denied. Its craving for a final satisfactory solution is at variance with its own vision of the ultimate and irremediable horror of much in life. Our civilization *is* "founded on the shambles." Evil has a final quality about it which we may yearn to see transcended. But the facts of this life do not show such transcendence. No eternal ideal order can atone for the agony of suffering experienced here and now.

The only way out is but incompletely satisfactory. *Some* of this misery can be alleviated. Some comfort is attainable through active energetic effort. So the solution, in so far as there is one, is practical. The absolute, with its aloofness from practical affairs here shows its impotence, its ineptitude for human service. As James observes, the absolute is beautiful aesthetically, intellectually, and morally (in so far as the desire for security is moral). But *practically* it is less beautiful. And the practical deficiency counterbalances the virtues. It is "from a human point of view" that its faults are most apparent.

So it was partly from "human" and "practical" considerations that James finally turned from the absolute. The indifference of the absolute to the problem of evil and human suffering and to the problem of freedom and human achievement furnished James with a pragmatic motive for rejecting it. The absolute satisfied some pragmatic demands but it failed to satisfy others which were more important. It simply was not verified in the actual experience of human living. As a postulate it did not have sufficient value, it did not work.

It was also partly from considerations of religious intimacy. As James shows in *A Pluralistic Universe* [36] absolutism furnishes a greater degree of intimacy with the Deity than does dualistic theism, but pluralism's intimacy is still more close. And religion with its experience of *salvation,* its testimony that real, not merely apparent, evil has been transformed

[35] P. 142.   [36] Esp. Chap. VIII.

into good through its " saving experiences " is witness to the working of a Power that cannot be absolute, or the evil would not have existed in the first place, but that is all the more god-like and worshipful because of the community of its interests and purposes with those of humankind. Religious experience, mysticism itself, take on meaning and significance if the religious Object be not an absolute but one to whom our human problems will be real.

Confirmation is brought to our contention that the way was logically open for James to accept the absolute in the fact that he himself calls it a possible hypothesis which must be taken into account, but as a hypothesis only. It is not a presupposition of our thinking. On this James insists most strenuously. It is not a necessary implication such that a person makes himself illogical or ridiculous by denying it. This dogmatic assertion of the absolute's necessity always aroused James's ire. Absolutism is a hypothesis, but not a presupposition. And anti-absolutism is another hypothesis equally worthy of a hearing. Reality may be one, but then again it may be of the " strung-along variety." And we observe at once that to admit other hypotheses as equally worthy of consideration is to take a position with which the strict absolutist can have little sympathy. The fact that James required *any* entity, even the absolute, to give a pragmatic account of itself shows at what a far remove from thorough-going absolutism was his personal position, and is further evidence that James entertained the notion of the absolute at all only because he was attracted by its religious value.

Even when the logical barriers were down, then, and when the absolute was admissible as a hypothesis, James refused to adopt it as his own. But although the rejection of the absolute *per se* is definite, we find up till the end concessions to the kind of religious Object of which the absolute was the most extreme example. We may set down these concessions in order. First, as noted, James admitted the absolute as a hypothesis. The absolute is not only true " so far forth " but it is available for certain uses. We may resort to it when we have occasion to. For example, it may be taken abstractly or concretely. " Abstractly, like the word ' winter,' as a memorandum of past experience that orients us toward the future, the notion of the absolute world is indispensable." The anti-absolutistic relativity of James's position comes out yet more clearly when we read that the absolute may be accepted by some and not by others: " Concretely it is also indispensable to some minds, for it determines them religiously, being often a thing to change their lives by." [37] And James gives some support for the extreme view that we may accept the absolute when it works and reject it when it does not, as the mood changes.

Second, we may note that of all the hypothetical absolutes he encountered, James found that of Royce the least uncongenial. Ever and again we find partial exception made for Royce in the midst of James's anti-absolutistic tirades. The reason seems to be not so much James's respect for the ingenuity of Royce's reasoning, though this is mentioned, as the almost pragmatic character of Royce's absolute. The ideas of which it was composed were defined in terms of purpose and a valiant effort was made to keep the absolute itself from indifference to human good and evil.[38]

Third, James suggests more than once that the absolute would be much more acceptable if it could only be transformed into an Ultimate. " The two notions would have the same content — the maximally unified content of fact, namely — but their time-relations would be positively reversed." [39] We are interested, that is, not so much in the rational unity of things as in "their possible empirical unification." This conception of the absolute as an " ultimate " suggests at once the pragmatic conception of truth as a goal that we approach rather than a relation that underlies our thinking. Truth is a process of verification. " Truth *happens* to an idea. It *becomes*

[37] *Pragmatism*, pp. 266–7.

[38] Cf. Royce's treatments of the problem of evil in *The Spirit of Modern Philosophy, Studies of Good and Evil* and in fact all through his work.

[39] *Pragmatism*, p. 159, cf. *ibid.* pp. 165, 280 ff., also *The Meaning of Truth*, pp. 266–7.

true, is *made* true by events." [40] Just as truth is what we work *toward,* a terminus, not a starting point, so the absolute has its desirable aspects if conceived as the ideal goal of our effort, the final synthesis which we ourselves help to establish. James refers us in this connection to Schiller's essay on " Activity and Substance " where reality is postulated as the summation rather than the substratum of experience. " To find true being we must look upwards to the Ideal, not downwards to the unknowable. Our true self is not what underlies thought, will, and feeling, but what combines them in a perfect harmony; Reality is not what transcends experience but what perfects it." [41]

Fourth, James did save the absolute's religious qualities. We cannot overemphasize the fact that to give up the absolute was not to give up the hope of satisfying his religious aspirations. James denied the absolute to affirm God. The absolute, as he often insists, is not the God of the prophets. " The absolute has nothing but its superhumanness in common with the theistic God." [42] The God to whom James did give his allegiance, as we shall see in another connection, was a God who could make a difference in the details of human living, for whom the particular facts of experience were matters of real concern, and who was able to grant to his worshippers mystical experiences of a " saving " nature.

James's final word on the absolute, then, was one of rejection, based chiefly on moral and religious grounds. Professor Hocking has said that " In *Pragmatism* and later works James became more or less tolerant of the Absolute," [43] but our evidence suggests that toward the end James's tolerance grew less instead of greater. At least it is true that only toward the end did he carry through a sustained argument whose object was the absolute's downfall. He seems to have been willing finally to do away with it because he had found such an adequate substitute. Fechner's over-soul, author of mystical experiences, plausible explanation of the way in which conscious-

---

[40] *Pragmatism*, p. 201.   [41] *Humanism*, p. 225.
[42] *Pragmatism*, p. 299; cf. *A Pluralistic Universe*, p. 134, Varieties, p. 522.
[43] *The Meaning of God in Human Experience*, p. 184n.

nesses can be compounded and the larger relations directly experienced, and truly intimate object of religious devotion, appealed to James both pragmatically and religiously. And it could only so appeal because it was in harmony with the philosophical belief a radical empiricist was compelled to hold, the belief in pluralism, which must now engage our attention.

III

THE PLURALISMS

I THINK it would have depressed him," wrote Professor Santayana of James, " if he had had to confess that any important question was finally settled. He would still have hoped that something might turn up on the other side, and that just as the scientific hangman was about to dispatch the poor convicted prisoner, an unexpected witness would ride up in hot haste, and prove him innocent." [1] But this conflict between the absolute and pluralism was full of issues which were too vital to permit a prolonged suspension of judgment. Pragmatism is introduced in the book by the same name as a method for settling just such metaphysical disputes, and James could not be expected to refrain from applying it to what was for him the most suggestive of all dilemmas. Bringing the pragmatic method and temper to bear on the problem, James finds that " with her criterion of the practical differences that theories make," pragmatism must " equally abjure absolute monism and absolute pluralism. The world is One just so far as its parts hang together by any definite connection. It is many just so far as any definite connection fails to obtain." [2]

This may be all very well speculatively, but does it settle our religious problem? Can we afford to wait until all the evidence is in before daring to give expression to religious feeling? Clearly we cannot, and James, author of *The Will to Believe* and champion of the view that faith may be necessary where assurance is impossible, knows that we cannot. So a

[1] *Character and Opinion in the United States*, p. 82.
[2] *Pragmatism*, p. 156.

more definite conclusion is reached a few pages further on, where James finds that "Pragmatism, pending the final empirical ascertainment of just what the balance of union and disunion among things may be, must obviously range herself on the pluralistic side. . . . [The] hypothesis of a world imperfectly unified still . . . must be sincerely entertained." [3] That is, pragmatism inclines to meliorism, a form of religious pluralism which insists that there is no assurance at present of the final salvation of the things that man holds dear, but that these things will be saved if at all by the joint effort of man and God in the quest for value.

James reaches a similar position in *A Pluralistic Universe.* The alternative is there drawn definitely between the "block universe" and the world composed of parts related in some ways and unrelated in others. These two "make pragmatically different ethical appeals." [4] We may choose either as we please, but the possibility of choosing either must be admitted. "Reality *may* exist distributively, just as it sensibly seems to, after all. On that possibility I do insist."

And for himself and his own view of life James insists on more than this possibility. The prodigal son attitude of monism is not the last word in philosophy, though it has its own pragmatic value and makes its own appeal. In the last analysis religion does not call us, as losers in the game of life, to weep on our Father's shoulder. Its message is much more adequately expressed in the words heard by Ezekiel: "Son of man, stand upon thy feet and I will speak unto thee." Life is real and life is earnest, its dangers and losses are real, as the "sick soul" knows only too well; but so are its victories and achievements.

So James is a pluralist. But what does this mean? Pluralism has stood for many different things in the history of philosophy. Atomism has been called pluralistic, and so has monadism. Yet James's philosophy does not read like that of either Democritus or Leibnitz. With Lotze James has more in common, particularly with Lotze's idea that reality is incomplete. With

[3] *Pragmatism*, p. 161.   [4] *A Pluralistic Universe*, p. 327.

Wundt's teleology and voluntarism there is also some affinity.
A less well known pluralist writer for whose views James professed sympathy is Lutoslawski. This author's theory of a
world of independent eternal spirits can be found in several
works.[5] Less individualistic, or, as the critics of pluralism
would say, less anarchical is the theory of James Ward, whose
pluralism shows its conservative nature in the fact that it finds
in theism its unified completion. Howison's *The Limits of Evolution* is an attempt to steer between what the author believed
was Royce's monistic failure to allow for individual freedom
and responsibility on the one hand, and what he considered
James's irrational chaos on the other. Dr. Hastings Rashdall
in his essay on " Personality: Human and Divine " also pleads,
in pluralistic fashion, for a system which shall insure each person's independence of his fellows, though not of God. Professor
McTaggart's pluralistic illustration is that of a " College "
which suggests a community of selves contained within an
absolute self.

Of that group of thinkers in whose theories of pluralism
James found a more direct confirmation of his own views, most
prominent is Professor F. C. S. Schiller, whose " humanism "
seemed to James to be pluralism of the right sort. Bergson's
ability to discover the constant working of a creative principle
by which circumstances apparently played-out and sterile were
made to yield an element wholly new James also welcomed
as supporting his own pluralistic view of the fact of novelty.
At times James refers to the individualism of Thomas Davidson, and quotes apparently with favor Davidson's view of the
universe as "a republic of immortal spirits." C. S. Peirce, who
influenced James along pragmatic lines, may also be called a
pluralist in his stress on the importance of the particular in
logical theory. B. P. Blood, whom James discovered and
brought before the public eye, claimed to be both a pluralist
and a mystic. Yet a study of his posthumously published *Pluri-
verse* suggests that his chief contribution to the philosophy of

[5] Cf. esp. *Über die Grundvoraussetzung und Consequenzen der individual-
ischen Weltanschauung*, p. 79.

pluralism lies in the attention he has called to the operation in the cosmos of a law which runs counter to the law of gravitation. If gravitation, the monistic principle which draws all things unto itself, were not counteracted, stars and planets would soon fuse in a conglomerate central mass. A pluralistic, divisive principle must be invoked to explain the fact that this does not occur. James seems to have been greatly attracted by Blood's unique and picturesque literary style. " Ever not quite " is a phrase of Blood's which James often quoted as expressive of the pluralistic position. But much more thorough-going was the influence of Gustav Fechner, whose panpsychism hinted at a solution of the psychological problems of mysticism, and whose attention to empirical detail suggested a pluralistic point of view. James often refers with approval to Fechner's theory of a hierarchy of selves which are independent yet members of one great cosmic consciousness.

The most important pluralistic influence on James, however, was undoubtedly that of Renouvier. This writer's pluralism may be called physical, metaphysical, and religious. So pervasive is it that one feels it can only be the product of a strong anti-monistic feeling. " Le monisme a pour invariable compagnon le determinisme," Renouvier tells us, and with a certain pluralistic vigor: " Ma conscience préfère cet individu misérable à toute la fantasmagorie des monismes." [6] The havoc that monism has wrought in the history of religion is graphically described in the *Psychologie rationnelle*.[7] Absolutism is an unworthy philosophy. The absolutistic habit of mind has led to intolerance and fanaticism. Freedom must be real and novelty must be also. There are many consciousnesses, not one all-embracing consciousness. And in the *Principes de la Nature* Renouvier explains that the physical world is made up of atoms and monads. But this means that, if we are not to be confronted with an infinity which is inconceivable and inconsistent, we must look on the world as made up of a limited number of separate units. Applied to the temporal sequence

[6] Cf. *Esquisse d'une Classification systématique*, 2: 241.
[7] In *Essais de Critique générale, Deuxième Essai*, 1875, 3: 253.

this suggests that instead of an infinite regress we must postulate a beginning in time. And if a beginning occurred once it can occur again, which means that novelty and freedom are not only demanded but entirely possible. And this in turn leaves room, as James explains, for " absolute novelties, unmeditated beginnings, gifts, chance, freedom, and acts of faith." [8]

This reference to writers who in one sense or another may be called pluralistic should be sufficient to suggest that the philosophy of diversity has itself been diversely interpreted. Pluralism has been defined by Professor John Dewey in Baldwin's *Dictionary of Philosophy* as " the metaphysical doctrine that all existence is ultimately reducible to a multiplicity of distinct and independent beings or elements." But as Professor F. J. E. Woodbridge shows, in his article in Hastings' *Encyclopaedia of Religion and Ethics,* pluralism in the past has been at times of the materialistic variety and at other times spiritualistic, while the newer pluralistic theories are better described as a philosophical tendency than as a definitely formulated system. In *The Persistent Problems of Philosophy* by Professor Mary W. Calkins we find a distinction made between numerical pluralism and the pluralism which is qualitative. Numerical pluralism regards the world as composed of many separate parts of the same kind. Qualitative pluralism denies the sameness of kind and asserts the existence of a distinction such as that between mind and matter. James was clearly a numerical pluralist. Yet his radical empiricism, the theory that " pure experience " is the only reality, would seem to make him qualitatively a monist. But right here the danger of overclassification, against which James warned so often and so vigorously, is apparent. James was a monist in his radical empiricism, but this statement should be followed immediately by the remark that very few have seen as clearly as he the distinctions between kinds of things and kinds of activities. His monism was limited to his theory of the knowing-process.

What, then, was James's pluralism? The best method for

[8] *Some Problems of Philosophy,* p. 164.

arriving at an answer to this question seems to be first to take the general connotation in James's mind of his conception of pluralism, then to note its more specific denotations as applied in differing situations, then to observe some of the corollaries of these specific conceptions, and finally to determine, if possible, whether there be order of importance among these conceptions themselves.

Taking the more general aspect first, then, we see at once that pluralism, if not chiefly, was in a very important way, a revolt against absolutism. James could not be an absolutist. If in order not to be one he had to be something else, then he was willing to be a pluralist, or almost anything. Much of the time this seems to be uppermost in his mind. Let us have done with absolutism, and let us espouse anything that will save us from it. James calls Paulsen a pluralist, for example, but, as is clear in his preface to the English translation of the *Introduction to Philosophy,* he is really referring to Paulsen's anti-absolutistic method and theory. With his ready and sympathetic interest in whatever was original and significant, James found the intolerance of the absolute itself intolerable. Setting itself up as the Whole of reality the absolute is at once too big for us to approach it intimately in religion, and too small to include all in itself. Some bits must always escape. With all its compromise and mediations, yes, because of them, pluralism is a finer and worthier and more virile conception, and as such must hold our allegiance.

Our contention that this general connotation of pluralism as an anti-absolutistic attitude loomed large in James's mind is confirmed by the fact that James seems to have been little attracted by anything that a strict pluralism had to offer *per se.* He was indeed an individualist, but individualism seems to be the application of pluralism to human relations, rather than itself a pluralism. James was not an atomist in the sense of having any theory as to the physical constitution of the universe. Nor was he a monadist. " I see you take pluralism as necessarily monadistic," he wrote to Professor Mary W. Calkins of Wellesley College (in an unpublished letter dated

May 20, 1907), " which I don't see as a necessity. The last two essays in Schiller's *Studies in Humanism* are a beginning of pluralistic evolutionism. If you start with tychism, you can have relations between terms vary, as well as terms, so you needn't remain monadistic." Nor did James have any interest in numbers for their own sake. His works give little evidence of any particular interest in mathematics. The Many had no mystical appeal for him such as the One at times actually did have. He was delighted to find a writer who claimed that the Many did exert such an attraction, but even in this case he had to admit that Benjamin Paul Blood's pluralistic mysticism was rather a " left wing voice of defiance " than an interest in the many on their own account.[9]

His own system in fact requires a universe as much as it does a multiverse. James is no exponent of a chaos. Time and again he inveighs against the criticism of his position which describes it as denying all connection between things. This very criticism, he claims, is a product of the absolutistic temper. It springs from the belief that what destroys some connection destroys all connection. James's demand is simply for *some* separation along with considerable connection. He asks for the " slightest wiggle of independence," anything to break up the awful and foreboding uniformity of the absolute. James does not even become as pluralistic as he might. In *A Pluralistic Universe* where he definitely champions pluralism he has much to say of a " continuum." Reality is a flux, there is a stream of consciousness, we must take account of the flow of time. And he points with approval to Fechner and Bergson, yet it could easily be argued that the monistic tendencies of both these writers were as important as the pluralistic.

Let us notice further that James does not use the conceptions of these men in a way which is unequivocally pluralistic. He drew from Fechner the conception of a great " mother-sea " or " fountain-head " of consciousness in which all our finite consciousnesses are confluent. But the use made of this conception in his Ingersoll lecture on *Human Immortality*

[9] Cf. *Memories and Studies*, p. 374.

actually gave rise as we have seen to the criticism that he left no scope for individuality. James clearly " abjured absolute pluralism," just as pragmatism did. He had none of the belief in pluralism as a goal to be attained at all cost which he accused monists of having with regard to their Absolute or their Unity. Pluralism has no intrinsic interest. Mystically it makes no appeal. Aesthetically it attracts only indirectly, as one may have an interest in a particular detail. Logically it presents itself as one among many hypotheses.

In its general aspect, then, pluralism is both a revolt against absolutism, and a means to moral and religious values. What more specific things does it denote? A few of James's definitions come at once to mind. Pluralism is the description of reality as of the " strung-along variety." It is a theory of " a world imperfectly unified still." [10] It is " the belief that the world is still in process of making." [11] It is the theory that " the sundry parts of reality may be externally related." [12]

These more specific definitions have many specific applications. The first to consider is the application to the theory of knowledge. Pluralistic influence here may be summed up in the statement that knowledge is incomplete. If it were not, we should not now be arguing about it. The world of experience is too indefinite in extent and too transient and growing in nature for the absolute or any one knower to know it all. But the fact that knowledge is incomplete should not discourage us. It grows, at least sometimes. And when it does, it grows in spots, — piecemeal, not all over. Some parts of knowledge are unrelated to other parts. There is no through-and-through relation. Relations are not constitutive, they are not integral to the terms related. One man's knowledge is independent of that of another man. And the objects of knowledge are as independent of each other as are the subjects. We know particular things. Concepts are nothing but means to more knowledge of particulars. This is what James calls the " additive " constitution of knowledge; or " noetic plural-

[10] *Pragmatism*, p. 161.
[11] *Meaning of Truth*, p. 226.
[12] *A Pluralistic Universe*, p. 321.

ism," a system of "concatenated knowing, going from next to next" which is "verified every moment when we seek information from our friends." [13]

But now, if knowledge be "additive" in this way, and if parts of it be relatively independent of other parts, what shall we say of the connections that we do find? Monism points to a relationship *durcheinander,* the meaning of each member implicit in the meaning of every other, each term determined by the sum of the relations into which it enters. For pluralism, however, the relations are external. The terms are not constituted by the relations, and are not touched at all by many relations which exist for other terms. "Each relation is one aspect, character, or function [of the term], way of its being taken or way of its taking something else; and . . . a bit of reality when actively engaged in one of these relations is not *by that very fact* engaged in all the other relations simultaneously. The relations are not *all* what the French call *solidaires* with one another. Without losing its identity, a thing can either take up or drop another thing like . . . [a] log." [14]

Relations and connections for pluralism, that is to say, are possible, not necessary. I may look to the right or to the left, and my looking is independent of the direction in which I look. Not being necessary, the relations are not constitutive. As J. S. Mill once observed, Newton is not prevented from being a mathematician by the fact that he is an Englishman. Relations imply not universal co-implication, but a "strung-along" condition. But if relations are external, how are they known? it may be asked. Relations there must be, to avoid chaos. Absolutism may give a closed system, but at least it lets us know that the relations are there. How can radical empiricism meet this difficulty? It can, says James, by finding that relations are as much objects of perception as are the terms related. The relations are given in experience. It is unnecessary to call on monism for aid in this relating process. Pluralism

[13] *Some Problems of Philosophy,* p. 129.
[14] *A Pluralistic Universe,* p. 323.

is thus not merely a general protest against the absolutistic
method. It is also a specific protest against what James calls
"vicious intellectualism," or "excluding from the fact named
what the name's definition fails positively to include," a protest against and remedy for the logical dilemma in which monism finds itself when it tries to explain how two things can
be related.[15]

So pluralism is a theory of the nature of reality as well as
of knowledge. Reality itself is additive. This is brought out
clearly by the emphasis James lays on selective activity. In
the *Principles of Psychology*,[16] James shows that selection is
the chief function of consciousness, just as he elsewhere shows
that it is the chief function of sensation. The importance of
selection is again seen in radical empiricism's world of pure
experience, where novelty consists in the new grouping of
elements already given. Biologically, it is the selective activity
of the human organism that gives meaning to life and that
makes it possible to call human activity purposeful. Cogni-
tively selection is a large part of the knowing process. It is
the chief part if we think, with radical empiricism, of consciousness as merely the regrouping of elements which are
already given.

Now this fact of human selective activity helps to explain
in what sense the universe may be of the growing or "additive" sort. We may choose [17] whether we shall regard a line
as running from east to west or from west to east — the line
itself remains passive. In a puzzle picture we pick out the
lines that are pertinent to our purpose. At night we observe
the heavens and select patterns which we call constellations.
But this is creation. This is humanly making an addition to
data already given. It is taking the world as formless yet
plastic and molding it to suit our purpose. As Lotze has said,
our descriptions are themselves important additions to reality.
We can contribute to reality and improve on it. " Our philos-

---

15 Cf. *A Pluralistic Universe*, p. 60.
16 Chap. IX on "*The Stream of Thought*."
17 *Pragmatism*, p. 252 ff.

ophies swell the current of being, add their character to it." [18]
So just as knowledge grows in spots, reality grows not integrally but piecemeal. Our human additions to reality suggest one of the ways in which it grows. And all the evidence
goes to prove that each bit of reality has its own external
environment. "Things are with one another in various ways,
but nothing includes everything, or dominates over everything. The word 'and' trails along after every sentence.
Something always escapes. 'Ever not quite.'" [19]

James sometimes tries to explain the pluralistic nature of
reality by contrasting a "concatenated" with a "consoli-
dated" union. The only example of true consolidation that
we know is gravitation. This is a truly monistic principle,
binding all matter together in an inexorable synthesis. But
there are many examples of concatenation. You can have wire
and copper without having a telephone system, but you can't
have a telephone without wire and copper. There is acquaintance without love, but there is no love without acquaintance.
These are concatenated relations — partially inclusive, partially exclusive.[20] The same thing can belong to many systems
without being "constituted" by any one of them, as when
"a man is connected with other objects by heat, by gravitation,
by love, and by knowledge."

This should be sufficient to show that James applies his
pluralistic conception to a wide variety of cases and finds it
vindicated in each instance. He cites, as we shall notice elsewhere in more detail, the moral consciousness with its demand for intimacy, the additive character of knowledge, the
selective nature of human activity, the apparent separateness
of terms and externality of relations, and all the evidences we
have of an imperfectly unified and growing world. He further
appeals, for confirmation of his pluralistic view, to what he
calls the perceptual flow of experience, and to this we must
now attend.

[18] *A Pluralistic Universe,* p. 317.
[19] *A Pluralistic Universe,* p. 321.
[20] Cf. *Some Problems of Philosophy,* p. 130.

A familiar contrast in James is that between percepts and concepts. Through the former we touch reality. The latter are inadequate in their representation of reality because they break it up into bits and fail to give an account of its continuousness. Now on the surface it would appear that a continuum which has been broken up into discrete bits has become more instead of less pluralistic, and since reality is plural it ought by this means to have become more real. James seems to have felt, however, that pluralism implied not so much discreteness as a growing, changing quality. A thing which grows must be many, even though it is a many-in-one.

But if we follow further James's idea of the flowing character of reality and his attempt to fit it to his pluralistic scheme we discover more difficulties. Professor Lovejoy [21] has shown that James really set forth three different and conflicting theories as to the nature of the perceptual flux of reality. In *A Pluralistic Universe* James insists on the " coalescence " and " compenetration " of the bits of experience. At the same time he describes perceptual reality as a " continuum." These two ideas are contradictory, Professor Lovejoy asserts, for if each pulse of experience completely coalesced with each other there could be no continuum, but all moments of time would be completely fused together in an eternal timeless moment. We may note in passing, however, that " coalescence " and " compenetration " need not mean *complete* merging of every bit of experience with every other bit. James's argument is directed, in fact, against precisely the sort of reasoning which tries to include too much in a definition. It seems wholly possible to assert that one moment blends into another without asserting that the blending is entire, with nothing left unblended.

However this may be, Professor Lovejoy's further criticism seems entirely valid. It is that James's assertion that reality is a continuum contradicts his statement that perceptual reality comes in bits. This latter view is clearly expressed in *A*

[21] Art. " The Problem of Time in Recent French Philosophy," *Philosophical Review,* 21: 538 ff.

Pluralistic Universe and also in *Some Problems of Philosophy.*
In this his last book James says, for example, " Either your
experience is of no content, of no change, or it is of a per-
ceptible amount of content or change. Your acquaintance with
reality grows literally by buds or drops of perception. Intellectually and on reflection you can divide these into components, but as immediately given, they come totally or not at
all." [22]

This it will at once be seen is much nearer a pluralistic theory
of reality than is the theory of the " experience-continuum "
which James also sets forth. A continuum can only with difficulty, accompanied by paradoxes and puzzles, be made a pluralism. But a reality growing by definite increments shows its
pluralistic affinities from the start. To our definitions of what
pluralism meant to James we must add, then, that pluralism
was for him a description of the way in which reality presents
itself to perceptual experience, and so, since percepts are our
most adequate means of knowing reality, it is a description of
reality as it is.

To recapitulate, pluralism is more than a general protest
against absolutism and a means to moral and religious value.
It is specifically a theory of the additive nature of knowledge,
of the disjunctive and external nature of relations, of the discreteness of parts of reality, of the finite numerical nature of
bits of the universe. But it is yet more. Pluralism is applied
by James, as it is by Fechner, to the realm of personal spirits.
James was interested not merely in showing that new beginnings happened in time, but in pointing out that they happened through the agency of persons. The independence and
creative ability of the personal individual are matters of extreme importance. In a passage in *Mind* for 1903 James says:
" Radical empiricism thus leads to the assumption of a collectivism of personal lives (which may be of any grade of
complication, and superhuman or infrahuman as well as
human), variously cognitive of each other, variously conative
or impulsive, genuinely evolving and changing by effort and

[22] Pp. 154–5, cf. Chaps. X, XI.

trial, and by their interaction and cumulative achievements making up the world." [23] And a later passage expresses the same idea: "If the ' melioristic ' universe were *really* here, it would require the active good-will of all of us, in the way of belief as well as of our other activities, to bring it to a prosperous issue. The melioristic universe is conceived after a *social* analogy as a pluralism of independent powers." [24] Elsewhere he carries further the notion that the universe may be peopled by an order of beings other than human with whom we may be in close relation as respectively objects and subjects of the religious experience. The universe might conceivably be a collection of godlike selves.[25] This is unblushingly called a " polytheistic " view [26] or " piecemeal super-naturalism." [27]

The final application of James's pluralism is made, then, in the world of spirit and personality. James believed, as did Fechner, in a " collectivism " of striving, coöperating beings, human and superhuman. This brings us at once to the most important corollary of James's pluralism, which was his individualism. It was because of its conflict with the rights of the individual that the absolute had to be discarded. James has been criticized for neglecting, in his book on religious experience, to treat institutions, forms, and observances of religion. But the reason for this neglect is clear and will be increasingly acceptable to the student of religion as the present wave of overemphasis on social institutions spends itself. It was quite rightly the individual, not the institution, that engaged James's attention, the *varieties* of religious experience, not their standardization. As James himself remarks, on the first page of his lecture on " Human Immortality," too often the institution defeats its own ends, and stands in the way of the individual wants it was organized to gratify. And again, " Surely the individual, the person in the singular number, is

[23] Reprinted in *Collected Essays and Reviews,* p. 444.

[24] *Some Problems of Philosophy,* p. 228.

[25] *Varieties,* p. 525.

[26] *Varieties,* p. 526.

[27] *Varieties,* p. 523.

the more fundamental phenomenon, and the social institution, of whatever grade, is but secondary and ministerial." [28] " There is very little difference between one man and another," he quotes from his carpenter friend, " but what there is is very important." James shares Carlyle's view that progress comes through individual rather than group activity.[29] And the absolute, as we have seen, is inadequate simply because "the facts and worths of life need many cognizers to take them in."

Closely related to James's individualism is his democracy. "Pluralism in philosophy," says S. Radhakrishnan, "is the logical development of the spirit of democracy; for he who has respect for sacredness of individuality will not be inclined to sacrifice this uniqueness for the sake of the absolute." [30] James's democracy included an interest in people of alien culture and traditions as having " insides of their own," and showed itself for example in many protests against the American occupation of the Philippines. In this imaginative interest, both in the rights of the foreigner and in his ability to reach universal truth, James shows his affiliation with the Romantic movement, though it must be said that he did not share the Romantic flair for the picturesque and exotic in itself. His interest was rather in the application of the philosophic principle that truth is not limited to the vision of one nation or race. Mention should also be made of the similarity of James's view to the Kantian maxim to treat " every human being as an end withal, and never as a means."

James strikes this note of sympathy for the point of view of the individual, wherever he may be found, time and again in his writings. In his lecture on immortality he reminds his hearers that the desires and aspirations after immortality of Chinese and Hottentots are as much to be respected as those of Bostonians. And in his " Talks to Students on Some of Life's Ideals " he reiterates the fact that the whole of truth is

---

[28] *Memories and Studies*, p. 102.
[29] Cf. Essay on " Great Men and Their Environment."
[30] *The Reign of Religion in Contemporary Philosophy*, p. 39.

not revealed to any one observer. Even prisons and sick rooms
have their special revelations. In *The Varieties of Religious
Experience* he stresses the fact that the mystic's vision is
authoritative for himself and unassailable. And in many ways
he makes it clear that not only truth, but value as well, grows
up inside finite experiences. The values which we know are
those achieved by individual striving human beings. As it is
expressed in the essay on " What Makes a Life Significant,"
" The solid meaning of life is always the same eternal thing,
— the marriage, namely, of some unhabitual ideal, however
special, with some fidelity, courage and endurance; with some
man's or woman's pains."

Allied to James's individualism was what might be called his
" particularism." Like many other pragmatists, he was a
nominalist. Truth grows by individual knowers; and the objects of the knowing process are as individual as its subjects.
One of the difficulties James found with the absolute was
that it precluded the possibility of knowing things separately.
In our discussion of the conflict in his mind we noted that
he makes a contrast between Hegel as an example of the
unifying and simplifying tendency and Renouvier as " the
greatest living insister that simplicity shall not overwhelm
clearness." " Clearness " in this context means careful attention to detail, regard for the integrity of the parts, and unwillingness to let them be swallowed up in the whole. Professor
Dewey has expressed a similar sentiment: " Philosophy for-
swears inquiry after absolute origins and absolute finalities
in order to explore specific values and the specific conditions
that generate them." [31] James's way of putting it is: " Acquaintance with realities' diversities is as important as understanding their connection." [32] " James maintained toward each
new fact an attitude of liberal expectancy," says Professor
Lovejoy in his article " William James as Philosopher " in the
International Journal of Ethics, Volume 21. His interest was
directed not merely toward the great uniformities and cate-

[31] *Influence of Darwin on Philosophy*, p. 13.
[32] *Pragmatism*, p. 130.

gories, but also toward the "unclassified residuum." No religious experience was too wild or too little amenable to conventional classification for him to examine and explore it. No "Spinoza of the Ghetto" or "rustic Hegel" was too uncouth to attract his eager interest.

But, as Professor Lovejoy also points out, James was not democratic enough to be over-tolerant. His liberal interest was not what Mr. William Archer has called "color-blind neutrality." He was too sensitive to life's contrasts. But this awareness of diversity is again a part of the pluralistic attitude. It is only the monist who ignores the distinctions and sees all as one completely luminous moment. The pluralist admits that good and evil are related, but he denies that good and evil are to be defined merely in terms of this relationship. Monism takes the relation as creating the term. But pluralism insists that goodness *quā* goodness is different from goodness defined simply as that which overcomes evil. It is another case of the externality of relations, for which pluralism contends. The claim that the relation between good and evil is definitive is a most glaring example of the vicious monistic belief in through-and-through relationship. Pluralism with its view that things may be related in external fashion again vindicates itself morally.[33]

This account of the corollaries of pluralism — individualism, democracy, particularism — serves to confirm the contention that pluralism in and for itself had little attraction for James and that its chief importance lay in its by-products, corollaries and results. James does not expound a consistent and definitive idea of what pluralism is. It may mean a collectivism of personal souls, or the additive character of knowledge, or the piecemeal nature of reality, or the coalescence of bits of perceptual experience, or the discreteness of these same bits. Pluralism signifies one of these at one time and another at another. And here, it may be suggested, James's procedure was truly pragmatic. Pluralism is interesting and important not so much for what it is in itself, for it is many and various

[33] Cf. Professor R. B. Perry's *Present Philosophical Tendencies*, p. 246.

things in itself. It is important, rather, for what it is " known as " in human experience. Its value can be reckoned in terms of particular experiences. Its truth or falsity " makes a difference " in human living.

This leads to the question of the value of the pluralism. It is easy to see that just as pluralism itself cannot be limited to one definition, so its values are many. The first is its consistency with phenomenal appearance. The world is changing. " Monism doesn't account for it." Pluralism is consonant with " this colossal universe of concrete facts, their awful bewilderments, their surprises and cruelties." [34] The world comes to us in pieces. " The parts seem, as Hegel has said, to be shot out of a pistol at us. Each asserts itself as a simple brute fact, uncalled for by the rest." [35] These parts are arbitrary, foreign, jolting, discontinuous. As contrasted with the great totality, " *prima facie* there is this in favor of the eaches, that they are at any rate real enough to have made themselves at least *appear* to every one, whereas the absolute has as yet appeared immediately to only a few mystics." [36] We must remember also James's contention that the presence of the least jot of evil was enough to put a blemish on monism's spotless appearance. As he expressed it once to his class, " if at the last day all creation was shouting hallelujah and there remained one cockroach with unrequited love, *that* would spoil the universal harmony." [37]

Occasionally James talks as though its consistency with appearance were its most important feature. " The only way of escape from the paradoxes and perplexities of monism . . . is to be frankly pluralistic." [38] " The absolute involves features of irrationality peculiar to itself." [39] But James shows that we

---

[34] *Pragmatism*, p. 22.

[35] Essay " On Some Hegelisms," *The Will to Believe and Other Essays*, p. 264.

[36] *A Pluralistic Universe*, p. 129.

[37] Quoted in Santayana's Chapter on Royce, *Character and Opinion in the United States*, p. 108.

[38] *A Pluralistic Universe*, p. 310.

[39] *A Pluralistic Universe*, p. 129.

must not take him too seriously when he talks of deciding on "rational" grounds, except as we understand that "rational" in large measure means "emotional." For, "what divides us into possibility men or anti-possibility men is different faiths or postulates. . . . Talk as we will about having to yield to evidence, what makes us monists or pluralists, determinists or indeterminists, is at bottom always some sentiment like this."[40] James admits that pluralism has its blemishes and does not present a wholly attractive appearance. He quotes the remark of a friend that pluralism reminds him of the motion of a mass of maggots in their carrion bed. "But while I freely admit," he says, "that pluralism and restlessness are repugnant and irrational in a certain way, I find that every alternative to them is irrational in a deeper way."[41] "No matter what the content of the universe may be, if you only allow that it is *many* everywhere and always, that *nothing* real escapes from having an environment; so far from defeating its rationality, as the absolutists so unanimously pretend, you leave it in possession of the maximum amount of rationality practically attainable by our minds. Your relations with it, intellectual, emotional and active, remain fluent and congruous with your own nature's chief demands."[42]

Much more important, however, than any conformity to the world of appearance is pluralism's agreement with "the moral and dramatic expressiveness of life." Pluralism means "real possibilities, real indeterminations," real beginnings, real ends, real evil, real crises, catastrophes, and escapes, a real God, and a real moral life."[43] It does make a "pragmatically different ethical appeal." Pluralism lets loose the strenuous mood "since it makes the world's salvation depend upon the energizing of its several parts, among which we are."[44] It is a stimulating view, for its "disconnections are remedied in part

[40] *The Will to Believe and Other Essays*, p. 152.
[41] *The Will to Believe and Other Essays*, p. 177.
[42] *A Pluralistic Universe*, p. 319.
[43] *The Will to Believe*, p. ix.
[44] *Meaning of Truth*, p. 227.

by our behavior." [45] This moral and melioristic value and advantage of pluralism is so prominent throughout James's work that it needs no emphasis here.

But a third value of pluralism has not received so much attention from commentators on James. This is the value of religious intimacy. " It surely is a merit in a philosophy," says James, "to make the very life we lead seem real and earnest. Pluralism, in exorcising the absolute, exorcises the great de-realizer of the only life we are at home in, and thus redeems the nature of reality from essential foreignness." [46] Pluralism makes the Deity more approachable. It is as we have seen a striking sign of James's interest in this religious value that he is willing to grant that because of it, even absolute pantheism has an advantage over what he calls the " older theism." For theism is dualistic. It makes man " an outsider and mere subject to God, not his intimate partner."

But while James gives pantheism credit for establishing intimacy, he does so only in order to give pluralism more credit for establishing a greater degree of intimacy. Pluralism banishes the foreignness which accompanied the older theism more effectively than pantheism can hope to do. When God is a part of the world instead of the whole of it, divinity and humanity have more in common. When he is thought of as having an environment, as purposeful, as working in time, as interested in causes for which we too can strive, he escapes the isolation which accompanies the uniqueness of the absolute.

The force with which this religious value of pluralism appealed to James comes out in some of his more informal utterances. "Make the world a Pluralism," he exclaims in the letter to G. H. Howison quoted above, " and you forthwith have an object to worship." And to N. S. Shaler he writes that polytheism makes for a " warmer " sort of religious loyalty. We worship, he says, " rather like polytheists . . . a collection of beings who have each contributed and are now contributing to the realization of ideals more or less like those

[45] *A Pluralistic Universe*, p. 330.   [46] *A Pluralistic Universe*, p. 49.

for which we live ourselves. This more pluralistic style of feeling seems to me both to allow of a warmer sort of loyalty to our past helpers and to tally more exactly with the mixed condition in which we find the world as to its ideals." [47]

Consistency with appearances, the demands of rationality, the moral need for freedom and the religious need of intimacy, — all these helped to determine James's pluralistic bent. Which of these is most important for him? Is there priority among them? We are on highly speculative ground here, yet the topic is so important for our purposes that it is worth while to give attention to it.

One of the ablest writers on James has said that his pluralism flows directly from his theory of knowledge. Yet many evidences seem to point to the religious pluralism as primary and its implications for knowledge as secondary both temporally and in interest. Attention may be called to the fact that James considered himself a pluralist for some time before the niceties of his theory of knowledge were worked out. The term pluralism occurs early in James's works. So does the term " radical empiricism," it is true, with its implications for a theory of knowledge. But radical empiricism does not specifically denote the doctrine of experienceable relations until after the publication of the *Varieties* in 1902, that is, until the last decade of James's life. It is the religious value of pluralism which holds his attention at the beginning. The claim is not made that it alone determined the pluralism of the theory of knowledge. But it is affirmed that with pluralism established in James's mind as, on religious and moral grounds, the only acceptable philosophy, his imagination, ever restless, played with the epistemological implications of the pluralism to which he had already been attracted, and produced the view of the knowing process set forth in *Essays in Radical Empiricism*. Credence is lent to this interpretation of the workings of James's mind by the fact that the data for the theory of knowledge lay, so to speak, ready at hand, and capable of being developed into an epistemological pluralism

[47] *Letters*, 2: 155.

if James had been interested in such a development. In 1884 James published in *Mind* the article " On Some Omissions of Introspective Psychology," parts of which were later incorporated into the *Principles*, in which he sets forth the importance of the "transitive" states of consciousness. The existence of these states he later took as evidence of the perceptual character of relations, which became one of the cardinal tenets of his pluralistic theory of knowledge. But if his original interest had been epistemological, and if he had been on the lookout for data on which to build an epistemological pluralism, is it not surprising that he waited twenty years before making these applications, especially since during all this period he was continually writing of pluralism and showing its advantages?

Again we may ask, if James's interest is chiefly epistemological, why is it that we find the importance of the individual stressed so continually? What place has the individual in " a world of pure experience " ? Consciousness *per se* does not exist in such a world, being merely a name for the grouping of elements. Even in the *Principles* consciousness is made to consist in the shifting memories of the past possessed by a succession of mental states. Yet we know that individuals and individual differences and achievements were for James the all-important things in life. This importance is intelligible only on the supposition that James's chief interest lay in the religious and moral significance of pluralism. A merely epistemological interest could not have produced such a result.

The conclusion seems to be forced upon us that pluralism took on life and vividness and meaning for James in its religious aspect. He was led to an interest in pluralism at the beginning by a pragmatic regard for its efficacy in making moral and religious values possible. This strong *moral* interest in pluralism is clearly indicated, as we have seen, in *The Literary Remains of Henry James* published in 1884. That an active, strenuous religion calls for a pluralistic belief is set forth in *The Will to Believe* and the essays which follow it. That the pragmatic philosophy, making truth dependent on value, must also take its stand with pluralism is set forth in the volume called *Pragmatism*. Finally, that pluralism satisfies the peculiarly religious demand for intimacy with the soul of the cosmos is brought out in *A Pluralistic Universe*. As an advocate of pluralism James thought in religious terms and of religious values. Its implications for a theory of knowledge followed both in time and in importance.

Of the criticisms of pluralism, and they have been many, the most important seems to be the claim that the pluralist gives up the intellectual battle when it is at its height, and so relinquishes his claim to be a thinker. After using the principle of internality, so runs the accusation, for his own purposes, the pluralist at last stops before a plurality of terms or categories and refuses to define further, thus betraying the cause to which his humanistic impulse to understand had committed him. Pluralism thus cannot be final, for it fails to satisfy the urge to comprehend.

Yet it seems wholly possible to argue that life presents itself to us in terms which are not wholly comprehensible. Pluralism leaves us with mysteries on our hands, but it cannot well do otherwise. To take merely one illustration, the future is a mystery, and it accords with our sense of the appropriate that it should be so. For we insist on believing that the future is undetermined, and so unknowable. It is worth observing that our practical attitude toward the future retains this belief in its undetermined possibilities, in spite of the definite tendency among the sciences of our day, especially the biological and psychological, to urge the opposite theory. And pluralism claims that its responsiveness to this practical attitude is evidence of a more thorough-going desire to be inclusive and to make the theory fit all the facts than is monism's laudable but sometimes formalistic tendency to push the defining process to the very edges of the cosmos itself.

The whole question of pluralism and its value will engage us again, but it may be well before leaving this discussion to suggest that pluralism in many respects has more in common with the traditional philosophy of religion than has the monistic view with which religion has been more commonly associated. Pluralism makes more direct connection with a conception of the Infinite. It suggests the venturesomeness of the human attempt to include all Being in one category. In this respect, and especially in its notion of the " unclassified residuum " it leaves room for just that kind of mystery with which religion has always been concerned. It represents a protest against the view that the world of fact is as small as monism would make it. The urge to classify is primal, but it may also be claimed that it is eternal, and hardly capable of being satisfied at the present stage of man's development. The very categories of the understanding by which the classifying process is carried on have come into being, according to James's view, by reason of the useful function which they perform in organizing our experience. And who shall say that our present form of experience may not at some time be superseded?

There are two kinds of unity which it is desirable to strive for but which it also is improbable that we shall ever attain. The first is that just hinted at, the unity of the external world as an object of the human knowing process. The second is the unity of each individual human life. The first kind of unity is elusive because the world itself suggests an infinite number of possibilities and also because, again from the human point of view, it contains so much that sticks out from any classification and refuses to be included in any harmonious, unified scheme. Insanity is a fact of human experience, yet insanity repels all attempts at inclusion in a " higher synthesis." And similarly in each individual life there are experiences which do not fit into a unified arrangement. Life comes to us as an opportunity to make the best of each situation as it arises. It simply will not submit to the monistic yoke. This does not mean that man goes from one circumstance to another, recognizing his helplessness before each. It merely suggests that the degree of unity which any one of us can achieve varies with his abilities and to some extent with conditions. There are circumstances, such as that of death, over which we have little control, and the kind of unity which in spite of them we are able to attain seems at times meagre in amount and indifferent in quality.

But pluralism, it cannot be too often asserted, so far from being chiefly a philosophy of weakness, is on the moral side a philosophy which lays great stress on human creative achievement. And the pragmatic pluralism of James, as we shall have occasion to observe, in its freedom from abstractness reaches a kind of unity which is impossible for monistic intellectualism itself. It denies the existence of a break between the active life and the theoretical description of the active life. Truth and value, it claims, grow together out of human activity situations. Knowing is a part of the practical business of living. All departments of human activity touch each other in the unity of the life-process.

To the monist's contention that anything else than an intellectualistic unity is inconsistent because unthinkable, the pluralist can reply that any philosophy which fails to take account of what James called the moral and dramatic expressiveness of life in its lack of inclusiveness is even more unthinkable. And in place of his demand for a final unity the pluralist can point to the only kind of unity which life as we experience it offers, the unity of an unfolding process rich in undetermined possibility.

IV

THE FREE WILL

AFTER pluralism, freedom. When we have once been released from what James called the "monistic superstition" the way is open to a belief in freedom itself. A free choice of freedom is indeed the first step along the voluntaristic path which pluralism points. In this and the two succeeding chapters we shall notice some of the results of the triumph of the active impulses in James's conflict of moods as they are shown in the operation of the free, believing, and purposive will. The goal achieved by this active aggressive quest for religious value will be discussed under the headings, "The Deity" and "Immortality." The passive counterpart, when the eager surge of the will is over, and the human spirit waits for the touch of a Power which it cannot control, will be treated in the chapter on "Mysticism."

In his brilliant study entitled *William James,* Captain H. V. Knox, whom James in one of his letters calls "an extremely fine mind and character," observes that the question of free will is for James the point of transition from psychology to the larger problems of philosophy. And James himself calls the question of the possibility of volitional attention the "pivotal question of metaphysics, the very hinge on which our picture of the world shall swing from materialism, fatalism, monism, toward spiritualism, freedom, pluralism, — or else the other way." [1]

In James's own philosophy the question is indeed a pivotal one. Some of his principal theories owe their inception to it.

[1] *Principles of Psychology,* 1: 448.

Pluralism, for example, is, in its most important aspect, hardly describable except in terms of free will. " The only consistent way of representing pluralism and a world whose parts may affect one another through their conduct being either good or bad is the indeterministic way," James tells us in the essay on " The Dilemma of Determinism." And the indeterministic way here means the way of free will, for " future human volitions are as a matter of fact the only ambiguous things we are tempted to believe in." Or, expressed in terms of novelty, which for James is so distinctly a pluralistic conception: " Free will means nothing but real novelty; so pluralism accepts the notion of free will." [2]

Just as important is the relation to free will of meliorism, the belief that man can coöperate with God in building a better universe. " Persons in whom knowledge of the world's past has bred pessimism . . . may naturally welcome free will as a *melioristic* doctrine. It holds up improvement as at least possible. . . . Free will is thus a general cosmological theory of *promise*." [3]

Radical empiricism both offers evidence for freedom, and finds in turn that the fact of freedom confirms its own postulates. Whatever is in experience is real. But volition is an indubitable fact of experience. The volition which is accompanied by effort makes its presence felt with especial emphasis. " The existence of . . . effort as a phenomenal fact in our consciousness cannot, of course, be doubted or denied." [4] Volition for James means attention, and of attention he says: " We *feel* as if we could make it really more or less, and as if our free action in this regard were a genuine critical point in nature." [5] And again " Our sense of ' freedom ' supposes that some things at least are decided here and now." [6]

But radical empiricism does not merely point to freedom as an object of experience. It finds in the fact of free will evi-

[2] *Some Problems of Philosophy*, p. 141.
[3] *Pragmatism*, p. 119.
[4] *Principles of Psychology*, 2: 535.
[5] *Talks to Teachers*, p. 191.
[6] *Some Problems of Philosophy*, p. 139.

dence for its own theory of relations. This theory is expressed in the statement that " the relations between things, conjunctive as well as disjunctive, are just as much matters of direct particular experience, neither more so nor less so, than the things themselves." [7] To support this theory radical empiricism is quick to seize upon any evidence it can find of conjunctive relations which are obviously experienced. But the very experience of change is clearly the experience of a relation which binds that which went before to that which is coming after. And where is the fact of change more distinct than in the experience of deciding between two alternatives? As James explains in the essay on " The Experience of Activity " that which transcendental idealists have called a category of causation and have found to exist only in the synthetic activity of the mind itself, is actually found in free will or spiritual causation, as a definitely experienceable relation.

And while radical empiricism thus finds in the study of the free will question valuable data for its controversy with idealism, pragmatism discovers in the problem of freedom one of its excuses for being. For the problem of freedom is one of those metaphysical disputes which when left untouched by the pragmatic temper are interminable. Again, the fact of freedom and of creative possibility furnishes pragmatism with the grounds for its opposition to " rationalism." " The essential contrast is that for rationalism reality is ready-made and complete from all eternity, while for pragmatism it is still in the making." [8] Finally, the importance of freedom for pragmatism is hinted at in the fact that according to pragmatism truth is a quality which happens to ideas. For if we are free and have some control over the circumstances of life, we can bring our ideas into a position such that truth will happen to them more easily than otherwise. The whole pragmatic philosophy must indeed be understood in the light of its belief in the ability of the human individual to choose, and through choice to create. There is a world of objective fact, to be sure, but even in the realm of truth we must not let the presence of the

[7] *The Meaning of Truth*, p. xii.   [8] *Pragmatism*, p. 257.

objective element weigh on us too heavily. Human creative achievement plays its part just as truly as does conformity. The future is not completely contained in the past.

But if the future is in any degree independent of the past there must be a point at which novelty enters. James's contention is that this novel element makes its appearance in the purposive activity of the human organism. Not in a metaphysical conception of the self, nor yet in a theory of reality and its tendencies in the large, apart from human interests, but in the choosing and " carrying-on " of the human individual do we find a break in the rigid deterministic sequence. Somewhat as Darwin, viewing the matter biologically, found the secret of progress in the fact of individual variation, James rests his case for novelty in the universe on the ultimate resistance to classification exhibited by each human being with his human and individual purposes. Yet the comparison with Darwin cannot be carried too far. The deterministic implications of the Weissmannian theory of the germ plasm point in another direction from that in which James was looking. For James each individual differs from his fellows not because of the nature of his protoplasmic substance but by virtue of his own interests and effort. And the difference shown by each individual multiplies itself in the free creative activity which each one exerts.

If novelty and freedom are to be found in the choosing and following of ends on the part of the human individual, we may expect that the problem of freedom will be at least in part a problem in psychology. How important it was for James's psychological theory is revealed in the fact that psychology was for James essentially a study of the mental process of selection. Human life is a continuous choosing between opposing interests. By giving our attention to certain things to the exclusion of others, we make them real — this is the theme of that remarkable chapter on " The Perception of Reality." So the study not only of human life but of reality itself is the study of the fact and meaning of the selective process by which the human organism is making its way in the world.

But while we here have evidence that the problem of freedom is as important for James's psychology as for his philosophy, it is instructive to observe that the solution, as James consistently asserts, will not be psychological, but ethical.[9] And often as he states that the solution is ethical, still more frequently does James suggest that the only way to get at whatever freedom there may be is freely to assume it. Like the person described in the diverting sketch by Principal L. P. Jacks published in the volume *Among the Idol Makers* James is suspicious of constraint even where its object be freedom. The early expression found in a note-book entry dated April 30, 1870, " My first act of free will shall be to believe in free will," [10] is repeated frequently in his published works.

So the problem of freedom is soluble only by an ethical process the first step of which is the practical one of acting on the basis of the theory. But before leaving the topic of the relation of the free will problem to the various facets of James's thought we should notice that specifically religious interests are also involved. " Not only our morality but our religion, so far as the latter is deliberate, depend on the effort which we can make." " Our religious life lies . . . on the perilous edge." " ' Will you or won't you have it so? ' is the most probing question ever asked." " We answer by *consents* or *non-consents* and not by words. What wonder that these dumb responses should seem our deepest organs of communication with the nature of things." [11]

The first move in the attempt to understand this " pivotal problem of metaphysics " whose ramifications affect so vitally James's ideas on pluralism, meliorism, radical empiricism, and pragmatism, and for whose solution we must ultimately look to the field of ethics and religion, is to take account of the psychological setting in which it is placed. A preliminary attack on the psychological problem is made in the chapter in the

[9] Cf. *Principles of Psychology*, 1: 454; 2: 573.
[10] *Letters*, 1: 147.
[11] *Principles of Psychology*, 2: 579.

Principles on " The Automaton Theory " where James explains in detail his notion of the selective nature of consciousness. " In the lowest sphere of sense, or in the highest of intellection " the function of consciousness is that of selection, emphasis, accentuation. The selective process is carried on in the pursuance of ends definitely established by consciousness itself. This is what makes it possible to call human life teleological. But if consciousness is useful and purposeful " it must be so through its causal efficaciousness, and the automaton-theory must succumb to the theory of common sense." We find, that is to say, that the organism in its conscious activity selects that part of its environment which leads to the ends that its own consciousness has in turn selected as desirable. To live at all is to choose.

But the highest forms of selection are carried on through *attending* to the desired object or course of action. Here the chapter on " Attention " takes up the thread of the argument. In this chapter James breaks definitely with the associationist school, and avows his belief in a spontaneously creative psychical power which uses the data of experience as its materials and impresses upon them its own desires and purposes. There is an interest that shapes our ends. For my experience is what I attend to, and I attend to the things in which I have an interest. But there exist contrasting kinds of interests, *e.g.* sensuous and ideal, and there are different kinds of attention, the most important distinction being that between passive and active attention. It is the active and creative attention which helps us to deal with the problem of freedom. Its importance cannot be overrated. " The faculty of voluntarily bringing back a wandering attention, over and over again, is the very root of judgment, character and will."

The attending process has two parts — sensory and ideational. The sensory process is always present, in " intellectual " as well as in " sensible " attention. In the former the sensory element consists in a " more or less massive organic feeling that attention is going on." Or, to be specific, while attending one has kinaesthetic sensations of movements in the head. During attention to an idea belonging to a particular sense sphere, this movement is related to the sense organ in question. Thinking in visual terms, for example, is accompanied by sensations in the eyeballs.

The reference to kinaesthetic sensations is of course wholly in line with James's marked sensationist tendency. In places he seems to fall in line with the thought of the associationist school. For example, he compares consciousness, at times, to a series of feelings in the throat, effort to a set of muscular sensations. But the tendency to break away from the sensationist view is just as marked. It appears here in the fact that James follows up this description of the sensory element with an account of the part which has to do with ideas. The intellectual experience of attending is of course nothing but idea. But the ideal element is also present in the sensory experience as an auxiliary, a means of making the sensation more distinct. Psychologically, this part of the experience which we call the idea may be described as a brain cell played upon from two directions. "Whilst the object excites it from without, other brain cells, or perhaps spiritual forces, arouse it from within." But which — brain cell or spiritual force? On this hinges the question as to whether attention is to be classed as a resultant or as in itself creative. But this is the question which psychology is not equipped to decide. " As mere *conceptions* the effect-theory and the cause-theory of attention are equally clear; and whoever affirms either conception to be true must do so on metaphysical or universal rather than on scientific or particular grounds." [12]

James leaves us in no doubt as to which way the question settles itself for him. He formulates the " effect " theory clearly and forcibly, and says frankly it *may* be true. But it is just as clear, he affirms, that it may *not* be true. Let us ask, for example, just what the effort to attend would accomplish if it were an original force. Briefly, " It would deepen and prolong the stay in consciousness of innumerable ideas which else would fade more quickly away. The delay

[12] *Principles*, I: 448.

thus gained might not be more than a second in duration —
but that second might be *critical*." In fact, " The whole
drama of the voluntary life hinges on the amount of attention,
slightly more or slightly less, which rival motor ideas may receive. But the whole feeling of reality, the whole sting and
excitement of our voluntary life, depends on our sense that in
it things are *really being decided* from one moment to another." And if you claim that this is basing the answer on
the excitement rather than on the evidence, James would reply
first that it is only rational to make your answer accord with
what he elsewhere calls the " dramatic expressiveness of
life," and second, as he does here, that what evidence there
is favors the cause-theory of attention as much as its rival
The latter is nothing but an argument from analogy, drawn
from fields where consciousness doesn't exist and applied to a
field where it *may* exist. Such a procedure can hardly claim
to be called either metaphysical or scientific.

In the chapter on " Will " James has much to say of the
ideomotor theory. An idea will inevitably reproduce itself in
action unless another idea occurs to combat it. A person
would lie in bed indefinitely unless the idea of getting up
came, at some moment, clearly and definitely into consciousness, free from the influence of all inhibiting ideas. But it is
just in this matter of preventing the interference of inhibitions
that the special fiat of the will is needed. We must *attend* to
the chosen idea in order to make it effective. And this attention involves deliberate rejection of other ideas. The necessity
for a particular creative fiat is especially evident in cases
where a " rarer or more ideal impulse " has to combat others
" of a more instinctive and habitual kind." In these cases
there is a distinct feeling of effort. The brave man conquers
his fear, but we do not hear a drunkard say that he *conquers*
his better impulses. To follow the more ideal aim is often the
line of greater, not less resistance. Here James definitely takes
sides with Aristotle, Ovid, and Paul, as against Socrates and
Plato. The idea of the action produces the action, but this
does not mean that wisdom, or the contemplation of the ideal,

and aggressively virtuous effort are one and the same thing. The facts of experience do not bear out such a theory. In a letter to Shadworth Hodgson [13] James cries out, after the manner of Paul, " I see the better, and in the very act of seeing it I do the worse." The fact is, as is shown in the *Principles,* that in order to produce conduct that is good, the idea must be *attended to,* that is, it must be held forcibly in the center of the field of consciousness, while inhibiting ideas are dismissed. But to talk of holding an idea forcibly is of course to depart decisively from the theories of the associationist school. Instead of leaving the matter to the passive play of ideas, James puts it squarely up to the human individual and his capacity to make an *effort*. Where the course of action to be followed is that of the greatest, not the least, resistance, a proportionate amount of effort must be brought into play. This means, of course, a denial of hedonism. That ideas of pleasure and pain play a large part in determining our conduct James admits. But this part is limited to the aid they can render the self in holding to some ideas and dismissing others. And in this their influence alone is not sufficient.

Thus " the whole drama is a mental drama " [14] and incidentally James here clearly contradicts what he had previously said of how " the only ends which follow *immediately* upon our willing seem to be movements of our own bodies." [15] The action takes place within our minds and the immediate result, the acceptance of one idea and rejection of others, seems to be wholly a psychical process. Effort of attention is the essential phenomenon of will. The desirable idea must be held steadily before the mind until it fills the mind. Moral effort consists in concentrated attention, and conversely " to sustain a representation, to think, is . . . the only moral act." But because attention often carries with it the element of " express consent to the reality of what is attended to," and because James does not find that this element of consent can be resolved into any more ultimate psychological components, he

[13] *Letters,* 1: 245.   [14] *Principles,* 2: 564.   [15] *Principles,* 2: 486.

comes to the conclusion that the problem of free will is insoluble psychologically.

But this is far from being the last word on the subject. Our psychological evidences are incomplete, but other data are not lacking. We have the feeling that we actually make an effort in the face of obstacles, and throw into our task more or less of energy as we choose. We also have an inescapable sense of responsibility. There are certain courses of action which we simply could not take and remain conscience-free. This is as indubitable a fact of experience as any. We have, furthermore, a clearly defined consciousness of the unpredictable character of all life. Human biographies will never be written in advance, of this we are sure. Obviously, it is our part to meet this situation with a true pragmatic sense of the values involved and in a manner which, pending the discovery of new evidence, will be helpful in meeting the problems of daily experience. Living in a world which demands moral and practical solutions for the very practical life that we lead, we find suspension of judgment impossible and an active attitude a necessity.

To get at James's moral solution for the problem of freedom we must leave his psychological work and turn to the essay on " The Dilemma of Determinism " now printed in *The Will to Believe and Other Essays*. In this essay James points out, as he does elsewhere, that the horrors of indeterminism are not as bad as they have been painted by those on the other side of the argument. Here, as in his defense of pluralism, James says he is not contending for complete separation between things, for a chaos or a nulli-verse. Even " chance," a word to which more opprobrium is attached than to the word " freedom," does not mean anything so very heretical. James takes up the cudgels for " chance " so vigorously that his philosophy has been called a "tychism " by some commentators, *e.g.*, Flournoy and W. K. Wright. But the word he himself used most frequently was " indeterminism." He chooses " chance " as opposed to "freedom " in order, he says, that the argument may stand on its own feet and not appeal unfairly to sentiment.

But now, following the thought in " The Dilemma of Determinism," suppose we admit chance into the world. Does the universe thereby fall to pieces? Certainly not, for as chance works out in our experience its effects are hardly noticeable to an outside observer. " Is anyone ever tempted to produce an *absolute* accident, something utterly irrelevant to the rest of the world? " All futures, whether made by chance or not, spring from the soil of the past. The chance that comes into our experience does not bring with it a complete break with all that we have known. A train is the same train, no matter which way the switch is turned. Similarly the world is just as continuous with itself for the believer in chance as for the strict determinist. Suppose one is faced with the alternative of walking home via Divinity Avenue or via Oxford Street. After the fact, either course appears as natural, as continuous with the past, as the other. So why this great outcry over the split-off nature of the undetermined future? If the results of chance appear no otherwise than the results of rational necessity, the difference between them cannot be so catastrophic. We have already seen that pluralism is much more innocent than its opponents have assumed. So, " make as great an uproar about chance as you please," says James, " I know that chance means pluralism and nothing more." [16] As a matter of fact, the word " chance " is merely a negative term, " giving us no information about that of which it is predicated, except that it happens to be disconnected with something else." [17] Or, looking at it in another way, the idea of chance is like the idea of a gift, " the one simply being a disparaging, and the other a eulogistic name for anything on which we have no effective *claim*." [18]

Chance is rendered still more innocuous when we understand how limited is the field of its application. Our experience reveals varying spans of activity with various degrees of independence of each other. In studying the psychology of the question we found, also, that freedom is limited to the func-

---

[16] *The Will to Believe, etc.*, p. 178.
[17] *The Will to Believe, etc.*, p. 154.
[18] *The Will to Believe, etc.*, p. 159, cf. *Essays in Radical Empiricism*, p. 274.

tion of conscious selection and voluntary attention. This makes absurd the contentions of some determinists that if man were free his life would be one series of wild and wholly unpredictable vagaries. For example, it is nonsense for Spencer to say that psychical changes either conform to law or they do not, and if they do not no science of psychology is possible. Or for John Fiske to declare in a similar strain that volitions are either caused, or they are not, and that if they are not caused, an inexorable logic brings us to absurdities. Or for Professor Fullerton to claim that if there be free will, a man's previous character can have no influence over his actions. Or for Mr. McTaggart to tell us that if Nero were " free " at the moment of ordering his mother's murder he could not be called a bad man, or that if there were freedom a majority of Londoners would burn themselves alive tomorrow. These violent caricatures of the free will position arise from their authors' failure to observe the narrowly circumscribed limits within which freedom can operate if it operates at all. Indeterminists do not claim that any conceivable act is possible for any man. Their claim is merely that among several alternatives which really *tempt* a man, more than one is possible.

So interpreted indeterminism appears less abortive, especially when we examine the grounds on which the other alternative is based. Consider the principle of causality: it is merely a postulate, a name which stands for the demand that there be something more fundamental in a sequence of events than mere contiguity and nearness. It is, says James, as much an altar to an unknown god as the one St. Paul found at Athens. In fact " All our scientific and philosophical ideals are altars to unknown gods. Uniformity is as much so as is free will." In the last analysis the principle of causality is merely one of the demands we human beings make upon the universe. Why should not our moral demands be as important as the demand for a uniform sequence? The one, says James, is quite as subjective and emotional as the other.

The fact is that it is determinism, not its rival, which is the monstrous conception. A world which contains such an event as a murder is a world which must be called on to explain its conduct. It is unthinkable that such an occurrence should be the goal of cosmic history up to that moment. But if you say this, or if you even show distress at the murder and confess that the world would have been better off without it, you are expressing a judgment of regret, — that is, you are saying that something ought not to have been, and that something else ought to have been in its stead. So determinism, denying that anything else could have taken place, plunges into pessimism. On a deterministic basis, regret for the murder leads to regret for the universe in which the murder was unavoidable. As James expresses it in the letter to Hodgson, quoted above, "The question of free will owes its entire being to a difficulty you disdain to notice, namely, that we *cannot* rejoice in such a whole, for it is *not* a palpable optimism, and yet, if it be predetermined, we *must treat* it as a whole. Indeterminism is the only way to *break* the world into good parts and into bad and to stand by the former as against the latter." [19]

In this judgment of regret lies the first dilemma of determinism. For if we try to escape from pessimism by calling our judgment of regret wrong, and take refuge in the idea of some higher synthesis in which the evil is atoned for, we find that we cannot transform our judgment to one of approval, since in our deterministic scheme the original quality of regret was determined. So we may rescue the event, but in so doing the judgment remains fast in the mire. If the murder is good, the judgment is bad; and if the judgment is good, the murder is bad. But both have been predetermined, so our determinism lands us in a dilemma as well as in pessimism.

One remedy for this dilemma is to adopt the point of view of subjectivism. If the world exists simply that we may know it, and that our consciousness of good and evil may be refined; if the purpose of the universe be not the creation of any external good but merely our own subjective growth in knowledge — then the regret and the deed may both be good at the same time. So here we have the second, and the really im-

[19] *Letters,* 1: 245.

portant dilemma of determinism. Pessimism or subjectivism, as determinists we must accept one or the other.

Naturally we do not expect James to accept either. Pessimism is intrinsically abhorrent. And the results of subjectivism have been in theology, antinomianism; in literature, romanticism; in practical life, sentimentalism.[20] James's escape from both horns of the dilemma is truly pragmatic, though this word does not appear. He quotes Carlyle as urging: " Leave off your general emotional tomfoolery, and get to WORK like men! " and continues the thought by saying that conduct and not sensibility is our chief interest. We see before us " certain works to be done, certain outward changes to be wrought or resisted." Like a Stoic or Kantian rigorist emphasizing the nobility of the daily task, James exclaims: " No matter how we feel; if we are only faithful in the outward act and refuse to do wrong, the world will in so far be safe, and we quit of our debt towards it." [21]

Significantly for our interest in James's religious attitude, he does not leave the matter here, but goes on to explain that this attempt on man's part to take care for the future is not irreconcilable with the notion of a governing Providence. Here he introduces the famous figure of two players before a chess board, a figure which once more suggests how near the absolute loomed in the background of his thinking. One of the contestants knows all the possibilities which confront the other, and is able to counter every advance that the other makes. Just so the finite player of the game of life may have real power of decision at each crisis, without interfering with the Divine power and plan. This arrangement would make possible the very thing that determinism denies, that is, actual decisions here and now. But if it all has been planned out in advance, says James, then may you and I have been determined to believe in liberty!

James often asserts that his general treatment of the prob-

<hr />

[20] Cf. review of Renan's " Dialogues et Fragments philosophiques," *Nation*, 1876, reprinted in *Collected Essays and Reviews*, pp. 36 ff.
[21] *The Will to Believe, etc.*, p. 174.

lem of freedom followed Renouvier [22] and once he mentions Lotze.[23] The " neo-critical " position of Renouvier is indeed similar to that of James on this subject [24] but any topic taken up by James's fertile imagination was endowed with new life and color, and was always treated in such a highly original manner that it became virtually a new contribution. Rarely has the age-old problem of freedom been given the vividness which it receives at James's hand. But for him it was a vital issue. Novelty, possibility, freedom, individuality, creative achievement — these are key words in James's philosophy. Paradoxical as it seems, there must be freedom. But " must " here suggests the compulsion of the moral life, not of a closed deterministic sequence. Freedom is necessary if moral and religious values are to remain attainable. The question is pivotal because its moral implications are so far-reaching. To the unusual and unacademic application of his theory to religious belief we must now turn.

[22] Cf. *Letters*, 1: 147, 163; *Essays in Radical Empiricism*, p. 185.
[23] *Collected Essays and Reviews*, p. 304.
[24] Cf. e.g. *Esquisse d'une Classification systématique*, 2: 396; also Arnal: *La Philosophie religieuse de Ch. Renouvier*, p. 72.

V

THE BELIEVING WILL

ON MORAL grounds James has established man's freedom to choose between alternative courses of action.
Does this freedom extend into the realm of beliefs?
We may have the power to decide how we shall act, but have
we any choice as to how we shall think? In our intellectual
life does not the whole world of objective, external fact stand
over against us to determine for us what our beliefs shall be?

Many framers of philosophical systems have not thought
so. The springs of belief are internal as external and both on
psychological grounds and as a matter of metaphysical theory
many thinkers have subordinated the intellectual to the volitional, conative aspect of life. The two contrasting positions
have often been found side by side in history. One may remark, for example, the difference in emphasis which in the
days before Socrates obtained between the philosophers,
largely of a rationalistic turn of mind, who lived on the shores
of the Aegean Sea and those of Pythagorean and Orphic per-
suasion who made their home in Italy. The contrast which the
Greek tradition as a whole, with its confidence in the ability
of the intellect, made with the moral conscientiousness of the
Hebrews has often been pointed out. A similar contrast is
found in the early days of Christianity between the Johannine
and Pauline systems of theology. In the Middle Ages the
difference crops up again in the contrasting views of Domini-
cans and Franciscans, or of Thomists and Scotists in philosophy, while in more recent times we have the Romantic movement growing out of the period of the Enlightenment.

James frequently expressed his lack of sympathy for Kant, yet it remains true that Kant's doctrine of the primacy of the practical reason over the reason that is theoretical had many points in common with James's notion of the will to believe. Fichte also makes the will take precedence over the intellect in his postulation of duty as an ultimate datum on which even the knowing process is dependent. Pascal, in a less formal manner, suggests the sure authority of religious faith in his much-quoted observation: " Le cœur a ses raisons, que la raison ne connaît pas." Like Pascal the Romanticists take a position of which James would approve in their insistence that reality itself is not knowable in intellectual terms exclusively. Schleiermacher in the *Reden* makes an especially forceful appeal for the non-intellectual character of religion and Ritschl, whose theology is based in part on Schleiermacher, makes close contacts with James in his discussion of value-judgments, his stress on the necessity of man's asserting his independence of the world of nature and creating his ideals in the world of the spirit, in his assertion that belief in God is necessary to bring about the victory of the moral ideal, and in his condemnation of the absolute as an idolatrous object totally unfit to be worshipped!

The line of influence from Pascal to James may be traced not only through the German Romanticists but also through the French neo-criticist, Renouvier. James's use of Pascal's famous wager, as an illustration of the way in which our desires may influence our beliefs, is well known. In *The Will to Believe* James argues, it will be remembered, that if the issue is a genuine one, is living, and forced, and momentous, then " Pascal's argument, instead of being powerless, . . . seems a regular clincher, and is the last stroke needed to make our faith in masses and holy water complete." [1] John Locke had used a similar illustration in his *Essay*.[2] Renouvier also shows an interest in Pascal's wager. In his *Esquisse d'une Classification systématique* [3] he represents a proponent for Pascal as saying: " Dieu est ou il n'est pas. Mais de quel côté pen-

[1] P. 11.   [2] 2: 21: 70.   [3] 2: 53.

cherons-nous? *La raison n'y peut rien* déterminer." Yet, as
Renouvier goes on to show, Pascal's setting of the conditions
is not wholly accurate. "Le vice radical du pari de Pascal,
c'est que ce pari porte sur la vérité ou la fausseté d'un dogme
trop défini." It is not a question of " Dieu est, ou il n'est pas,"
it is rather, as he shows clearly in *La Nouvelle Monadologie,*
a question " du monde moral et de la vie future." " Dans ces
termes, la correction du *pari moral* ne serait pas facilement
contestée, comme elle a pu l'être, sous d'autres formes." [4] And,
as Renouvier later shows us, his chief objection is that " ce
dilemme, l'argumentation de Pascal le fait, au fond, porter
sur la foi et le culte catholiques, d'une part, et sur la vie hors
de cette religion, de l'autre." [5] Pascal has argued, "Vous êtes
embarqué." You are placed here, and the conditions are
forced upon you. But you are not forced, Renouvier replies,
to choose between the Catholic faith and utter darkness. The
issue is a moral one. The question as to whether or not there
is a moral order cannot be answered with apodictic knowledge,
but must be settled by belief. And, " l'intérêt " is a legitimate
factor in belief. Just as he freely chose to believe in freedom, so Renouvier postulates a moral world-order, " taking a chance " in each case, and allowing what James later
called " our passional nature " to have a voice in the
decision.

In England also we find an anticipation of James's views in
the tendency of some British thinkers to lay stress on the
claims of " belief " as opposed to those of " reason." Thomas
Reid, for example, maintained that life is more fundamental
than reason or logic, that beliefs grow directly out of the
needs of life and furnish the basis for arguments instead of de-
pending on them. Sir William Hamilton also has a part in this
" anti-intellectualist " movement by virtue of his attempt to
show from the contradictions in our notions of the infinite and
the absolute that religious belief must rest on faith rather
than on logic. What cannot be known must, where the great
issues of life are at stake, be believed. Dean Mansel in his

4 Pp. 457–8.   5 P. 523.

Bampton lectures on *The Limits of Religious Thought* also deals rationalism a blow by maintaining that the truths which guide our practice cannot be reduced to principles which satisfy our reason, in the religious or in any other realm.

In recent years Mr. Balfour has taken these philosophically agnostic conclusions of some of his countrymen and attempted, as he says, " to develop the negative speculations of philosophic doubt into a constructive, if provisional, system." At least one of his conclusions seems to have been in agreement with those of his predecessors, namely, that the system of axioms and postulates on which science is based is as tentative as the similar system underlying religious belief, the chief difference being that Balfour was interested in the postulates of science, while the others, working before the present era of pervasive scientific activity, were interested rather in comparing the truths of religion with " intuitive " truths about knowledge and about practical life. But Balfour's scientific interest does not prevent him from having an interest also in the demands of the practical life. Science demands a practical working faith and indeed the mere process of living from day to day demands it as well. Most important is it that man keep his faith in ethical as well as scientific ideals. Like James in his most pragmatic moods Balfour makes much of the inadequacy of any system of belief which fails to substantiate and make legitimate man's moral aspirations. For him as for James the intellectual demand for consistency is only one human demand among others and does not take precedence over the rest.

Mr. Balfour's work shows many interesting parallels to James's thought, notably in his demand for concreteness in religion, and especially for a limited God,[6] in his assurance that the hypothesis of a personal deity satisfies the largest number of moral and religious requirements,[7] but in nothing more than in his conviction, already referred to, " that in accepting science, as we all do, we are moved by ' values ' not

---

[6] E.g. *The Foundations of Belief,* pp. 359–60.
[7] Cf. *The Foundations of Belief,* p. 344; *Theism and Humanism,* pp. 125–34.

by logic." [8] So it is interesting to find this passage in a letter written by William James to his brother Henry, dated April 26, 1895 (a few months before the address on " The Will to Believe " was first delivered): " I have been reading Balfour's *Foundations of Belief* with immense gusto. It almost makes me a Liberal-Unionist! If I mistake not, it will have a profound effect eventually, and it is a pleasure to see old England coming to the fore every time with some big stroke. There is more real philosophy in such a book than in fifty German ones of which the eminence consists in heaping up subtleties and technicalities about the subject. The English genius makes the vitals plain by scuffing the technicalities away. B. is a great man.' '

Some parts of Royce's work exhibit a striking similarity to James's theory of the will to believe, particularly the ninth chapter of Royce's *The Religious Aspect of Philosophy*. We may recall that in " The Dilemma of Determinism " James had said that our moral demands on the universe were as authoritative as our intellectual demands. And Royce tells us that if a man abandon religion's postulate that goodness is at the heart of things he ought also to abandon the postulate of science that order and reason are the truth of things. But to do either is to be cowardly. For, says Royce, you are placed in a world of confusion, yet you assert that ultimately it must meet your intellectual needs and be a world of order. Is it any more presumptuous to assert that it must meet your ethical needs and have righteousness at its heart? Why is one postulate not made as readily as the other? Is the ethical need the less important? Postulates are voluntary assumptions of a risk for the sake of a higher end. They take a chance, but they do it courageously and intelligently, whereas mere blind faith is unintelligent and cowardly. The sea-captain postulates that he will get to harbor, the general that he will beat the enemy. We all postulate that our lives are worth the trouble. Indeed the wise live by postulates.

[8] Art. " Creative Evolution and Philosophic Doubt," *Hibbert Journal,* October 1911, p. 5.

We hear men say, Royce goes on, that they will believe what the facts force on them. But each of us determines what he will believe by determining what he will give his attention to. A foreign language may be mere jargon, or it may be made intelligible by our attention, as we listen. Through our attention we exert an active force on experience, and this active element in knowledge is fully as much to be reckoned with as is the passive play of sensations and ideas. As for prejudice, we all have it, because we all *create* experience in addition to receiving it. The great question is simply: " In what sense, to what degree, with what motive, for what end, may I and should I be prejudiced? " So we go on living with faith that the highest reality is with and not against us, just as we try to understand the world with the faith that the highest reality conforms to reason. The risk in both cases is one which it would be ignoble to avoid.

In Friedrich Paulsen we find nearly as intimate a relation to James's thought as is exhibited in Royce. James and Paulsen believed in each other. James wrote an introduction to Thilly's translation of Paulsen's *Einleitung in die Philosophie* and praised Paulsen for his anti-absolutism. Not to be outdone, Paulsen wrote a *Geleitwort* for Lorenz's translation into German of the *Will to Believe* as *Der Wille zum Glauben* (1899) in which he placed James in the Kantian succession, saying: "Professor James steht in einer Reihe, deren Richtungslinie durch die Namen Hume, Kant, Fichte, Carlyle bezeichnet ist; auf positivischer Unterlage eine idealistische Weltanschauung mit energistischer Tendenz." Then in explanation: " Der Wille bestimmt das Leben, das ist sein Urrecht; also wird er auch ein Recht haben, auf die Gedanken einen Einfluss zu üben."

And not only in this *Geleitwort* but in the *Einleitung in die Philosophie* also one feels the spirit of James, especially in the section on " Knowledge and Faith" which sets forth Paulsen's own will-to-believe theory. In the seventh (German) edition Paulsen mentions James's view in this connection as similar to his own. Philosophy, Paulsen says, is not a product of the understanding merely, but of a man's entire personality. The will, the revolt against the miserable present, determines the direction of the personality and arouses its passions. The origin of our convictions is to be sought in our own experience. You cannot prove the truth of your view to one who does not share your loves, your hates, your hopes, and your ideals. Paulsen is truly pragmatic in his criterion, for he leaves the decision as to the correctness of one's view to the future. But the peculiarity of the future is that it is accessible through faith, not through knowledge. Faith is in this sense the formal principle of every philosophy.

Faith, will, future verification, empirical approach, subjective convictions, temperamental passional decisions! With these as a sympathetic avenue of approach we should be ready for a discussion of James's own theory.

The tendencies which later found expression in the famous " Will to Believe " doctrine are clearly seen in some of James's earlier work. As early as the '70s he was actively rebelling against the notion that the truth ideal, " Truth with a capital T," was something which required only passive obedience on the part of humankind. In contrast to this he seemed eager to bring out the active nature of the knowing process and the creative part played by man, both in the fact that by paying attention to the flux of experience he creates order out of chaos and also in the fact that man in a sense creates his own environment by following his interests and desires and insisting upon the reality for himself of their objects. And James also seems to have been impressed by the importance of man's contributions to other ideals beside the intellectual. There are as many ideals, as many " goods," as there are human desires. The only question is, when they conflict, what standard is one to apply in order to determine which should have precedence? The answer is not far to seek, however, for evolution is showing us that the cosmos itself is revealing a standard. When man judges rightly, among his conflicting desires, he succeeds in the game of life.

In this sense, all human activity is intensely practical. In fact, " the theorizing faculty . . . functions exclusively for the sake of ends that . . . are set by our emotional and practical subjectivity." [9] The truth-attaining end is one of a number of such ends and must compete on equal terms with the others, the standard by which its claims are judged being that of practical utility. Humanity is caught in the onward rush of a biological process, of which the ultimate tests are practical. But "practical" must not be interpreted too narrowly. Activity which serves the highest interests of the race is practical, but not invidiously so. Considered from the point of view of racial aims and interests, there may be practical purposes which are at the same time ideal. But their ideal quality is transfused with the conditions and objectives of the context of human experience out of which they have sprung. Apart from the larger human concerns they can have no meaning.

These two ideas, that truth-attainment is one of many human interests all arising out of man's subjective nature, and determined ultimately by the practical character of the biological process, and that in truth-attainment the active element with its attendant risk is as important as the passive, were joined with a third idea, that belief in a certain outcome helps to effect that outcome, to form the nucleus of the essay on " The Will to Believe" and the other essays in the same volume which express a similar attitude.

" The Will to Believe " begins with a discussion of hypotheses, showing that a hypothesis to be eligible for free choice must be living, forced, and momentous. When a hypothesis conforming to these conditions is present, our non-intellectual nature is sure to influence our decision. Now, argues James, it is true not only that our passional nature may enter into certain decisions, it is also true that in many cases it is the only deciding factor. Many and many a time we simply cannot wait for complete knowledge. The evidence will not be in during our span of life, or perhaps not until the life of the race is over. So, since we cannot have all the evidence, we

[9] *The Will to Believe, etc.*, p. 117.

must decide on other than purely evidential grounds. For to refuse to decide is itself a decision. To wait is not to act. To hesitate is to make a passional decision as truly as to act without waiting for all the evidence.

James goes on to claim that this necessity for a passional decision is empiricism's view of the whole matter. Objective evidence is a fine thing to have, but how can we know surely when we have it? The absolutist thinks that he does know when his evidence is infallible, but for the empiricist it is impossible to be certain when one has attained certainty. " There is but one indefectibly certain truth, and that is the truth that pyrrhonistic scepticism itself leaves standing, — the truth that the present phenomenon of consciousness exists. That however is the bare starting point of knowledge, the mere admission of the stuff to be philosophized about." This, however, is not saying that truth is unattainable; it is merely transferring truth from the past to the future. Here James gives us a clear forecast of pragmatism, in this volume which appeared ten years before the book by that name was written, especially when he says of the empiricist and his hypothesis, " if the total drift of thinking continues to confirm it, that is what he means by its being true."

But now what are some of these questions which we cannot wait to decide? Well, all moral questions, all value judgments as Ritschl or Lotze would say, being decisions not as to what is, but as to what ought to be, are questions involving something more than merely intellectual evidence. " If your heart does not *want* a world of moral reality, your head will assuredly never make you believe in one." Such a matter demands the attention of the whole nature and is not satisfied with a judgment of the intellect alone. And beside general questions of value there are certain questions as to future fact, cases where faith in a certain outcome helps to bring it to pass. You win promotions if you believe that you can win them, you jump to safety if you don't doubt your own ability.

In religion all these cases are found. Religious faith offers an option that is forced and living and momentous. Yet who can ever attain to a knowledge of all the evidence? The emotions are bound to play their part in this decision, the only question is, which emotion shall it be? Shall we allow ourselves to be influenced more by our hope for religion's benefits, or by our fear that we may make a mistake? " Dupery for dupery, what proof is there that dupery through hope is so much worse than dupery through fear? " And here James takes a more radical step. May we not, he asks, help to create the truths of religion by believing them?

" This feeling, forced on us we know not whence, that by obstinately believing that there are gods (although not to do so would be so easy both for our logic and our life) we are doing the universe the deepest service we can, seems part of the living essence of the religious hypothesis. If the hypothesis *were* true in all its parts, including this one, then pure intellectualism, with its veto on our making willing advances, would be an absurdity; and some participation of our sympathetic nature would be logically required. I therefore, for one, cannot see my way to accepting the agnostic rules for truth-seeking, or wilfully agree to keep my willing nature out of the game. I cannot do so for this plain reason, that *a rule of thinking which would absolutely prevent me from acknowledging certain kinds of truth if these kinds of truth were really there, would be an irrational rule.*" [10]

So the kind of rationality to which as empiricists and anti-absolutists we must come, thinks James, is the rationality of religious belief, and since all belief is measured by action, we must come to religious activity. Realizing the risk, but realizing also that there is a risk whichever way we turn, is it not the part of courage as well as of rationality to champion the positive alternative, postulate a religious reality at the heart of things, and let loose in ourselves the activity which only a religious environment can call forth? Is it not clear that this is both the creative and the reasonable decision, since the event may depend upon our choice? Shall we not seize the alternative of promise, glorying in our ability to do so! In later

[10] *The Will to Believe*, p. 28.

works James twice alludes to what he calls a " faith ladder," showing the series of steps, not one of them logical, by which beliefs enter the mind:

" A conception of the world arises in you somehow, no matter how. Is it true or not? you ask.

It *might* be true somewhere, you say, for it is not self-contradictory.

It *may* be true, you continue, even here and now.

It is *fit* to be true, it would be *well if it were true*, it *ought* to be true, you presently feel.

It *must* be true, something persuasive in you whispers next, and then — as a final result —

It shall be *held for true,* you decide; it *shall be* as if true for *you*.

And your acting thus may in certain special cases be a means of making it securely true in the end." [11]

One of the features of this whole discussion which James was most eager to emphasize, and which he felt his critics overlooked, was the circumscribed region in which the " will " or the " passional nature " can operate. His critics, he often claimed, seized upon what he called the catchpenny title " Will to Believe " which should have been " The Right to Believe," and without paying any attention to his real argument had accused him of making such foolish assertions as that a person may believe anything he wishes and make it the truth. Whereas the argument strove to show that *in certain cases* the unaided intellect fails us, since the means for a purely intellectual decision are simply not at hand. In such cases we actually do make a passional decision, whether or not we realize that we are doing so. In fact, the intellectualist critics of the theory are themselves making " passional " decisions and exercising their " will to believe " in their very choice of a philosophic standpoint.

This brief sketch of the essay on " The Will to Believe " should serve to bring out its three distinctive emphases mentioned above: the stress on the importance of the subjective

[11] *A Pluralistic Universe*, pp. 328-9.

factor in beliefs and in truth itself, on their practical nature, and on the creative part which man himself plays in the making of truth. We are so accustomed to the notion of truth as having to do only with the world of objective fact, and of beliefs as acceptable only if based on evidence which is entirely external to the believer, that the possibility of subjective evidence is likely not to occur to us. Yet James has just at this point made a most important contribution to the philosophy of religion. This question of objective, external evidence must not be made too much of a fetish — such seems to be James's idea. Obviously it is all-important when we have it. But when the question is one of religious belief science does not carry us very far either way. And why should we be afraid, in such a case, to trust what we call our subjective impulses, our faiths and aspirations? Why should we not recognize at the outset that they are no more subjective than our desire for intellectual consistency itself? " Hardly a law has been established in science, hardly a fact ascertained, which was not first sought after, often with sweat and blood, to gratify an inner need." [12] " But the inner need of believing that this world of nature is a sign of something more spiritual and eternal than itself is just as strong and authoritative in those who feel it, as the inner need of uniform laws of causation ever can be in a professionally scientific head." [13] Our moral demand on the universe is as trustworthy as is our requirement that there be a uniform sequence, " the one demand being, so far as I can see, quite as subjective and emotional as the other is." [14]

Clearly we are well on the way to religious belief if our right to draw on our subjective life for evidence is vindicated. To trust his aspirations and hopes is just what the religious man has always been eager to do. But too often he has been fearful or cautiously meticulous about a complete and final consistency, something which in the nature of things, with our limited span of life and exceedingly slight knowledge of the universe, may never be possible. It is important, indeed, to be consistent, but it is also important to weave as many

[12] *The Will to Believe, etc.,* p. 55. [13] *Ibid.,* p. 56. [14] *Ibid.,* p. 147.

as possible of the facts that do enter our experience into our consistent web. The pragmatic philosophy, in James's hands, has from the beginning emphasized the need of taking account, in all our intellectual analyses, of other elements than the purely formal, and of realizing that analysis itself is a less complete thing than life in its fullness and richness.

No less unavoidable than the subjective factor in religious belief is the practical. Subjective demands are but practical postulates. They are demands made on life in the interests of the human organism, a part of its attempt not merely to adapt itself to the environment, but to adapt its environment to itself. One test of the legitimacy of these demands is their efficacy in this adjusting, creating process. Ideas, according to the pragmatic view, are but means to practical adjustment. Consciousness itself functions for practical ends. The line traditionally drawn between theory and practice is an artificial one. Metaphysically there is no convincing evidence for pointing to the experience of an absolute as distinct from that which comes to us in practical life here and now. Ethically there are many evidences against the belief in anything which minimizes the reality of the moral struggle. Psychologically we find the fact that consciousness is an instrument of adaptation. Our religious beliefs function in a practical manner and are tested by their results only in the sense in which all intellectual activity is ultimately practical. And since all our beliefs are being refined in the furnace of experience, and since the truth or falsity of our ideas is known by their ability or lack of ability to help us, it is accurate to say that truth itself is being built up as a body of ideas which prove themselves by their working.

But "practicality" here leads to creativity. For if in the case of beliefs we make success, or practical working out, the criterion of adequacy we put a part of the responsibility for the success of the belief squarely on the shoulders of the believer. If, for example, the alternative be that between optimism and pessimism, an enthusiastic advocacy of the former may help to justify the belief in it. The world is good,

we may say, for it shall be made good by our efforts. There
are cases where belief in a possibility helps that possibility to
realize itself. Your active attitude may be instrumental in
creating the reality of the thing that you postulate. But, if
this be so, is it not wholly absurd to accept any theory of
truth which prevents you from assuming the attitude by which
alone the possible is brought to actuality? In a case like this
the more creative attitude is the *truer* since it is the realizer
of greater possibilities. For truth, in any important and significant sense, must be distinguished from mere correctness by
the criterion of utility. If you think you cannot jump the
chasm, and, so thinking, you fall in, your previous judgment
was correct, but it was not useful. Before the event the truth
of the matter lay either in the chasm or on the other side. It
is impossible to say that the truth was already *established* in
either place. There was no absolute truth at the time, truth was
being created by your act. And the tragedy of it is that you
might have created a useful truth by your willingness to believe in it. The possibility of falling was the alternative which
should have been rejected; the other possibility was just as
ready at hand. The real, in the sense of the important and
relevant fact in the whole situation was the fact that you
might succeed. To grasp such a potential truth and force
its verification is a moral duty.

It must be remembered that belief is an active assertion as
to what shall be real for us. Psychologically it is a similar
activity to that attention which in making one possibility more
real than others actually brings new reality into being. Experience in its active aspect is conscious experimentation.
Believing is part of the whole selective process and it creates
as it selects and holds. This is not true in all cases, of course,
for the environment is not by any means entirely pliable, and
the world cannot be molded to accord with all our desires.
But within a restricted sphere, choice and creation do operate.
And religious beliefs lie in this sphere.

James always maintained that this position was compatible
with the point of view of realism. The creation of reality

through attention, for example, is not purely a subjective process. We do our part in the attending process. " The rest is done by nature, which in some cases *makes* the objects real which we think of in this manner and in other cases does not." [15] And pragmatism is far from indifferent to the existence of an external world of fact. " Pent in, as the pragmatist more than anyone else sees himself to be, between the whole body of funded truths squeezed from the past and the coercions of the world of sense about him, who so well as he feels the immense pressure of objective control under which our minds perform their operations? If anyone imagines that this law is lax, let him keep its commandment one day, says Emerson." [16]

And in a letter to Professor Dickinson S. Miller, dated August 5, 1907, James says, " I am a natural realist. The world *per se* may be likened to a cast of beans on a table. By themselves they spell nothing. An onlooker may group them as he likes. He may simply count them all and map them. He may select groups and name these capriciously, or name them to suit certain extrinsic purposes of his. Whatever he does, so long as he *takes account* of them, his account is neither false nor irrelevant. If neither, why not call it true? It *fits* the beans-*minus*-him and *expresses* the *total* fact, of beans-*plus*-him. Truth in this total sense is partially ambiguous then. If he simply counts or maps, he obeys a subjective interest as much as if he traces figures. Let that stand for pure "intellectual" treatment of the beans, while grouping them variously stands for non-intellectual interests. All that Schiller and I contend for is that there is *no* " truth " without *some* interest, and that non-intellectual interests play a part as well as intellectual ones. Whereupon we are accused of denying the beans or denying being in any way constrained by them! It's too silly! " [17]

There is constraint enough, in the world of sense-percep-

---

[15] *Principles of Psychology,* 2: 320.
[16] *Pragmatism,* p. 233.
[17] *Letters,* 2: 295–6.

tion, in that of " intellection," in the very rush of the biological process. But pragmatism focuses its attention on that portion of experience where problems and crises and decisions are real. These are the significant parts of life. And it is with these that truth itself has to do. So when James finds a man faced by an option, saying: I choose this course of action, but this is a practical decision, having to do with matters of conduct and remote from the abstract world of truth, he protests. Truth is what you are making here and now by this decision, he says. It is not something aloof from your daily interests. Truth is the most vital and practical thing we know. It grows up inside our finite experiences. Truth is a process. It is being made by our actions. It is not a prior static relationship, but *it is the success* of our decisions and activities.

This is merely taking the human activity-situation and saying that truth is in and of it. Truth had always been considered valuable, but James saw that it did not degrade truth to say that it is the valuable, and the valuable is the true. And his constant defense against his critics is: What else can the truth be? If you say it is " correspondence," then where is the correspondence? What corresponds, and to what does it correspond? To say " to reality " is too vague. Is there a pre-established world to which every detail of our lives must conform? To say so would be to deny the dramatic quality with which life seems to be invested. Novelty is real, new situations come, and truth is implicit in them. Instead of calling them " merely " practical let us realize that the problems of theory itself are set by practice. Consciousness is the middle term between sensation and reaction. It is grounded in practical interest.

What shall we say, however, as to truth about the past? Here James's theory strikes a difficulty. When an event has once occurred, we cannot unmake it or change it. On that reality we cannot, seemingly, exert creative influence. Nor do we appear to have much to do with the " verification " of a truth about an event in history. When this criticism is made, by Dewey, Russell, Hawtrey and others, James resorts to the

rather arbitrary procedure of distinguishing between the givenness of a fact and the truth of a belief about the fact. To con-
vert a fact, Caesar is dead, into a proposition, " That Caesar
is dead," is to make room for all sorts of evasions, James says.
Having done so, intellectualists are prone to confuse their
belief that Caesar is dead with the fact, and so, James tells us,
they try to make out a case for the " absolute " nature of
their belief.

James's theory, however, is in essence a protest against the
notion of irrelevant truth. Past events are past facts; truth
should be concerned with things that are verifiable and relevant. And there is a sense in which James's treatment even
of past events is more objective than is that of his critics. We
find a suggestion of it in his claim that the empiricist, unlike
the absolutist, does not know certainly when truth is in his
grasp, and is consequently unwilling to posit any truth as
absolute and final. But this means that he leaves room for
future verification even of past events. Does the empiricist
then not appeal to a higher standard even than the absolutist?
For the empiricist, verification is never complete, a higher
verification is always possible. Truth itself advances with the
novelty that keeps coming into the world. It seems possible
to argue that James saw the nobler and more inclusive nature
of this truth whose verification was never finished. The absolute is incomplete until it has become the Ultimate.

But when all is said and done, the pragmatic theory does
seem to be inadequate on the side of its treatment of events in
the past. Of them it can only say that the truth of my belief
about past events is susceptible of verification in so far as my
future experiences may bring me into situations such that these
past events have a bearing on my conduct. Yet this is of course
to neglect an important part of the truth about the past. Pragmatism, being a forward-looking theory, neglects the past because of its lack of interest in it. We live forward but we
understand backward, Kierkegaard has said, and pragmatism,
with its emphasis on the finding of truth in human living as
much as in human understanding, directs its whole attention

to fields of new discovery. This lack in pragmatism is, however, a point in favor of our argument. Pragmatism's interests and emphases are pre-eminently those of religious faith,
its attitude is pre-eminently that of the will to believe. Belief,
for pragmatism, is not belief about the past. That is unessen-
tial and irrelevant. Pragmatism's beliefs are postulates in the
sense of Kant's and Royce's and Schiller's postulates — forward-looking demands made upon the universe for the satisfaction of subjective needs, among which the moral and religious needs are prominent. Pragmatism clearly has much more
in common with the religious view, where the objects of belief
must always remain unknowable, than with the scientific view
where the correspondence relation may be the thing of chief
importance. Religion will always require postulates, faith, the
will to believe, and pragmatism's fitness for this type of thinking is significant evidence for the fundamental character of the
religious strain in James's philosophy.

Criticisms of James's whole point of view have been offered
in abundance. And in the endeavor to meet them it seems to be
necessary always to keep in mind James's insistence that life
and experience are richer than theories about them can possibly be. One critic, for example, makes much of the " problematic " attitude on which what James calls a passional decision
is based. That a problematic attitude, so runs the argument,
involves a theoretic judgment is agreed by logicians even when
they differ as to the content of the theoretic judgment. For
example, Sigwart claims that the problematic or hypothetical
judgment, " A may be B," contains a theoretic assertion as to
the uncertainty of the A-B relation, while Windelband says
that the theoretic judgment is a negative one, the denial that
anything is known definitely about the A-B relation. In either
case, when James asserts: This belief may be true, let us affirm
it and make it true, he is really involved in a theoretic judgment which must vitiate his whole procedure.

But in the light of the pragmatic theory of life and of truth
this argument does not carry much weight. The judgment " A
may be B " can be said to involve a theoretic judgment in the

sense that from any human situation certain features may be
singled out and a theoretic judgment made concerning them.
But pragmatism sees life as a more complex affair than a
succession of theoretic judgments. Because life is more than
theory, because " reality overflows logic," certain occasions do
come for which our theoretic knowledge is inadequate. In such
cases our activity cannot wait for our knowledge, because our
knowledge is incomplete. Decide we must, for even vacilla-
tion is one kind of decision. And pragmatism can affirm that
this is not acting in a manner unworthy of the truth because
of its view that truth is dynamic and " grows up inside our
finite experiences." Logical statements of insufficient evidence
are not the whole of life. The Kingdom of Heaven cometh
not by syllogisms.

The same critic and others have maintained that there are
really no " forced options." The possibility of doubting and
continuing to inquire is still open. But the reply is of course
that doubt is itself one alternative of a forced option. As
James shows in the *Principles of Psychology,* the opposite of
belief is not disbelief but doubt. And as he shows in *The Will
to Believe,* the religious question usually presents itself not so
much as a choice between faith and atheism as between faith
and skepticism. Doubt cuts us off from the privileges of belief as surely as a negative decision does. And James's argument is simply that when such a forced option comes we are
justified in accepting the immediate evidences which the positive alternative brings and need not feel compelled to go grub-
bing through logical processes for mediate ones which can be
no more satisfactory if indeed they are even found. The vision has its claims upon us as well as the argument. " The
essence of the whole experience, when the individual swept
through it says finally ' I believe,' is the intense concreteness
of his vision." [18]

Another criticism maintains that it is inaccurate to say that
in any sense belief or faith creates its own verification. If we
are bailing out a leaky boat, we succeed not because of the

[18] *The Meaning of Truth,* p. 258.

truth of our belief, but because of the effectiveness of our bail-ing. But James's theory, as we have abundantly seen, is in the first place a protest against the notion that the truth of the success or failure is established already. We make the truth along with our faith and effort. In the second place, psycholog-ically it can hardly be denied that belief in success is a stimu-lus to greater effort. To say that the truth causes the success sounds like an intellectualist's account of truth as already or-dained in the nature of things. But to say that the belief brings about the success is to talk not like an intellectualist but like a psychologist. In the third place, this example brings out one of pragmatism's chief claims to advantage. Its theories are pertinent to just such situations as these; it has a mes-sage for the difficult and crucial places in life, the message of courage.

The appeal to courage is one of the greatest assets of James's whole argument. Undoubtedly our intellectual life has too often been regarded as wholly passive, a process of meas-uring and conforming after the fact. Its adventurous and creative aspect has been understood well enough by those who have engaged in the intellectual life for themselves, but others have been slow in realizing it. This is reflected far too clearly in our educational process, which is often regarded by the student as a process of absorption rather than creation. James's pragmatic emphasis brings out the mistakenness of this point of view and also brings out the peculiarly creative part which thought plays when it is directed toward the sub-ject of religion. Aside from its experiential aspect religion seems to afford an especially good example of the will to realize value. Much of our thought life, historical, scientific, analytical, is concerned with the world of description. Our passion for unity and continuity, well enough in itself as an aid in classifying, is apt to lead us to the view that the world of fact and the world of interpretation are one and continuous. It requires creative effort and imagination to see that they are not. The science of anthropology may give us the facts of the origin of religion but it cannot dictate or throw light on the question of the values of religion. These values exist in potentiality, ready to be created by our recognition of them. But to recognize them we must have energy and courage. Our recognition must include a definitely creative factor. In his famous essay on "Axioms as Postulates" Professor F. C. S. Schiller insists that, in large measure, our perceptions depend upon what we come prepared to receive, and that in religion one can go further than this, for "nothing is more reasonable than to suppose that if there be anything *personal* at the bottom of things, the way we behave to it *must* affect the way it behaves to us." [19]

So in religious faith the courageously creative factor in the intellectual process attains its highest degree of worth. For faith means analysis of and discrimination between values, but it also means thorough-going insistence that values *shall* exist even at the heart of the universe. Faith is a postulation, a demand that the universe itself recognize the eternal worthwhileness of the moral quality of every-day life. This is what is meant by the comparison often made of faith and courage. In an epigram of Professor Kirsopp Lake's, "Faith is not belief in spite of evidence, but life in scorn of consequence." [20] In James's words: "Faith means belief in something concerning which doubt is still theoretically possible; and as the test of belief is willingness to act, one may say that faith is the readiness to act in a cause the prosperous issue of which is not certified to us in advance. It is the same moral quality which we call courage in practical affairs." [21] And "if religious hypotheses about the universe be in order at all, then the active faiths of individuals in them, freely expressing themselves in life, are the experimental tests by which they are verified, and the only means by which their truth or falsehood can be wrought out." [22]

So it is in religious faith that we have the most clear-cut example of the worth of the creative factor in the situation

[19] *Personal Idealism,* p. 63.
[20] *Landmarks of Early Christianity,* p. 74.
[21] *The Will to Believe, etc.,* p. 90,
[22] *Ibid.,* p. xii,

out of which that relation which we call truth arises. And in
the series of essays published with "The Will to Believe"
and written, as James tells us in the preface, in defense of religious faith we have a clear anticipation of the distinctive
elements in James's later theory of truth. In these essays
James brought together several ideas which found expression
in the *Principles of Psychology* and in some of the earlier reviews and essays, such as the practical function of consciousness, the interdependence of the thinking, willing, and feeling
processes, the purposive nature of all human activity, the psychological kinship of belief and volition, and combined with
them an emphasis on the need for postulates or the importance
of passional decisions, the unavoidableness of risk, and the
notion of verification as a process awaiting completion in the
future. These are all important ideas in James's pragmatic
philosophy, and it is instructive to notice that we find them
assembled here in defense of religious faith.

The threads of our argument here begin to come together.
James, we see, had to solve his conflict in favor of pluralism
to be consistent with the thought of the will to believe. Yet
the conflict was a real one, for monism appealed on the very
subjectivistic and pragmatic grounds we have been outlining,
especially as they merged in the demand for religious well-
being. But the problem of freedom is also a crucial one. It
must be solved in a way such that the experienced reality of
the moral struggle will not be denied. And freedom holds in
the world of belief as in that of action. "The Will to Believe" is the point of clarification and crystallization of
James's pragmatic theory. And as the main lines of his
thought converge here for clearer definition, so do they
broaden later into a more inclusive view, in which the attributes of religious faith are seen to be in greater or less
measure applicable to the problem of truth in general.

VI

THE PURPOSIVE WILL: VALUES AND TELEOLOGY

OUR study so far has brought out the central position which values occupy in James's philosophy. Life, as James conceived it, is full of valuable and desirable things, and its aim is to bring to pass as many of these as possible. These values are empirical, that is, they are found in experience and tested by experience. They arise out of human desires and are justified in the fact that they fill human needs. This is sufficient authority, it is indeed the highest possible authority, for there can be no *a priori* or transcendental justification. Truth is a relation in which the element of value is important. Its authority, like that of values themselves, rests on its pertinence to human situations. In fact, truth may almost be called a corollary of value. If a belief or idea is valuable it is true " so far forth." Truth has to do with the " relevant," the " meaningful," the " important." James's whole philosophy may indeed be described as centering in the notion of the humanly significant.

Since Plato, at least, all philosophers have been interested in values, but not all have stressed, as does James, the human origin of values and their empirical criteria. Nor do all philosophers make these immediately experienced values and their postulated criteria the basis on which to build a theory of the nature of truth and its relation to human living. Many modern philosophers of religion in their insistence on the reality of a world of interpretation as contrasted with the scientific world of description seem to be taking their cue from Kant and his theory of the primacy of the practical reason. The world in which we live and work and envisage better things must provide an environment for the values for which the spirit yearns. Let values live though the heavens fall. Our faith in the reality of moral and spiritual worths is as justifiable and its objects as sure as any factual data which science can discover. So reasons much of modern religious thought, going Kant one better in its attempt to stress the autonomy of the world of ideals.

Ritschl, in his *Justification and Reconciliation,* was one of the first to bring out the importance for religion of the value-judgment. According to him both philosophy and religion make use of value-judgments, but their use by religion is more consistent than their use by philosophy. For philosophy professes complete disinterestedness, while religion acknowledges a supreme interest in values from the beginning.[1] This absorption by religion in the concerns of value is emphasized by modern writers on religion like Höffding, W. K. Wright, and the late Professor G. B. Foster who make religion consist in the faith that there is an integral connection between fact and value, and the belief that lasting values can be achieved. A spirited defense of religion as bound up with our understanding of values is made from the idealistic position in the final chapter of Professor R. A. Tsanoff's recently published book, *The Problem of Immortality.* Professor W. D. Sorley in his *Moral Values and the Idea of God* argues from the possibility of finite error in moral judgments to the existence of a transcendent standard, a Supreme Worth, which is God.

James starts, however, not from the possibility of error in judgments of value, but rather from the possibility of success in the value-attaining process. Values are dependent on human interests. A thing is valuable in so far as it is desired by some sentient being. Is this to say that values are subjective? Yes, in a sense, but not in a bad sense. For in the first place to affirm that values are relative to and dependent on our interests is not to say that they are dependent on our opinion about them. The interest and the consequent value

[1] P. 210, Eng. tr.

are empirical facts. The judgment may not be a judgment of fact at all, it may be an error. We must distinguish carefully between desire itself and judgment concerning desirability. The desire is subjective in the sense that an individual finds it emanating from himself, but objective in the sense that it is an empirical datum. Again, it must be remembered that in James's philosophy the opposition between value and fact is beginning to break down, since facts themselves are known only by a process in which the valuing element is prominent, a process of selective attention taking notice of those facts which fall in line with its interests. Every fact is in a sense a judged fact, and into any judgment of fact the evaluating element enters. When we remember James's distinction between fact and truth it is not difficult to see how far from being a term of reproach " subjective " is when applied to value. Truth is a relation between mind and fact which brings out the significance of the fact. Truth and value join hands in their essential quality of significance for human life.

Values then, are subjective in the sense that they are personal. They are, in the second place, individual rather than social. Royce once said that the greatest difference between his religious philosophy and that of James lay in his emphasis on the social aspect, as contrasted with James's individualistic interest. Not that James was blind to the demands made upon the individual by society. The ultimate goal of all activity is the good of the greatest number of individuals. " There is but one unconditional commandment," James wrote in " The Moral Philosopher and the Moral Life," " which is that we should seek incessantly, with fear and trembling, so to vote and act as to bring about the very largest total universe of good which we can see." And in a more concrete sense, James had emphatically what would be called a " social outlook." We have commented before on his activity in behalf of the Philippine Islanders, as well as on his democratic instincts. " On a Certain Blindness in Human Beings " is an eloquent appeal for tolerance of other ideals and ideas and for non-interference with other lives. In the essay on " What Makes a

Life Significant " he remarks that he sometimes thinks " not to our generals and poets, but to the Italian and Hungarian laborers in the Subway, ought monuments of gratitude and reverence to be raised." From Europe he writes to his wife in glowing terms of the unobtrusive and unappreciated virtues so widely prevalent in peasant life. And as for his attitude toward those of his own circle of acquaintance, no one can read the two volumes of published letters without realizing how true and warm a friend he must have been, and how largely the welfare of his friends determined his own happiness.

Yet it remains true that in his religion, as in his philosophy, it is the individualistic note that is struck. James does not share the interest of the French school of sociologists or even of his fellow partisans the Chicago pragmatists, in the social origin and sociological significance of religion. Social ceremonies are hardly mentioned in all the twenty lectures which make up the volume on *Varieties of Religious Experience.* Mysticism is treated not as a precipitation of ideas gained from the social milieu, but as the point at which the individual's vision brings its own authority. Similarly James does not have Rauschenbusch's interest in formulating a theology for the social gospel any more than he catches Royce's vision of the Beloved Community. His is not primarily a gospel of social righteousness or of service. Both follow from his theory, but they follow *implicitly.* They are not James's point of approach or his final goal. His writings in this respect furnish a refreshing contrast to the prevalent over-emphasis on the social origin and social values and functions of religion.

In his entire theory of values James is consistently individualistic. What is the purpose of a college education? he asks in the essay on " The Social Value of the College-Bred." [2] It is to help you to know a good man when you see him! Our colleges should teach biographical history. Perhaps it is James's early artistic training which makes its influence felt here, for just as the greatest art finds universal qualities in

[2] *Memories and Studies,* pp. 309 ff.

the individual, so James seems to discover universal values in the whole-hearted aspirations of the human individual spirit. College should teach us, he says, what it is that makes a superior individual superior: " The feeling for a good human job anywhere, the admiration of the really admirable . . . this is what we call the critical sense, the sense for ideal values. . . . Our colleges ought to have lit up in us a lasting relish for the better kind of man, a loss of appetite for mediocrities, and a disgust for cheapjacks."

And seeing in what superiority consists we should strive to attain it for ourselves. More abundant living, on the part of each man and woman, — that is James's ideal for us. The satisfaction of the greatest number of desires of the greatest number of individuals is the goal. Let each individual make life as rich and complete as he can, let him satisfy as many of his own ideals as possible, always remembering the other person's freedom to determine his own ideals for himself. For " neither the whole of truth nor the whole of good is revealed to any one observer."

Values are thus linked with personality as it expresses itself in individualistic and distinctive desires and purposes. Another requirement of values is that they shall fill the needs of the whole man rather than those of the theoretic consciousness exclusively. Consciousness itself functions, as we have seen in detail, for the sake of ends that are set by our practical and emotional nature. In Goethe's words, which James often quoted:

" Grau, theurer Freund, ist alle Theorie
Und grün des Lebens goldner Baum."

The nature of values may be further explained by noticing how the interested, purposeful individual not merely finds them, but brings them into being. In a previous chapter it was observed that we invest with reality the objects to which we attend. To this statement must now be added another, that our attention, itself determined by emotional and volitional interests, has the power to invest its object with *value*. If we were ourselves devoid of interest, and viewed the world with a complete absence of emotion, we should find the world it-self to be empty of value. " Significance " and " importance " would then be meaningless terms. So we may say that " What-ever of value, interest, or meaning our respective worlds may appear endued with are thus pure gifts of the spectator's mind." [3] Here is summed up at once the subjective, individual, and emotional-volitional character of value. Or, to take a dif-ferent context, Walt Whitman's ecstasy may seem absurd, says James, " yet in what other *kind* of value can the precious-ness of any hour, made precious by any standard, consist, if it consist not in feelings of excited significance like these, en-gendered in some one, by what the hour contains? " [4]

These experiences of " excited significance " seem to have come most often for James when the element of aggressiveness was present. When the active part of man's nature is work-ing effectively, when it is strongly aroused by a combative or recalcitrant element in the experiential material which must be bent to its purpose, then life takes on zest and meaning. The ideal must be there, but it must be coupled with effort. This is divertingly illustrated in a letter to Mrs. James written after he had attended a Chautauqua conference. Such a " mid-dle class Paradise " was too lacking in vigor to hold his enthusiasm: " Now for Utica and Lake Placid by rail, with East Hill in prospect for tomorrow. You bet I rejoice at the outlook — I long to escape from tepidity. Even an Armenian massacre, whether to be killer or killed, would seem an agree-able change from the blamelessness of Chautauqua as she lies soaking year after year in her lakeside sun and showers. Man wants to be *stretched* to his utmost, if not in one way then in another." [5]

To mention strain and effort is to suggest moral values and their place in the scheme. The first question which occurs is: What is their origin? This subject James takes up in the final chapter of the *Principles of Psychology* but he does not find an answer which entirely satisfies him. The last paragraph of

[3] *Varieties of Religious Experience*, p. 150.
[4] *Talks to Teachers*, p. 247.
[5] *Letters*, 2: 43.

the book leaves the question undecided. However, if we do not know whence moral ideals came, we do at least know something about the manner of their coming. They seem to correspond to changes of brain structure which in turn have come as spontaneous variations. Certainly some of them have nothing to do with immediate utility. But like our sensitiveness to the charm of a sequence of sounds or of a design or of an arrangement of colors, many of our ideals seem to have arisen from certain inborn feelings for the fitness of things, which themselves are inexplicable except as variations of organic structure.

This is true alike of intellectual, moral, and aesthetic ideals. We are inclined to think of the desire for scientific accuracy as something which the race has always possessed; but actually, " few even of the cultivated members of the race have shared it; it was invented but a few centuries ago." [6] But with the intellectual ideal once established, the " subjective need for uniformity " or the felt necessity for relating and classifying, we find that the environment lends itself to its requirements more readily than it does to aesthetic or moral needs. Science finds its postulates justified fairly readily, much more readily than are those of art, and still more than those of morality. The external order does not yield easily to the demands of our moral nature. When it does yield, our moral postulate becomes a moral proposition, but accepted propositions of ethics are today even less in number than those of aesthetics, as the latter are less than those of science.

The account of the origin of these ideals given by the associationist school in psychology is correct to a certain extent. Some of them are determined entirely by habitual association with ideas of pleasure and pain. But just as clearly others are independent of habit or of immediately felt utility, and these we can only refer to spontaneous physiological variations in ourselves. In the intellectual realm we accept much as a matter of experience — that fire burns, that motion is communicated from one object to another, etc. But the ulti-

[6] *Principles*, 2: 640 n.

mate postulate of the rational mind, that the universe must be through and through intelligible, is not a product of any experienced effects. Similarly in the moral realm the individual takes his own rights as a matter of course, but the more subtle details of social ethics are not explicable so easily. " They present themselves far less in the guise of effects of past experience than in that of probable causes of future experience, factors to which the environment and the lessons it has so far taught us must learn to bend." [7]

The question of origins, however, is not the most important question of ethics. James is throughout consistent with the standard which in the *Varieties* he sets up for the study of religion. Not by their roots, but by their fruits, ye shall know them. The question of how obligation arises must defer to the question of its practical meaning for us. Moral and other values, as we have seen, do not exist except in a world of sentient beings. In a universe constituted merely of physical and chemical elements it is impossible to say that one state of affairs is better than another. But as soon as even one sentient being is introduced, a standard of value enters. " Good " and " bad " now have meaning, for any thing or event may further the interests of this being. In so far as any phenomenon does so, it is absolutely good. Any conflict has to do simply with the interests of this being, there is no standard external to him. Of the various ideals with which he is confronted, some " will no doubt be more pungent and appealing than the rest, their goodness will have a profounder, more penetrating taste; they will return to haunt him with more obstinate regrets if violated. So the thinker will have to order his life with them as its chief determinants, or else remain inwardly discordant and unhappy." [8]

This inward lack of concord is all that immorality means so far, but the situation is greatly complicated if another person or a number of persons be introduced. Then we should have as many worlds as persons, each with its demands gradually becoming internally unified and developing its own indi-

[7] *The Will to Believe, etc.,* p. 189.   [8] *Ibid.,* p. 191.

vidual ideas of truth and value, but with as yet no common criteria. There is a great deal of goodness in the world thus described because there are many desires and demands. The method of determining *betterness* is not so clear. But James sticks to his guns. Nothing is good except as some consciousness feels it to be good, and there is no obligation except as some personality makes a claim. The converse is true as well. Obligation is felt only where there is a claim, and wherever there is a claim there is an obligation. There is nothing external to our human wants which swoops down and infuses them with validity. Our wants carry their own obligation. " Take any demand, however slight, which any creature, however weak, may make. Ought it not, for its own sole sake, to be satisfied? If not, prove why not. The only possible kind of proof you could adduce would be the exhibition of another creature who should make a demand that ran the other way. The only possible reason there can be why any phenomenon ought to exist is that such a phenomenon actually is desired. Any desire is imperative to the extent of its amount; it *makes* itself valid by the fact that it exists at all." [9]

What a confusion! is our first reaction. Desires everywhere making claims, yet no way of telling which claim has precedence. But just here the religious view shows its superiority. For religion postulates demands which are both personal and authoritative. The claims which God makes are as genuinely personal as any claims can be and at the same time more compelling than anything human. So a man who believes in the existence of a great universal consciousness and who believes he knows the desires of this consciousness has a sure standard of moral values. But he must not appeal over the head of the Deity to any *a priori* ethic, any transcendental Reason or Justice. And even his recognition of the divine will must be kept concrete. It is not *abstractly* right that he should respect God's commands. God's own standard of right must find confirmation in the believer's desires before it is final for him.

So personal desires determine values. With a true scientific,

[9] *Ibid.*, p. 195.

realistic interest in the concrete, James regards human interests the surest things we know and the most satisfactory determinants of whatever values there may be in life. And where human desires fail to provide a satisfactory standard there is always the tempting possibility of bringing in divine desires to fill the gap. The religious conflict which has taken so much of our attention was itself a conflict between claims arising from conflicting desires. The problem of the absolute James settled on the basis of comparative values. And conversely the problem of absolutism seems to have helped him to a theory of value. Ever and again in his writings we find evidence that the question of absolutism was lurking in James's mind and influencing his decisions. He adopts a radical notion of truth largely because he cannot allow himself to be committed to an absolutistic, static universe. And similarly his aversion for the determined and the compulsory seems to have had a part in his decision for a theory of value in which man plays a creative rôle.

A characteristic touch is found in James's statement that the postulation of God is not necessary to give validity to the ethical claim. For himself it is the most satisfactory method but he does not wish to force his method on others. It is necessary that the belief in God should not be necessary. The one thing we must not accept is compulsion in our beliefs or in our actions. Whether or not God exist, human life affords a basis for an ethical code. The only question is whether the *philosopher's* demand for ethical stability is adequately met in a system which leaves religion out. But since human life does afford such a basis there must be some strictly human method of distinguishing what is truly good. " The best, on the whole, of these marks and measures of goodness seems to be the capacity to bring happiness. But in order not to break down fatally, this test must be taken to cover innumerable acts and impulses that never *aim* at happiness; so that, after all, in seeking for a universal principle we inevitably are carried onward to the *most* universal principle — that *the essence of good is simply to satisfy demand.*" [10]

[10] *Ibid.*, p. 201.

Yet even this brings out the tentative character of ethical theory. Which demands are satisfied in truly lasting and effective fashion? In the chapter on *Mysticism* we shall take up one possible way of answering the question. Here let us notice that in the essay on " The Moral Philosopher and the Moral Life," which has furnished the material for the present discussion, James definitely gives evidence of the longing which we have noticed in him before for that peace of finality which transcends all experimentation. " It would seem, too, — and this is my final conclusion — that the stable and systematic moral universe for which the ethical philosopher asks is possible only in a world where there is a divine thinker with all-enveloping demands. If such a thinker existed, his way of subordinating the demands to one another would be the finally valid casuistic scale; his claims would be the most appealing; his ideal universe would be the most inclusive realizable whole. If he now exist, then actualized in his thought already must be that ethical philosophy which we seek as the pattern which our own must evermore approach. In the interests of our own ideal of systematically unified moral truth, therefore, we, as would-be philosophers, must postulate a divine thinker, and pray for the validity of the religious cause." [11]

Religion thus satisfies the need for final authority but the conflicting need is ever present. Even in this essay the part that it also plays in calling up the strenuous mood is emphasized. In religion " the more imperative ideals . . . begin to speak with an altogether new objectivity and significance, and to utter the penetrating, shattering, tragically challenging note of appeal. They ring out like the call of Victor Hugo's alpine eagle, ' qui parle au précipice et que le gouffre entend,' and the strenuous mood awakens at the sound. . . . The capacity of the strenuous mood lies so deep down among our natural human possibilities that even if there were no metaphysical or traditional grounds for believing in a God, men would postulate one simply as a pretext for living hard, and getting out of

[11] p. 214.

the game of existence its keenest possibilities of zest. . . . Every sort of energy and endurance, of courage and capacity for handling life's evils, is set free in those who have religious faith. For this reason the strenuous type of character will on the battle-field of human history always outwear the easy-going type, and religion will drive irreligion to the wall." [12]

This stirring passage should be convincing on the score that moral values reach their consummation in a religious environment just as the philosophic demand for a unified ethical theory is most easily satisfied on a religious basis. From whatever angle we view it, morality points to religion. Deeply intrenched as is James's scientifically realistic urge, just as deep is the impulse to peer out beyond the world of phenomena to find a transcendent reality which shall give human values the highest kind of validity.

A teleological view of human life finds its completion in religion in a similar way. Like his ethics, James's teleology has a psychological basis, and starts by stressing the volitional nature of human activity. It appears early in his writings, notably in his " Remarks on Spencer's Definition of Mind as Correspondence," first published in 1878 and now reprinted in *Collected Essays and Reviews,* pp. 43 ff., where the purposive character of thought is clearly stated. Human interests and desires, one discovers in this article, are not only the determinants of our ethics, they furnish both the power and the direction for our thinking. Thought is carried on for the benefit of specific interests. All intellectual activity is definitely purposive. James's teleology, that is to say, is not the kind which has reference to a universal, cosmic plan which the whole creation travaileth together to achieve. It is not the Platonic or Leibnitzian variety, but one allied in some respects to that of vitalism. It is not like the " radical finalism " which Bergson repudiates [13] but bears resemblance to the *élan vital* which he postulates. Or, using Professor McDougall's ter-

[12] P. 213.
[13] *Creative Evolution*, p. 39.

minology, it is a kind of " hormic " theory.[14] James has himself hinted at the difference in a letter to N. S. Shaler.[15]

Teleology as expressed in the *Principles of Psychology* makes consciousness an organ functioning for the sake of emotional and volitional needs. Mental activity is a means to practical adjustment. Pragmatism recognizes anew the importance of this practical adjustment and makes it a criterion of the correctness, that is, the success, of mental activity. The teleological view finds in the practical differences made by consciousness the fulfillment of the organism's purpose. Pragmatism finds in them a clue to the meaning of truth as well. Truth itself resides in the satisfaction of those interests which consciousness, following its volitional leading, says must be satisfied.

In the essay on " Reflex Action and Theism " James uses his teleological theory in the interests of religion. The reflex theory of mental action, he says, the theory that all intellectual activity is a middle term between the incoming currents of sensation and the outward active discharges from the nervous centres, forces us to regard the mind as a teleological mechanism. The middle department, the theorizing part of the mind, functions in the interest of what James calls our emotional and practical subjectivity. Our minds receive a sense impression, define it, decide on a course of action, and then react. But the defining and deciding are carried on for the sake of the action, they are purposeful. And when the object that confronts us is not an individual sense-object but the whole of experience, when we are forced, that is, to decide on our attitude toward life and its values, then again our decision is made for and known in terms of its practical consequences. I may refuse to decide or may decide that " All is vanity," but the consequences are significant in any case.

A decision as to the universe, then, like a decision as to anything else, must satisfy each of the three departments of the mind. It must not contradict what we learn through the senses, it must not be internally inconsistent, or conflict with

[14] *Outline of Psychology*, p. 71.   [15] *Letters*, 2: 154.

other mental conceptions, and finally it must be consonant with our active impulses. This last requirement, thinks James, is the one that needs the most emphasis. And in it is found one of our surest leadings towards a theistic decision. The solutions to the riddle of the universe which are offered by materialism and agnosticism are wholly out of accord with our active demands. Our volitional nature demands something to do. But what? Remain in ignorance and act on the hypothesis that you don't know, says agnosticism. React to atoms, says materialism. But how can this satisfy our active needs? Theism, however, " always stands ready with the most practically rational solution it is possible to conceive. Not an energy of our active nature to which it does not authoritatively appeal, not an emotion of which it does not normally and naturally release the springs. At a single stroke, it changes the dead blank *it* of the world into a living *thou,* with whom the whole man may have dealings. . . . Our volitional nature must then, until the end of time, exert a constant pressure upon the other departments of the mind to induce them to function to a theistic conclusion." [16] Anything short of a theistic view therefore will always be irrational, using the word rational, as James always does use it, to mean satisfactory to the whole nature of man. Theism, in making the universe personal, makes possible vigorous and satisfactory action. Like pluralism it gives a man "something to worship and fight for."

But if anything which falls short of theism is irrational, anything which goes beyond theism is impossible. We may change the " it " of the universe into a " thou," but we are not justified in turning the " thou " into a " me." To do so is to follow the gnostic tendency to bridge the gap between subject and object, as in the Hegelian system. An unwarranted and undesirable monism is the result. The fact that James could not tolerate a conceptual identity of Deity and devotee must not be construed, however, as a rejection of the possibility of mystical union. Theistic mysticism, he says,

---

[16] *The Will to Believe, etc.,* p. 127.

does not try to transcend the dualism of worshipper and Object of worship; it simply is not interested in speculating on whether there is a dualism or not. The mystic (or the theist) decides that a religious reaction to the world is appropriate, " and into that reaction he forthwith pours his soul. His insight into the *what* of life leads to results so immediately and intimately rational that the *why*, the *how* and the *whence* of it are questions that lose all urgency. . . . Happiness over the fact that being has made itself what it is, evacuates all speculation as to how it could make itself at all."[17] Thus if we accept the teleological view of human life which James thinks psychology forces us to accept, we are led inevitably to theism. Anything less than theism is irrational, anything greater is impossible. Again philosophy finds its completion in religion.

The more one studies James the more vivid becomes the impression of the keenness and liveliness of his sense for value. He was awake, as only the most gifted spirits are, to the richness and beauty and worth-whileness of life, and one of his outstanding characteristics was his ability to find desirable and noteworthy objects in the most surprising and out-of-the-way places. He had a full share of those "piercing intuitions" which in one passage he mentions as necessary for the discernment that makes possible the good life. The more intimate of his letters fairly breathe this quality, and it is found to a marked degree in the talks to students and in the biographical sketches published in *Memories and Studies*.

The conflict between this eager, appreciative type of mind intent after realizable values and insistent that these values may justifiably be taken as an index of ultimate reality, and the other type which prides itself on its purer, in the sense of more disinterested, intellectualism has been commented on before. James, as we have seen, has been taken to task by a host of critics for his supposed failure to recognize that the student should aim to envisage the truth as it is in itself rather than as he wishes it to be. This criticism is made with peculiar force by Professor Santayana in his brilliant essay in

[17] *The Will to Believe, etc.*, p. 136.

Character and Opinion in the United States. " James," he
says,[18] " fell in with the hortatory tradition of college sages;
he turned his psychology, whenever he could do so honestly,
to purposes of edification. . . . He seems to have felt sure
that certain thoughts and hopes — those familiar to a liberal
Protestantism — were every man's true friends in life. . . .
But what is a good life? Had William James, had the people
about him, had modern philosophers anywhere, any notion of
that? I cannot think so. They had much experience of personal goodness . . . but as to what might render human existence good, excellent, beautiful, happy, and worth having as a
whole, their notions were utterly thin and barbarous."

A touch of severity, this, which seems hardly called for. In
the first place, James's outlook was clearly not limited by
Protestantism any more than it was by the point of view of
any other confession. In the second place, not merely as a
doer, but also as a discoverer of what is good, he seems to
have established a place in the minds of thousands of his
readers. It is true that James was, to use Matthew Arnold's
terms, as much of a Hebraist as he was a Hellenist. A seeker
after truth he was indeed, but one who found both value and
indications as to truth in the doing of the immediate task.
The good life is not discovered *merely* by speculating concerning it. Thought and speculation there must be, most assuredly, but meanwhile there are tasks to be done, friendly
services to be performed, beautiful things to be appreciated.
Life includes all these things, and the good life is the one
which is more richly endowed with them than any other.
And if we say that life offers us these things must we add
that in doing so it breaks with truth? Is not even truth made
up of elements which the active life brings and joins to the
contemplative? Ideas themselves are, psychologically speaking, in large part the product of motor reactions. Consciousness is impulsive. And truth is dynamic, individual, and in
part, perhaps the most important part, being created by
human effort.

[18] P. 84.

The criticism of James's right to turn his psychology "to purposes of edification" seems to rest on the supposition that he should not have tried to edify unless he had an assurance which neither he nor any other human being can hope to have as to the final adequacy of his premises. Instead of commenting on this rather remarkable assumption that science is never justified in pointing a moral, one may indicate the extraordinary response which James evoked by his use of psychology for moral admonition. His chapters on "Habit" and on "Will" are recognized as remarkable for their ethical insight. The former has been published separately, and widely used for ethical instruction. It seems a trifle far-fetched to claim that its "hortatory" and "edifying" qualities *per se* interfere with its scientific standing. Is it not rather the case that its ability to meet the needs of so many persons is an evidence of its claim on the truth? It may be the fact in actual experience that the preacher often does not share the investigator's clear vision of reality. But if so, he fails not because he is a preacher but simply because he is not an investigator as well. And the most adequate research worker in the field of ethics and religion would seem to be the one who has the most complete vision and the broadest sympathies, who understands the practical implications for human living of his scientific vision and uses that understanding to arrive at the most complete, most synthetic truth. James has done just this. And it is noteworthy that his use of the evidence of value and purpose in human life to suggest the nature of ultimate reality pointed the path which is today being followed in many of our contemporary attempts to bring science and religion closer together.[19] James's description of human life in its cosmic environment in terms of will and purpose is a moral and spiritual tonic, and may be trusted to make its appeal to readers as a true account as long as men think of experience in terms of effort and combat.

[19] Cf. the arguments of Dean Shailer Mathews in *Contributions of Science to Religion* and of Professor Arthur Thomson in his *Science and Religion*.

James's whole philosophy may thus be described in terms of its insistence on the reality of human values in themselves as defined by human desires and purposes, and on the right to consider them as indices of whatever higher realms of being may exist. The real is the rational, truly enough, but the rational must include the humanly desirable. No definition which leaves this out is thinkable. And the humanly desirable can be brought into existence if our will be sufficiently strong. In religion we are dealing with the realm in which what *ought to be* can, with certain limitations, be identified with what *is*.

In concluding this chapter let us once more notice the important supplementary part which religion plays in James's theory of values. Whether there be a God or not, moral values endure. Yet James seems hardly to have arrived at a satisfactory human standard for appraising them. Utility, pungency, lasting quality, — these are not easy to apply. If, however, we can believe in a God, a clear and authoritative standard appears. And the presence of a God not only satisfies our desire for finality, it makes the values themselves more compelling. Finally, it is in the religious realm, if anywhere, that we begin to see how value can be identified with validity. For here we are dealing with postulates and creative hypotheses. The active will in its freedom and its purposefulness asserts its right to believe and in so doing creates the appropriate conditions for the operation of the objects of its belief. To two of its beliefs, in God and in immortality, we must now turn.

VII

THE DEITY

"ANY author is easy," said James, "if you catch the centre of his vision." From it his ideas radiate and in it the main lines of his thought converge. Nearly all the paths in James's thought led to a conception of the Deity. James was attracted to the absolute in so far as he could conceive it as an Object of worship. The insight of the passive mood brought by suffering and discouragement revealed the deeper levels of experience. But the way to God indicated by the active impulses was just as sure. Our volitional activity may be our deepest organ of communication with the nature of things. Ethics points to a Deity both in order to realize the most stable and systematic code of rules, and also to call forth the most thorough-going allegiance to the moral ideal. While the moral aim remains dominant, "religion will drive irreligion to the wall." Similarly, the teleological view of human activity makes anything less than God irrational, anything greater impossible. The testimony of mysticism, which we shall later examine in greater detail, lends probability to the notion of a Deity; our subjective nature, which we have a right to trust, demands one; and pragmatically the value of the God-idea for life encourages us to a positive belief. That God exists is thus the testimony of many different elements in James's philosophy.

James's conception of God seems to have undergone a fairly clear line of development, marked by three stages. The distinctions between these stages are not absolute, and frequently the difference is only a matter of emphasis. But that the distinction, at least of emphasis, is there it seems impossible to deny. The first position is found in the volume called *The Will to Believe and Other Essays,* including articles originally published from 1880 to 1895. The second is set forth in *The Varieties of Religious Experience* published in 1902. The final statement is found in *A Pluralistic Universe* published in 1909.

In the first stage God is conceived primarily as a postulate necessary for the letting loose of the strenuous mood, an essential stimulus to the most vigorous and most highly moral life. Other ideas of God are mentioned. As we have already seen, " The Sentiment of Rationality," written before 1880, the earliest of the essays published with " The Will to Believe," makes favorable references to " ontological emotion " and " the peace of rationality." But a careful reading will show that the emphasis in this and later essays in the same volume is the other way. " ' Son of Man, stand upon thy feet and I will speak to thee! ' is the only revelation of truth to which the solving epochs have helped the disciple." And " that has been enough to satisfy the greater part of his rational need." [1] All great periods of intellectual expansion have taught the lesson: " The inmost nature of reality is congenial to *powers* which you possess." [2] To be acceptable a philosophy must indeed to some degree determine expectancy, but it must to a greater degree make an appeal to our capacities for effort. Here in " The Sentiment of Rationality " as in the essay on " The Will to Believe " James uses the call to activity as an argument for faith in God. In the interests of our active nature a God must be postulated. Inferentially, God is that which calls forth our latent energy.

The next essay, on " Reflex Action and Theism," an address delivered in 1881, brings this out as clearly as the first. Any conception which falls short of God is irrational because any conception less than God is an inadequate stimulus to our practical nature. But, as we have seen, theism is always ready with " the most practically rational solution it is possible to conceive. Not an energy of our active nature to which it does

---

[1] *The Will to Believe, etc.,* p. 88.   [2] *The Will to Believe, etc.,* p. 86.

not authoritatively appeal, not an emotion of which it does not normally and naturally release the springs." [3] And elsewhere in the same essay James defines God as " A power not ourselves . . . which not only makes for righteousness, but means it, and which recognizes us." [4]

Energy, power, moral activity, for these things we must have God, and the most important definition of God is that formulated in terms of his function of arousing them in us. The essay on " The Moral Philosopher and the Moral Life," written in 1891, carries this thought on consistently. A world without a God lacks the power to appeal in the most stimulating way to our moral energy. If there were no other grounds for belief men would postulate a Deity simply as a pretext for living hard. We need God for this kind of stimulation, we postulate him to fill this need, and we define him as the one who does so fill it. Our moral and volitional response to life seems to be our deepest organ of communication with the nature of things, our clearest source of revelation as to that nature.

" Is Life Worth Living? " written in 1895, continues in the same key. Life *is* worth living, James says, since it is what we make it, from the moral point of view. By exerting ourselves we can force it to be worth living. Our moral activity is the determinant. We must believe that our life is worth while, and our belief will help to create the fact. Religious faith is belief of this sort. We know nothing positive of the unseen world, but we believe that the significance of our present life consists in our relation to it. This is our nearest clue to a knowledge of its nature. Any definition which we make of this unseen world or of God must be in terms of significance for human life, especially significance in calling forth our most strenuous moral powers. Life is a real fight, and ultimate reality must be understood as taking cognizance of and even having a part in it.

To this first stage in James's thought about God belongs an illuminating unpublished letter to Thomas Davidson. In this

[3] *The Will to Believe, etc.,* p. 127.   [4] *The Will to Believe, etc.,* p. 122.

letter the idea of a finite God and a pluralistic melioristic world scheme is clearly suggested, though the date of the letter is as early as 1882. But the interest here also is in defining God in terms commensurable with human purposes. Our strivings must have an outward warrant, God must be that which gives meaning to our moral activity. The " address " referred to in the first paragraph is apparently that on " Reflex Action and Theism " ; the " squib on Hegel " seems to be the paper written for Professor Palmer's Hegel class which, on Professor Palmer's suggestion, was published in *Mind* for April, 1882, and later republished along with " The Will to Believe " under the title " On Some Hegelisms."

CAMBRIDGE
January 8, 1882

My dear Davidson:

Your letter, just rec'd, makes glad my heart. Next to a good Theist, give me a good Atheist; and that you seem to have become, — whether in spite or in consequence of Rosmini, ignorance prevents me from deciding. To speak seriously, your blame is more agreeable to me than most all the praise I've got for that " address." The latter left me with my bad conscience increased; for the address was a curious composition on my part, the conclusions I believed in being enforced by arguments which I cared little about and which were used merely on account of their availability and *ad captandum* power. I wanted to show that psychology could send out an anti-materialistic blast as well as she had been supposed to emit materialistic ones. I wanted too to give popular form to my hobby of the ubiquitousness of emotional interests in the mind's operations. So I rather deliberately sacrificed accuracy to effectiveness in taking the reflex triad ready made from the psychologists, as if it were a truly *mental* analysis, — and I reaped my reward in much applause. I have felt constrained to explain my errors to such correspondents as Hodgson and Renouvier. But you don't attack me for them, but for my conclusions, which I hold to. It is a curious thing,

this matter of God! I can sympathize perfectly with the most
rabid hater of him and the idea of him, when I think of the
use that has been made of him in history and philosophy as a
starting point, or premise for grounding deductions. But as an
Ideal to attain and make probable, I find myself less and less
able to do without Him. He need not be an *all*-including
"subjective unity of the universe," as you suppose. In fact
there is nothing I clasp hands with you so heartily in, as in
defying the superstition of such a unity. It is only one possible hypothesis amid many — and becomes (d — n my eyes, I
must call my wife to write for me!) a pure superstition the
moment it is treated dogmatically. All I mean is that there
must be *some* subjective unity in the Universe which has purposes commensurable with my own and which is at the same
time large enough to be, among all the powers that may be
there, the strongest. I simply refuse to accept the notion of
there being no purpose in the objective world. On the other
hand, I cannot represent the existence of purpose except as
based in a mind. The not-me therefore, so far as it contains
purpose must spring from a mind; but not necessarily a *One
and Only* mind. In saying " God exists " all I imply is that my
purposes are cared for by a mind so powerful as on the whole
to control the drift of the Universe. This is as much polytheism as monotheism. As a matter of fact it is neither, for
it is hardly a speculative position at all but a merely practical
and emotional faith which I fancy even your Promethean
Gemüth shares. The only difficulties of theism are the moral
difficulties and meannesses; and they have always seemed to me
to flow from the gratuitous dogma of God being the all-inclusive reality. Once think possible a primordial pluralism
of which he may be one member and which may have no
single subjective synthesis, and piety forthwith ceases to be
incompatible with manliness and religious " Faith " with intellectual rectitude. In short the only theism I defend is that
of simple unphilosophic mankind, to which numerical mysteries are added corruptions. If there be a God, how the devil
can we know what difficulties he may have had to contend

with? (This last remark is from my amanuensis spouse.) *Darauf kommt es an!* Possible difficulties! they save everything. But what are they but limitations to the all-inclusiveness of any single being?

January 9th. Since last night we have finished reading aloud your article on Rosmini which we began some days back. It amused me to find how some of your phrases at the end agree with those I have used in this letter. It is a strong article both in style and matter, and ought to produce an impression; but what will your Rosminian friends think of you after reading your *Auslassungen* against their religion? I wish I could get a glimpse of the meaning of R's system. Not a line of the *Psicologia* I hoped to read this winter has been looked at yet — So runs the world away!

What news can I tell you? Nothing in the college, where the old routine prevails. Harris has founded a weekly Saturday afternoon Hegel Club where he expounds the third volume of the *Logik* to ten of us, Palmer, Cabot, Hall, Everett, Emery and some others. I am much won by his innocence and apostolic disposition, but not a word has he said that has any magic for me. I rather shrink from hurting his feelings by my squib on Hegel and have left the decision in the hands of Robertson. I am sorry you find Hodgson confused. To not many of us is it granted to be confused on such a scale!

Dr. Gibson, who I think must have been a rather big, modest, silent bearded man, with whom I dined at Hodgson's one day, I supposed to be himself an Hegelian from the manner of his review of Sully's *Illusions* in Harris' *Journal.*

Addio, Davidson mio. If there *is* a God, where will you be on the day of judgment? The immortality of which you are so certain will keep you forever exposed to his wrath. Write again soon to yours ever

WM. JAMES

The contention that at this time in his life James was interested in defining God chiefly in terms of his function as a
stimulus to men is confirmed by the realization that these essays and this letter were written during a period when the
theory of pragmatism was beginning to take on interest for
James. Charles S. Peirce had printed his " Illustrations of
the Logic of Science " the year before " The Sentiment of Rationality " appeared, the famous second paper in Peirce's
series, called " How to Make Our Ideas Clear," having been
published in the *Popular Science Monthly* for January, 1878.
" Consider what effects," Peirce had written, " which might
conceivably have practical bearings, we conceive the object
of our conception to have. Then, our conception of these effects is the whole of our conception of the object." [5] This defining a conception in terms of its effects is just what James
has done here. Pragmatism, at this period of his life, meant
this kind of procedure. It was a theory of the definition of
conceptions in terms of their practical consequence, and it was
not the elaborate theory of truth and value which James afterwards made it. Even in 1898, in the Berkeley address on
" Philosophical Conceptions and Practical Results," where he
first uses the word " pragmatism," James applies it only to
this kind of case, using it to define ideas in terms of consequences. It is interesting to notice further that two of the
ideas prominent in the essays we have been discussing, the
subordination of conceptual to volitional activity, and the interdependence of belief and action, are found in Peirce's
article.

What we have called the first stage in James's developing
conception of God is therefore the stage in which, using his
earliest version of the pragmatic theory he defined God in
terms of his function as releaser of man's active energies. The
case is different when we come to the second stage, set forth
in *The Varieties of Religious Experience.* Here the interest
shifts from man's active energies to God's saving power.
Throughout the *Varieties* James seems ever to be impressed

[5] *Popular Science Monthly,* Vol. 12, p. 293.

anew by the *power* of the religious Object. God comforts the sick soul, encourages the healthy-minded, knits up the divided self, accomplishes conversion, leads on to saintliness, communicates with mystics, and is the author of saving experiences in which work is undeniably accomplished. These experiences are so real that their cause must be real. So much work must require a Worker. To say that the kind of cause to which those who have religious experiences almost unanimously testify is imaginary is to be untrue to the empirical ideal. Accepting the data given, we find work being done which does not readily lend itself to analysis according to our usual human categories. No more do we need to postulate, we have merely to describe what we see going on. The interest, it seems fair to say, is no longer anthropocentric but theocentric.

Correspondingly, while in the *Varieties* the active energies are not neglected, it is the passive mood which receives the greater amount of attention. On the whole it is not man's active energy, but his capacity to receive help from on high which is stressed. The moment of discouragement may bring the deeper insight. " Morbid-mindedness ranges over the wider scale of experience," and life's ills may be " possibly the only openers of our eyes to the deepest levels of truth." The deepest need of the human heart may be not for combat but for assurance and peace.

James announces at the beginning of the *Varieties* that his criterion of value is results, not origins, and the book as a whole is largely a description of the results for life of religion. One of the early chapters treats of the reality and objective quality of the unseen presence immediately experienced in religion. The two following explain how religion brings serenity, poise, and immunity to certain kinds of disease, and show that in the deliverance which it brings lies religion's chief claim to our interest. The next three chapters describe the remarkable phenomena attending conversion, including spiritual activity of a highly dramatic nature. Following this comes a discussion of " Saintliness " with its fruits for life, and here James says explicitly that the value of results is a determinant of the objective reality of the agency which produces the results. Since saintliness tests high ethically the beliefs which inspire it stand accredited. Mysticism, likewise, brings its own unimpeachable authority to the person to whom it comes, and prayer is a condition in which spiritual work is really accomplished.

Finally, in his conclusions, James comes out unequivocally for the significance of the spiritual activity which all these experiences describe, and for the reality of the agency by which they are produced. All religions are capable of description, he says, in terms of: (1) An uneasiness, and (2) Its solution, *i.e.*, by the sense that there is something wrong about us as we stand, and the sense " *that we are saved from the wrongness* by making proper connections with the higher powers." Man becomes conscious of a " more " which is conterminous and continuous with the higher part of himself " which is operative in the universe outside of him, and which he can keep in working touch with, and in a fashion get on board of and save himself when all his lower being has gone to pieces in the wreck." [6]

He then goes on to his famous theory that " whatever it may be on its *farther* side, the ' more ' with which in religious experience we feel ourselves connected is on its *hither* side the subconscious continuation of our conscious life." [7] Whether or not this be a satisfactory way of describing our means of contact with the Object of religious experience we are not here interested in deciding. The point to be stressed is that in this book the actual power of the religious experience was uppermost in James's mind. It is this which leads to statements like the following: " we have in *the fact that the conscious person is continuous with a wider self through which saving experiences come,* a positive content of religious experience which, it seems to me, *is literally and objectively true as far as it goes.*" [8] And James does not hesitate to identify the source of these saving experiences with God. " I will call this higher part of the universe by the name of God. We and God

<hr />

[6] *Varieties*, p. 508.   [7] *Varieties*, p. 212.   [8] *Varieties*, p. 515.

have business with each other; and in opening ourselves to his influence our deepest destiny is fulfilled." [9]

The difference between this and the first stage is readily apparent. No longer is it *our* active energies which need a postulated God to call them forth. Here the emphasis is all on the active energies of God, on God's power to produce real effects. And along with the change of emphasis from the powers of men to the power of God goes a change of scene. We are no longer in the world of moral postulates, but have entered the field of psychological description. Our part here is to describe rather than to postulate. " Over-beliefs " may enter, we may have postulates in that sense, but they take the form of hypotheses as to probable causes rather than demands made on the basis of some subjective interest.

Let us notice also that the transition between these two stages in James's conception of God is paralleled by a development in his pragmatic theory. If the first stage is marked by a pragmatism which is directly influenced by Peirce, and finds its chief interest in defining concepts in terms of their practical consequences, this second stage is marked by a tendency to define truth itself in terms of value. A reference to their practical consequences helps not only to make our ideas clear, but to determine their truth, or the reality of their objects. Both kinds of pragmatism do, as a matter of fact, enter the *Varieties*. In the chapter on " Philosophy " James invokes pragmatism by name (which he did not do in the volume on *The Will to Believe*) to test the significance of God's metaphysical attributes. Finding that they have no pragmatic meaning, he rejects them. But it is particularly interesting to note that James did not stop with this attempt to extract a pragmatic meaning for God's attributes as traditionally enumerated. God is more than the attributes which have traditionally been predicated of him, and pragmatism is equipped to discover this more. In attempting to do this pragmatism is but making explicit use of what has always been an implicit popular means to the discovery of truth. Religions have always

[9] *Varieties,* p. 516.

approved themselves to mankind by their fruits for life, and it is reasonable that we should set up value as a standard of truth now. " How can any possible judge or critic help being biased in favor of the religion by which his own needs are best met? "[10] As we saw above, if religion commends itself as a desirable kind of human activity, " then any theological beliefs that may inspire it will stand accredited. If not, then they will be discredited, and all without reference to anything but human working principles." [11]

This, it will be observed, is a clear reference to the determination not only of clearness and meaning, but of truth, on the basis of value and " working," and this procedure is characteristic of James throughout the *Varieties*. Values point the way to truth, and particular facts indicate underlying ultimate principles. " Both instinctively and for logical reasons," he writes, " I find it hard to believe that principles can exist which make no difference in facts. But all facts are particular facts, and the whole interest of the question of God's existence seems to me to lie in the consequences for particulars which that existence may be expected to entail." [12] There is no difference of theory without a corresponding difference of practice and of fact. So much Peirce had said. But now, at least implicitly, James applies the converse of this proposition and, finding marked differences in fact and practice, he makes a difference in his theory to fit them. In two ways, then, we see an advance from the earlier position. Formerly he had said that a need justifies a postulate. Now he suggests that an empirical value points to an ultimate truth. And secondly he is here not content to say that clear definitions of ideas can be made only in terms of consequences. He goes on to the further position that there is no difference among particular facts without a corresponding difference in theory; his interest is not in the clarity of ideas so much as in the new principles which particular facts suggest.

It is evident that we have here a parallel development of James's religious theory and his pragmatic theory in which we

[10] *Varieties*, p. 333.   [11] *Varieties*, p. 331.   [12] *Varieties*, p. 522.

can see mutual influences at work. Clearly James's developing sense of a pragmatic standard had something to do with his belief that religion could claim objective truth as well as subjective value. And it seems just as clear that James's investigation of religion, bringing him into touch with such a mass of testimony as to the existence of a kind of value to which he was himself not at all insensitive, played its part in helping him to the realization that worth for life must be a criterion of truth. Not only is the rational the real, but the truly valuable is the real, the belief that brings truly valuable consequences must have some hold on reality. Such important differences in concrete fact must point to an important speculative element of which our theory should take account. In this book, published in 1902, James appears to be approaching the more radical statement of pragmatic theory which found expression in the volume *Pragmatism,* published in 1907, and which, significantly, was not included in his first utterance on the subject, the Berkeley address delivered in 1898. We have thus found another place where James's religious philosophy takes an influential place in his thought. The study of religious phenomena and the conclusions which it was necessary to draw from that study appear to have influenced his conception of truth itself.

Turning now to what we have called the third stage in the development of his conception of the Deity, we find that it combines the chief characteristics of the other two. To begin with, in *A Pluralistic Universe,* where this third position is set forth, James repeats his comment in the *Varieties* that the testimony of experience to the working of power from on high must influence our notion of the existence of a religious Object. God works in a mysterious way. Religious experiences are of a specific nature and not deducible from our other sorts of experience. Examining religious experience we find " possibilities that take our breath away, of another kind of happiness and power, based on giving up our will and letting something higher work for us." [13] Reasoning in *a priori* fashion we should never

[13] *A Pluralistic Universe,* p. 305.

have suspected the working of this higher power, but proceeding empirically we must take these experiences into account. " As they actually come and are given, creation widens to the view of their recipients." [14] " We inhabit an invisible spiritual environment from which help comes, our soul being mysteriously one with a larger soul whose instruments we are." [15]

But along with this emphasis on God as saving *Power,* characteristic of what we have called James's second position, we find in *A Pluralistic Universe* a similar emphasis on the fact that God's nature is such as to call forth *our* most active response. We live in a *pluralistic* world, for any other kind would take away all life's zest and meaning. Pluralism means real losses as well as real achievements, and it stimulates us to real effort, where monism sets up merely a thin abstraction. God is a part of this pluralistic world and so he is finite, but on that very account more approachable and more of a real leader and inspirer. " Having an environment, being in time, and working out a history just like ourselves, he escapes from the foreignness from all that is human, of the static, timeless, perfect absolute." [16] If God be working out a history " just like ourselves " we enjoy an intimacy with him and respond to his will in a way impossible under any other system. Our whole active nature is quickened by the thought that we are co-laborers with God, aiding him in the realization of purposes that are ours as well as his.

In the autumn of 1904, that is, between the publication of the *Varieties* and *A Pluralistic Universe,* or at the beginning of this third period in the development of his conception of God, James answered Professor J. B. Pratt's questionnaire on religious belief. In his answers we find indications of the attitude which was to become so prominent in *A Pluralistic Universe.* God carries our ideals to fruition and we share in his purposes. But we touch him in our weakness as well as in our strength.

[14] *A Pluralistic Universe,* p. 306.
[15] *A Pluralistic Universe,* p. 308.
[16] *A Pluralistic Universe,* p. 318.

There is a " wider universe of experiences " which ministers to our needs. Some of the replies were as follows:

Q. What do you mean by God?

    A. A combination of Ideality and (final) efficacity.

Q. Is He a person — if so, what do you mean by His being a person?

    A. He must be cognizant and responsive in some way.

Q. Or is He only a Force?

    A. He must *do*.

Q. Or is God an attitude of the Universe toward you?

    A. Yes, but more conscious. " God," to me, is not the only spiritual reality to believe in. Religion means primarily a universe of spiritual relations surrounding the earthly practical ones, not merely relations of " value," but agencies and their activities. I suppose that the chief premise for my hospitality towards the religious testimony of others is my conviction that " normal " or " sane " consciousness is so small a part of actual experience. What e'er be true, *it* is not true exclusively, as philistine scientific opinion assumes. The other kinds of consciousness bear witness to a much wider universe of experiences, from which our belief selects and emphasizes such parts as best satisfy our needs.

Q. Why do you believe in God? Is it . . . because you have experienced His presence?

    A. No, but rather because I need it so that it " must " be true.

Q. Or do you not so much *believe* in God as want to *use* Him?

    A. I can't use him very definitely, yet I believe.

Q. Do you accept Him not so much as a real existent Being, but rather as an ideal to live by?

A. More as a powerful ally of my own ideals.[17]

Thus the two conceptions, God as Power, and God as inciter of our powers, are combined in this third and last stage in James's progress toward a satisfactory conception of God. We have seen that the other two stages marked points of advance in James's pragmatism as well as in his religious theory. Correspondingly we find in this third stage an echo of one of the latest developments of pragmatism, the doctrine of meliorism. This doctrine is explicitly set forth only in the book *Pragmatism,* and in any detail only in the last chapter of that book. It is a theory of the nature of reality and of man's ability to coöperate with God in effecting changes in reality. James describes it as standing midway between optimism and pessimism. It offers a social scheme of coöperative work to be engaged in by God and man together. It realizes, that is to say, the intimacy between God and man which James finds possible in a pluralistic universe, and it calls on the Power of God and the powers of man to effect real changes for the better in a growing world.

The description of these three stages in James's theory has not by any means exhausted the kind of God or Gods which James suggested as possible objects of belief, or their attributes. Nowhere does James's imagination play more freely than on this subject. He always professed himself as particularly interested in " over-beliefs." He found them " the most interesting and important things about a man." His own over-beliefs as expressed in different places in his writings are many and various, and at times border on the grotesque. His pluralistic bent, particularly, at times carried him to extremes. That he himself may have felt this is indicated by his calling his own position that of " crass " or " piecemeal supernaturalism." One of the most curious possibilities is described in the much quoted " Postscript " to the *Varieties* where he suggests that " beyond

[17] *Letters,* pp. 213–4.

each man and in a fashion continuous with him " there may exist a larger power which is friendly to him and to his ideals. ". . . It need not be infinite, it need not be solitary. It might conceivably even be only a larger and more godlike self of which the present self would then be but a mutilated expression, and the universe might conceivably be a collection of such selves. . . . Thus would a sort of polytheism return upon us. . . ." [18]

Much in James suggests that he was drawn at times to some such polytheistic view. The lecture on immortality hints at the possibility of many orders of beings. Fechner's hierarchy of spirits he seems to have taken half seriously as a hypothesis. The earth soul he calls something to which we can pray as men pray to their saints. Monism is a lifeless conception. " Ordinary monistic idealism leaves everything intermediary out. . . . First you and I, just as we are in this room; and the moment we get below that surface, the unutterable absolute itself! Doesn't this show a singularly indigent imagination? Isn't this brave universe made on a richer pattern, with room in it for a long hierarchy of beings? " [19]

This extraordinary " piecemeal supernaturalism " represents the extreme to which James's pluralistic imagination led him. Alongside of this pluralistic extreme should be placed the pragmatic extreme to which some writers have been driven, though James himself seems to have been on his guard against it. This is the position that while the idea of God is a useful one in human experience it is useful only as idea and has no objective reality. Frazer's famous definition of religion as propitiation of superior powers with a view to their use [20] opened the way to this type of thinking, and Professor Leuba brought the idea into prominence in his much-quoted article in the *Monist* [21] where he said: " God is not known . . . he is used . . . sometimes as meat purveyor, sometimes as moral support." Professors Irving King and E. S. Ames are sometimes interpreted as emphasizing the usefulness of the God idea and

[18] P. 525.
[19] *A Pluralistic Universe,* p. 175.
[20] *Golden Bough,* 1: 63.
[21] 11: 571.

minimizing its objective validity, while in writers like Feuerbach and Vaihinger God becomes a useful product of the imagination or " fiction." But James's pragmatism is careful to avoid this extreme position. The constant argument of the *Varieties* is that the activity observed in religious experience presupposes an objective agency, mysticism is treated as definitely a perceptual experience and express care is taken that God shall not be identified with the subconscious self. " If you, being orthodox Christians," he writes, " ask me as a psychologist whether the reference of a phenomenon to a subliminal self does not exclude the notion of the direct presence of the Deity altogether, I have to say frankly that as a psychologist I do not see why it necessarily should." [22]

God exists, or some Power or Powers exist, and whether Deity be one or many, pluralism and pragmatism as well as ordinary common sense require that it be *finite*. " God, in the religious life of ordinary men, is the name not of the whole of things, heaven forbid, but only of the ideal tendency in things. . . . He works in an external environment, has limits, and has enemies." [23] Monism, as we have seen in detail, is internally inconsistent and externally indifferent to human moral value. It interferes with human freedom and it fails to meet the problem set by the existence of evil. " My ' God of things as they are,' " wrote James, " being part of a pluralistic system is responsible for only such of them as he knows enough and has enough power to have accomplished. . . . The ' omniscient ' and ' omnipotent ' God of theology I regard as a disease of the philosophy-shop." [24] " The line of least resistance, then, as it seems to me, both in theology and in philosophy, is to accept, along with the superhuman consciousness, the notion that it is not all-embracing, the notion, in other words, that there is a God, but that he is finite, either in power or in knowledge, or in both at once." [25]

James has often been pointed to as a radical on this question

[22] *Varieties*, p. 242.
[23] *A Pluralistic Universe*, p. 124.
[24] From a letter to C. A. Strong, *Letters* 2: 269.
[25] *A Pluralistic Universe*, p. 311.

of a limited God, yet the fact is that in this particular he has only been following one of the distinctive tendencies of Western religious philosophy as compared with that of the Orient. The absolute and the infinite have always been more at home in the East. The West, with its interest in practicality, personality, and purpose has been driven to a different kind of thought. It is easy enough to sympathize with absolutistic attempts to satisfy both the intellectual and the mystical cravings for unity, and the absolutistic systems of our own day meet the philosophical and religious needs of many people. But there is apparent a growing tendency among writers on religion to show how much better other systems are able to meet the demands, especially the moral demands of our generation.

Sir Charles Eliot in *Hinduism and Buddhism* has effectively contrasted the Western insistence on the reality of evil, of time, of change, purpose, conflict, and achievement with the Eastern view of the monistic Being for whom there is no purpose, just " sport," no goal but only an endless and aimless round of existences. It seems clear that one of the motives which led Eastern thinkers to this position was the urge to free the Deity from limitations. What could be less hampering than the condition of Brahman? Nothing else exists but Maya, and it is illusion. Or what more ultimate than the Thibetan Adi-Buddha in whom all other Buddhas have their origin, or than the Chinese Tao, the very way of the cosmos itself, or than the Bhutatathata, translated in English by the expressive title " Suchness," of which Asvaghosa exhorts us to " think joyfully " ?

But in both East and West these attempts to reduce all to one underlying principle have failed to be satisfactory because they have made distinctions, the most necessary things in our every-day experience, ultimately unreal. Sankara's pantheism was not far removed from the nihilism of Nagarjuna. And the scholastic attempt in the Middle Ages to protect the Deity from limitations only succeeded in limiting him completely. To ascribe infinity to him was to deny all else including all that was worth while. Hume in his essay on *The Natural History of Religion* observes that theism developed out of polytheism by increasing " adulation." That is to say, men vied with each other in ascribing greatness to the Deity until he finally became as great as their words could make him. And in the *Dialogues Concerning Natural Religion* he hints that absolutism may have come about in much the same way, and that both philosophy and religion would be better off if the conception of an infinite God were superseded by " a more accurate and moderate " idea.

Obviously enough the modern conception of a limited God traces its ancestry back to the beginnings of thought. The gods of primitive man, being many, were limited. Even the " Mana " conception had pluralistic implications.[26] For the Greeks life was too full of things both beautiful and ugly to be reducible to a monotonous unity. Chaos produced gods and men, Xenophon was told, but he received no answer to his question: Who produced Chaos? As far back as the Milesians there was speculation about an ultimate " physis " and also about the gods, but little attempt to combine the two and think out a Deity who should be ultimate. Later on, Plato could not refer to God the origin of evil, and Aristotle found form struggling with matter.

Theological development among the Hebrews followed similar lines. In the beginning, God, said the authors of the Pentateuch, yet the rhythmically powerful Elohim was even in the beginning a limited God, hampered by the materials with which he worked if not by his own purposes. Yahweh's limitations appear even more clearly. But while they are clear to us they were either not clear or not important to his worshippers. It is not until the time of Marcion that the difficulties inherent in the notion of a redeeming Creator come to consciousness. With the rise of scholasticism a desperate attempt is made to remove all inconsistencies by careful definition. It is difficult to imagine any improvement in this direction on Anselm's statement that God is that than which noth-

[26] Cf. Hopkins, " *The History of Religions,*" pp. 18, 67 ff.

ing greater can be conceived! In Anselm's time and later, the dualism inherited from both Greece and Persia seems paradoxically to have come to the aid of the monistic metaphysician, enabling him to place the supernatural realm so far above the natural as to make all human categories and predicates inapplicable to Deity.

But when God is so far removed that the only statement which can be made about him is that no statement can be made, we may well ask what need, religious or other, he can fill. This question, as we have seen, was raised in emphatic form by Hume and in even more trenchant fashion by J. S. Mill in his *Three Essays on Religion*. No reader of Mill can forget the graphic illustrations he uses to show the frustration of any imagined benevolent Omnipotence, or the forceful manner in which he turns the argument from design back upon its proponents, insisting that design means contrivance, *i.e.*, lack of power. Arguments similar to those of Mill were used in a book published in 1822 purporting to come from a " Philip Beauchamp " but now supposed to have been written by Bentham and Grote. Samuel Butler in the last chapter of his *God the Known and God the Unknown* calls his Deity only " quasi-omnipotent and quasi-all-wise." Among modern contenders for a limited God one of the most outstanding is Professor Schiller, who claims in *Riddles of the Sphinx* that as applied to God or to any other reality the epithet "infinite " has no meaning. Professor J. M. E. McTaggart concludes in *Some Dogmas of Religion* that we save God's moral character by limiting his power. Professor L. T. Hobhouse, in *Development and Purpose,* finds that the presence of mechanism, discord, and evil prevents one from identifying the object of contemplation with the whole of things and from ascribing omnipotence to it. Mr. Balfour in *The Foundations of Belief* discovers that the Christian conception of God as one who took on human limitations satisfies the deepest ethical need. Professor G. H. Howison believes that minds must be independent of God. " In no other way am I able to conceive how, at once, God can be good, and there can be in the imperfect and catastrophic world an order really moral."[27] Professor James Ward in *The Realm of Ends* claims that "Oriental servility and *a priori* speculation have made God synonymous with an ' Infinite and Absolute,' " and that the traditional conception must be revised in such a way as to afford autonomy to men, making them co-workers with God. Dr. Hastings Rashdall in *The Theory of Good and Evil* suggests that the term infinite can more properly be applied to that which includes God and other spirits than to God himself, and that to avoid limiting God's goodness a definite restriction must be placed on his power. A popular statement of the conception of a limited God is H. G. Wells's *God the Invisible King,* made apparently on the basis of a convincing religious experience.

The indictment of an absolute and infinite God by all these writers is made on grounds that are practically unanimous. God must have personality and purpose, man must have freedom and capacity for moral achievement, theology must face squarely the problem of evil. The results of this attack are seen in such philosophical works as Professor Pringle-Pattison's *The Idea of God* where omnipotence is made to consist of a continuous process of redemption, and absolutism is re-interpreted so as to contain " all the strenuousness, the sense of uttermost reality in the struggle, on which James rightly insists."[28] And we notice its influence in the work of a theologian like Bishop McConnell who in *Is God Limited* admits that the word absolute may hardly express the idea at which the religious person is aiming when he uses it, and professes indifference as to whether the " metaphysical quality " of omnipotence be retained. Perhaps as satisfactory a synthesis of the two views as any is that of Professor D. C. Macintosh, who reaches the absoluteness of God by way of experience rather than the high *a priori* road. " He is great enough to be absolutely dependable and the adequate Source of inner preparedness for anything that can happen, and the Source of actual salvation, deliverance from evil, for all who

[27] *Hibbert Journal,* 1: 121.   [28] P. 413.

persist in the right religious adjustment." God is the absolute of experimental religion, " the absolutely dependable Object of dependence and Source of salvation." [29] Professor Macintosh meets the problem of evil by insisting that while this is not the best possible world it is the best possible *kind* of world. We must have law though it be accompanied by suffering.

James uses practically all the arguments for a limited God which we have noticed in these other writers and combines with them an especially emphatic insistence on the need for intimacy with the Deity. God must be limited to be approachable. We must be able to share his purposes. The closest intimacy is effected by thinking of God as continuous with us spiritually while at the same time we are morally independent, — the synthesis of the best in both pantheism and dualism which James thinks a spiritual pluralism brings.

The view of a continuity of consciousness between God and man is one to which James gave frequent expression. It is believed by some of his former pupils that toward the end of his life James was coming to a belief in a form of panpsychism.[30] Radical empiricism seems to be capable of interpretation along panpsychical lines, and problems as to the relation of man to any possible religious objects are hinted at in the questions raised by radical empiricism about the influence on each other of narrower and wider spans of experience (*e.g.*, in the essay on " The Experience of Activity "). For if there be a God, he is not the all-knower or the experiencer of all reality, but simply " the experiencer of widest actual conscious span."

This suggestion of spiritual continuity between Deity and worshipper, the last feature of James's discussion of God which we shall take up, is important and finds expression in many different places. In the essay, " Is Life Worth Living? " James suggested that our whole physical life might be soaking in

---

[29] *Theology as an Empirical Science,* pp. 176 ff.

[30] Cf. also " William James and Panpsychism " by Professor Wendell T. Bush in the recently published second volume of the Columbia University *Studies in the History of Ideas.*

a spiritual atmosphere, a dimension of being that we at present have no organ for apprehending. The lecture on *Human Immortality* looked to Fechner and his theory of continuous consciousnesses for analogies, though James does not have as much to say as does Fechner about man's opportunity on his own account to start currents which work toward the Deity. In the *Varieties*, as we have seen, much is made of man's capacity to receive spiritual power from an agency apparently outside but continuous with himself. In 1906 James wrote: " It is high time that the hypothesis of a world-consciousness should be discussed seriously." [31] Finally, in the last two chapters of *A Pluralistic Universe* he definitely places his theory of the continuity of experience at the service of religion. A single field of consciousness shades off into other fields — larger, more extensive fields which suggest a higher than human experience. " Every bit of us at every moment is part and parcel of a wider self, it quivers along various radii like the wind-rose on a compass, and the actual in it is continuously one with possibles not yet in our present sight. And just as we are co-conscious with our own momentary margin, may not we ourselves form the margin of some more really central self in things which is co-conscious with the whole of us? May not you and I be confluent in a higher consciousness, and confluently active there, though we now know it not? " [32] We may indeed, and we may know of our own " confluence " if we will only listen to the testimony of experience. " I think it may be asserted that there *are* religious experiences of a specific nature. . . . I think that they point with reasonable probability to the continuity of our consciousness with a wider spiritual environment." [33]

The approach to God through James's philosophy is then as sure as it can be made in a philosophy which has forsworn apodictic certainty. Pragmatically we both test and postulate him, through pluralism we provide for a community of interest with him, empirically we know him.

[31] *Collected Essays, etc.,* p. 469.   [32] Pp. 289–90.   [33] Pp. 299–300.

VIII

IMMORTALITY

I T HAS commonly been supposed that James's interest in immortality was not very great, — "relatively slight" one commentator has called it. As a consequence little has been written on this phase of James's belief. Where the topic has been treated at all the approach has usually been in one of two ways. The first way has been to quote from the Ingersoll lecture on *Human Immortality* the statement: " I have to confess that my own personal feeling about immortality has never been of the keenest order," [1] or from the concluding chapter of *The Varieties of Religious Experience:* " I have said nothing in my lectures about immortality or the belief therein, for to me it seems a secondary point," [2] and to leave the matter there. The second way has been to point to James's researches among psychical phenomena and to say that whatever view he did hold was determined by his investigation of mediums and their trances.

Both of these supposed clues seem, however, to be misleading. The expressed lack of interest is belied by too much else in James to be taken at its face value. And we must remember his imaginative and lively interest in all objects of human regard and aspiration. " Overbeliefs " always attracted his attention. It would surely be surprising if James with all his human sympathy and his willingness to allow hope a part in the formation of belief should not himself have cherished any overbeliefs on a question of such recurrent interest as that of life after death.

[1] P. 3.   [2] P. 524.

James's expression of his own overbeliefs does not always occur in the place where we should expect to find it. For example, in his book on religion where we might suppose the hopeful note would be dominant, he dismisses the question of immortality as " eminently a case for facts to testify." [3] And on the other hand, in the midst of a psychological discussion we come upon the remark that "the surest warrant for immortality is the yearning of our bowels for our dear ones." [4] Because the alternation of these two attitudes, the purely scientific and the more personal, is so constant in James it is necessary for a discussion of his belief in immortality to touch on each point of view in turn. For a clear understanding of his personal attitude it will be necessary first to make a brief review of the result of his scientific research.

James's interest in the English and American Societies for Psychical Research is well known. In 1884, two years after its organization, he became a member of the English Society, and he was active in helping to found the American branch. An unpublished letter to Thomas Davidson is interesting in this connection.

BELLEVUE COURT,
NEWPORT, R. I.,
February 1, 1885

My dear Davidson:

Your letter has been forwarded to me here, arriving Saturday P.M., so my answer cannot be " immediate " as you desire.

I suppose the meeting of " Psychicals " to which you are invited tomorrow is in New York. I know nothing about it, not even whether it consists of members of our Society. I have seen no " report of proceedings " of our society, so think it may be something else. As for any " anti-spiritual basis " of our society, no theoretic basis, or *bias*, of any sort whatever, so far as I can make out, exists in it. The one thing that has struck me all along in the men who have had to do with it is their complete colourlessness philosophically. They seem to have no preferences for any generalism whatever. I doubt if this could be matched in Europe. Anyhow, it would make no difference in

---

[3] *Varieties*, p. 524.   [4] *Principles of Psychology*, 2: 308.

the important work to be done, what theoretic bias the members had. For I take it the urgent thing, to rescue us from the present disgraceful condition, is to ascertain in a manner so thorough as to constitute *evidence* that will be accepted by outsiders, just what the *phenomenal conditions* of certain concrete phenomenal occurrences are. Not till that is done can spiritualistic or anti-spiritualistic theories be ever mooted. I am sure that the more we can steer clear of theories at first the better. The choice of officers was largely dictated by motives of policy. Not that scientific men are necessarily better judges of all truth than others, but that their adhesion would popularly seem better evidence than the adhesion of others, in this matter. And what we want is not only truth, but evidence. We shall be lucky if our scientific names do not grow discredited the instant they subscribe to any " spiritual " manifestations. But how much easier to discredit literary men, philosophers or clergymen! I think Newcomb for President was an uncommon hit — if he believes he will probably carry others. You'd better chip in, and not complicate matters by talking either of spiritualism or anti-spiritualism. " Facts " are what are wanted. . . .

WM. JAMES

In the course of his investigation of psychical phenomena certain things particularly attracted James's attention. In the first place he became much interested in hallucinations. He conducted a census of these, devoting considerable attention to the reports he received, and he records as especially noteworthy the conclusion of Mr. and Mrs. Henry Sidgwick in England that the number of instances where the apparition of a person was seen on the day of that person's death was over four hundred times too great to be ascribed to coincidence.[5] Secondly, James seems to have been inclined to believe in the fact of telepathy in certain instances.[6] Third, in his study of mediums James was impressed by the genuineness of the external urge whose power the medium felt. Fourth, he was particularly in-

---

[5] *The Will to Believe and Other Essays*, p. 312.
[6] *Proceedings American S. P. R.* 1909, p. 506.

terested in Frederick Myers's suggestion that the hypothesis of a " subliminal self " might be used to relate the phenomena of hypnotism, automatism, and double personality.

Yet none of these appears to have influenced him toward a belief in the existence of departed spirits. Hallucinations and telepathy in themselves had no direct bearing on the problem. The urge felt by the medium might be real yet its source a matter of serious question. And the conception of a " subliminal self " which interested Myers chiefly because of its suggestion as to personal survival of bodily death James found useful only in another field, and employed it as a means of explaining certain phenomena connected with religious experience. More germane to the whole question of immortality James found two other matters, one an empirical datum, the other a hypothesis. The first of these was the apparent presence in the minds of mediums of knowledge attained in a supernormal way. The second was the possibility of the existence of a spiritual environment of consciousness, " diffuse soul stuff," or a cosmic reservoir of memories.

The supernormal knowledge of the medium presented a puzzling problem. James discusses it in several papers, two of which are now printed respectively with *The Will to Believe* and in *Collected Essays and Reviews*. His final opinion is summed up in a letter about Mrs. Piper, with whom he had had the most positive results obtained in all his research: " Mrs. Piper has supernormal knowledge in her trances; but whether it comes from ' tapping the minds ' of living people or from some common cosmic reservoir of memories, or from surviving ' spirits ' of the departed is a question impossible for *me* to answer just now to my own satisfaction. The spirit theory is undoubtedly not only the most natural, but the simplest, and I have great respect for Hodgson's and Hyslop's arguments when they adopt it. At the same time the electric current called *belief* has not yet closed in my mind." [7]

[7] Dated April 21, 1907, *Letters of William James*, 2: 287. Cf. *Collected Essays, etc.*, p. 490.

Why did this electric current not close in James's mind? With his readiness to find truth in the novel and the unconventional why was James left unconvinced by the same kind of evidence which had satisfied some of his colleagues? It could not have been on account of any *a priori* objection to finding proofs for immortality in this field. James was perfectly willing to examine any messages which purported to come from his friends. It is interesting to know, also, that James did as Myers and Hodgson had done before him, and said that he would communicate after death if he were able. But although many mediums have published messages which claimed to come from him, those who knew James intimately and who have examined the messages say that nothing which could possibly be considered authentic has ever been received.

Yet though James had no *a priori* objection to receiving or giving messages in this fashion, he seems to have had an *a posteriori* objection to believing that his friends were leading the kind of life which these " spirit-returns " claimed to reveal. The picture they drew of an attenuated sort of existence and confused mental processes was not either a pleasant or a convincing one. Previous investigators had explained that the messages were conveyed through the subconsciousness of the medium and were confused and thinned-out in transit. But the suggestion is not a wholly plausible one. Unclear lines of communication cannot explain banality. James recognized the seriousness of this objection and commented on it by saying: " The spirit-hypothesis exhibits a vacancy, triviality and incoherence of mind painful to think of as the state of the departed; and coupled therewithal a disposition to 'fish' and face round, and disguise the essential hollowness, which are, if anything, more painful still." [8]

Here as so often in James the personal and intimate feeling, the " passionate vision " which suggests the philosophical position, has close affinity with the religious view. It is impossible not to feel that James rejected the immortality sug-

[8] *Collected Essays and Reviews,* p. 438.

gested by psychical research partly because it did not satisfy his sense for the religiously appropriate. For James religion was a means to more abundant living just as ethics was a call to the satisfaction of the greatest number of legitimate human desires. To harmonize with the demands of his robust religious faith a conception of immortality would be forced to postulate a richer and more complete life than the present, not the impoverished one suggested by the mediums. James seems indeed to have found much that was revolting in his psychical research and to have been correspondingly disinclined to look to it for light on such a problem as that of life after death. He once remarked on " the cabinet, the darkness, the tying, suggesting a sort of human rat-hole life," [9] and again on the fact that these phenomena are " smothered in the mass of their degenerative congeners," [10] while in one of his unpublished letters he calls his contact with mediums " a strange and in many ways a disgusting experience."

The supernormal knowledge in the minds of mediums James thus found interesting in itself but not finally suggestive as to immortality. The other interest mentioned above, however, seems to have occupied his mind for a considerable period of time. That was the interest in the possibility of the existence of a spiritual environment of consciousness connecting all individual lives in one great cosmic continuum. Frequent references are made to this idea in James's works, but in most of the places where it is mentioned it is applied, as we have observed before, not so much to the problem of immortality as to the question of the nature of God.

The application of this conception to the problem of life after death is made most specifically in the Ingersoll lecture on *Human Immortality*. Here James combats the notion that to make thought a function of the brain is to make it depend exclusively on the brain. Consciousness may be a function of the brain in one of two senses. It may be produced by the brain or it may pre-exist and receive from the brain merely its form. The latter alternative has an interesting bearing on

[9] *Memories and Studies*, p. 197.   [10] *Proceedings Eng. S. P. R.* 18: 33.

the problem of immortality. The whole material realm may be " a mere surface-veil of phenomena, hiding and keeping back the world of genuine realities." It may be that, as Shelley suggests,

> Life, like a dome of many-colored glass,
> Stains the white radiance of eternity.

This means that certain parts of the phenomenal world may be more permeable than others, and at these parts "gleams, however finite and unsatisfying, of the absolute life of the universe, are from time to time vouchsafed." Our brains may be these translucent places. They may be the individualizing organs by which the cosmic consciousness is divided into finite streams of thought. If this were the case consciousness would be dependent upon the brain in a sense, but the brain's function would be transmissive, not productive. The brain would exercise a regulative influence, arranging and giving form to thought, at the same time that it helped partially to obscure the divine effulgence.

A beautifully symbolic passage expressing the same idea is found in the article entitled " Final Impressions of a Psychical Researcher." ". . . we with our lives are like islands in the sea, or like trees in the forest. The maple and the pine may whisper to each other with their leaves, and Conanicut and Newport hear each other's foghorns. But the trees also commingle their roots in the darkness underground, and the islands also hang together through the ocean's bottom. Just so there is a continuum of cosmic consciousness, against which our individuality builds but accidental fences, and into which our several minds plunge as into a mother-sea or reservoir. Our 'normal' consciousness is circumscribed for adaptation to our external earthly environment, but the fence is weak in spots, and fitful influences from beyond leak in. . . ." [11]

Another unpublished letter to Davidson is interesting here:

[11] *Memories and Studies*, p. 204.

CAMBRIDGE,
October 20, 1898

Dear Thomas:

If you had the slightest spark of scientific imagination you would see that the mother sea is of a glutinous consistency and when she strains off portions of her being through the dome of many colored glass, they stick so tenaciously that she must shake herself hard to get rid of them.

Then, as there is no action without reaction, the shake is felt by both members, and remains registered in the mother sea like a " stub " in a check book, preserving memory of the transaction. These stubs form the basis of the immortal account which we begin when the prismatic dome is shattered.

These matters, you see, are ultra simple, and would be revealed to you if you had a more humble and teachable heart. Your whole lot of idle and captious questions proceed so obviously from intellectual pride, and are so empty of all true desire for instruction that I will not pretend to reply to them at all. I am glad that my poor little book took them out of you, though. You must feel the better for having expressed them.

I have sent the letter to Alice, who is in the country having a chimney, alas! rebuilt.

In great haste,
Yours affectionately,
WILLIAM JAMES

On the whole James seems to have found the conception of a great " mother-sea " of consciousness most fruitful when applied to other religious problems than that of immortality. Even in the Ingersoll lecture where immortality was the topic under discussion he arrived at conclusions which were not wholly satisfactory either to himself or to his hearers. Indeed, so many criticisms were received after the publication of the lecture in book form that James was forced to write a preface to the second edition admitting that the theory did not necessarily provide for personal individual immortality and that it merely lent itself to such an interpretation along with other possible alternatives. As a matter of fact, his whole study of psychical phenomena he found not only unconvincing, but hardly even suggestive. " For twenty-five years," he once wrote, " I have been in touch with the literature of psychical research. . . . Yet I am theoretically no ' further ' than I was at the beginning." [12]

More fruitful was the more personal approach to the problem through the demands of the moral and religious consciousness. In the second half of the Ingersoll lecture James drops the point of view of the scientist and turns from the discussion of a psycho-physical theory to take up an argument based on human desire and its right to be satisfied. His way of introducing the question is indeed a little startling. We must not be prejudiced against the idea of immortality, James here says, on account of any fear we may have that Heaven will be overcrowded with undesirable citizens! Surely only in a truly " Brahmin " environment could such a proposition be seriously set forth! Yet James seems to have been half in earnest about it. The idea of value at the bottom of his ethical theory shows that he had a hatred of the commonplace, and that the notion of spending eternity surrounded by mediocrity would have been repulsive to him. James often used to remark, Professor George Herbert Palmer has told the present writer, " Heaven would be an awfully crowded place! " But the conclusion to which the argument of the lecture leads is as characteristic as is this outburst. Just as he had written elsewhere that the cardinal sin is blindness to the significance of other lives than one's own, so here he refers again to Stevenson's " The Lantern Bearers " and comments that we who miss the inner joy of these alien lives miss all. Consistently with the position taken in his ethics that every desire has a right to be fulfilled except as it conflicts with other desires, James argues here that our indifference to another's yearning for immortality is no evidence of the unreality of that yearning nor against its right to be satisfied. And the fundamentally

[12] *Memories and Studies*, pp. 174-5.

religious character of his argument is shown by his reference to the desires of the Deity as a court of last appeal. " The Universe, with every living entity which her resources create, creates at the same time a call for that entity, and an appetite for its continuance — creates it, if nowhere else, within the heart of the entity itself." It is absurd to suppose that " in the heart of infinite being itself there can be such a thing as plethora, or glut, or supersaturation." [13]

Some of the most interesting and pointed utterances are found, however, outside the Ingersoll lecture. A few of them seem to reveal the deepest searchings of his own heart. Many of them are vague and not at all positive in tone. But, to use James's own expression, " weak sticks make strong faggots," and the total impression which they convey when grouped together is of a strong undercurrent of feeling on James's own part. A twofold division may be made here similar to that which we have seen should be made in his religious philosophy as a whole. At times James wants and believes in immortality for the sake of more activity, while at other times the need for comfort and assurance is paramount.

As an example of the former attitude the following may be cited from the *Principles of Psychology:* " The demand for immortality is nowadays essentially teleological. We believe ourselves immortal because we believe ourselves *fit* for immortality." So even a " stream of consciousness " should be immortal if it can believe itself "fit " to be, for

" A ' substance ' ought surely to perish, we think, if not worthy to survive, and an insubstantial ' stream ' to prolong itself, provided it be worthy, if the nature of Things is organized in the rational way in which we trust it is. Substance or no substance, soul or ' stream,' what Lotze says of immortality is about all that human wisdom can say:

" ' We have no other principle for deciding it than this general idealistic belief: that every created thing will continue whose continuance belongs to the meaning of the world, and so

---

[13] *"Human Immortality,"* p. 40. Cf. *Collected Essays, etc.,* p. 132.

long as it does belong; whilst every one will pass away whose reality is justified only in a transitory phase of the world's course.' — *Metaphysik*, Sec. 245." [14]
With this published in 1890 it is interesting to compare James's replies in 1904 to the questionnaire sent out by Professor J. B. Pratt:

> *Q*. Do you believe in personal immortality?
>   *A*. Never keenly; but more strongly as I grow older.

> *Q*. If so, why?
>   *A*. Because I am just getting fit to live.[15]

A remark made by James referring to Professor F. J. Child fits in with this train of thought: " I have often said that the best argument I knew for an immortal life was the existence of a man who deserved one as well as Child did." [16]

Of the second group, where the longing for assurance dominates, one of the earliest recorded is found in a letter to his father after he had received word that the latter's death was imminent. Under date of December 14, 1882, he writes from London:

" We have been so long accustomed to the hypothesis of your being taken away from us, especially during the past ten months, that the thought that this may be your last illness conveys no very sudden shock. You are old enough, you've given your message to the world in many ways and will not be forgotten; you are left here alone, and on the other side, let us hope and pray, dear, dear old Mother is waiting for you to join her. If you go, it will not be an inharmonious thing. . . . In that mysterious gulf of the past into which the present soon will fall and go back and back, yours is still for me the central figure. All my intellectual life I derive from you; and though we have often seemed at odds in the expres-

---

[14] *Principles of Psychology*, 1: 348–9.
[15] *Letters*, 2: 214.
[16] *Proc. Amer. S. P. R.* 1909, p. 580.

sion thereof, I'm sure there's a harmony somewhere, and that our strivings will combine. . . . As for the other side, and Mother, and our all possibly meeting, I *can't* say anything. More than ever at this moment do I feel that if that *were* true, all would be solved and justified. And it comes strangely over me in bidding you good-bye how a life is but a day and expresses mainly but a single note. It is so much like the act of bidding an ordinary good-night." [17]

Nine years later he was writing to his sister in similar circumstances, and in the course of his letter he alluded to the relation of psychological investigation to his father's Swedenborgian belief:

" . . . Your fortitude, good spirits and unsentimentality have been simply unexampled in the midst of your physical woes; and when you're relieved from your post, just *that* bright note will remain behind, together with the inscrutable and mysterious character of the doom of nervous weakness which has chained you down for all these years. As for that, there's more in it than has ever been told to so-called science. These inhibitions, these split-up selves, all these new facts that are gradually coming to light about our organization, these enlargements of the self in trance, etc., are bringing me to turn for light in the direction of all sorts of despised spiritualistic and unscientific ideas. Father would find in me today a much more receptive listener — all *that* philosophy has got to be brought in. And what a queer contradiction comes to the ordinary scientific argument against immortality (based on body being mind's condition and mind going *out* when body is gone), when one must believe (as now, in these neurotic cases) that some infernality in the body *prevents* really existing parts of the mind from coming to their effective rights at all, suppresses them, and blots them out from participation in this world's experiences, although they are *there* all the time. When that which is *you* passes out of the body, I am sure that there will be an explosion of liberated force and life till then eclipsed and kept down." [18]

[17] *Letters*, 1: 219–220.   [18] *Letters*, 1: 310–311.

Here and there the reader finds hints that the notion of a future life was one upon which James's mind often dwelt. For example, one letter mentions the death of John Ropes, then turns to other matters, and then at the end of the letter says: " John Ropes, more than most men, seems as if he would be natural to meet again." [19] And in a letter to his son, speaking of scenery he says: "I have often been surprised to find what a predominant part in my own spiritual experience it has played, and how it stands out as almost the only thing the memory of which I should like to carry over with me beyond the veil, unamended and unaltered." [20]

In the memorial address for Francis Boott now printed in *Memories and Studies* there are some beautiful passages concluding with the words: "Good-by, then, old friend. We shall nevermore meet the upright figure, the blue eye, the hearty laugh, upon these Cambridge streets. But in that wider world of being of which this little Cambridge world of ours forms so infinitesimal a part, we may be sure that all our spirits and their missions here will continue in some way to be represented, and that ancient human loves will never lose their own."

Suggestive also is the testimony of a group of unpublished letters recently found. They were written by James to a cousin, Mrs. Kitty James Prince, at a time when she was living at the home of President Julius H. Seelye of Amherst College. In several of them James refers to the Society for Psychical Research, and in one he asks: "Will President Seelye join this ghost investigating society?" Quotation is made here from some of the letters which reflect James's interest in immortality, the entire letter being given in some cases on account of its interest.

The first two contain references to James's work on his father's writings published in the fall of 1884 as *The Literary Remains of Henry James.*

[19] *Letters,* 2: 109. [20] 2: 175.

15 APPIAN WAY
CAMBRIDGE, MASS.
Oct. 20th (1884)

Dictated

My dearest Kitty

All summer long I deferred writing to you because I expected to pay you a visit toward the end of September. When that time came however I found I had just enough money to bring me home from the Adirondacks by way of Vermont — not enough to return by the Boston and Albany Road. It was lucky it was so for I had a fever attack immediately after my return which would have caught me at Amherst had I gone round through Albany and stayed over with you. I had three of them this summer, one keeping me in bed eight days, and the effect on my eyes etc. has not yet worn off — one more reason why I have not written. It was delightful to get your long letter the other day, and hear you speak as if in such good spirits — though Heaven knows, Kitty, you never let yourself speak otherwise however you may feel in the secret fastnesses.

From not having heard from you so long I had begun to be a little anxious as to whether you were keeping up well. The place you have got in Amherst, with the friendly Mrs. Scott, seems indeed providential. We are embarking on what promises to be a much easier winter than the last — the house more furnished, two hours less of lecturing, some pieces of work done which is a relief to my mind, etc., etc. — you see the prospect. I succeeded during the summer in doing my part of the work on father's literary remains. The book will appear in two or three weeks. I made a lot of extracts from his previous writings some of which I think you will enjoy.

My Alice will have told you all the *news* such as the going of Alice to Europe — Bob's being here, Howard's histrionic success, etc. Bob is my amanuensis now and will add a word for himself. I need not tell you, dear Kitty, how often and with what affection I think of you. Though separated here below, we shall in that future life have many active doings together which will last for an indefinite period. Pray give my best regards to the Seelyes and believe me your most affectionate

(Signed)   W<small>M</small>. J<small>AMES</small>

C<small>AMBRIDGE</small>, Dec. 24 (1884)

My dear Kitty,

I mailed you yesterday a copy of poor dear old Father's " Literary Remains " which you are not bound to read if your head disagrees, but which I know you will like to see and possess. The autobiography will, however, interest you, and perhaps parts of the introduction, in the writing of which all alone here last summer I seemed to sink into an intimacy with Father which I had never before enjoyed. I trust he takes cognizance of it somewhere. Vacation began yesterday, and I am going for a change to N. Y. and Philadelphia, and hope to spend at least a week away. We are founding here a " Society for Psychical Research " under which innocent sounding name ghosts, second sight, spiritualism, and all sorts of hobgoblins are going to be " investigated " by the most high-toned and " cultured " members of the community; and my business in Philadelphia is partly to confer with some of the leading spirits in the movement there. A society in London of the same name has put the *evidence* for these things on a most respectable footing. We are all well — Alice busy-*issima* with the housekeeping and the babes. We are thinking of building a house out Mount Auburn way, in which there will be a good room for *you* whenever you please to come. The thing isn't settled yet fully, but soon will be. I send you also from Alice a little " individual " salt and pepper caster, which she trusts may be useful. With warmest love, and a merry Christmas to you from both of us, I am ever your affectionate Cousin

W<small>M</small>. J<small>AMES</small>

The next two letters refer to the loss of his infant son, Hermann.

CAMBRIDGE, *July 12,* '85

My dear Kitty,

Our little Humster, whom you never saw since his first babyhood, has also gone over to the majority. We buried him yesterday, under the young pine tree, at my father's side. For 9 days he had been in a desperate condition, but his constitution proved so tenacious, that each visit of the doctor found him still alive. At last his valiant little soul left the body at about nine o'clock on Thursday night. He was a broad, generous, patient little nature, with a noble head who would doubtless have done credit to his name had he lived. It *must* be now that he is reserved for some still better chance than that, and that we shall in some way come into his presence again. The great part of the experience to me has been the sight of Alice's devotion. I thought I knew her, but I didn't, nor did I fully know the meaning of that old human word *motherhood*. Six weeks with no regular sleep, 9 days with never more than 3 hours in the 24, and yet bright and fresh and ready for anything as much on the last day as on the first. She is so essentially *mellow* a nature that when the excitement is gone and the collapse sets in, it will be short and have nothing morbid about it. We are all pretty tired, and as I write this, I can hardly keep my eyes open.

We leave for Jaffrey in a day or two, little Billy staying here so as not to catch the whooping cough from his mother. He has been kept three weeks in the neighborhood of Jaffrey by Margaret Gibbens, and the climate doesn't seem to agree. What more permanent plan for the summer we shall make, I don't know, but will let you know when it is made. Dear Kitty, I have thought of you often, with the Angel of Death near by. It brings one closer to all mankind, this world old experience. Yours ever, with Alice's warm love,

WM. JAMES

JAFFREY, N. H., *Aug.* 11, '85

My dearest Kitty,

I have been on the point of writing you every day for the last 12 — having been at home in Cambridge in Mrs. Gibbens's house, whilst she took my place with Alice. But the divine afflatus kept me going on my work all the time, rousing me once as early as 2.30 A.M. to write, and keeping me going usually till 5 in the afternoon. Under these conditions, much as one may wish to write a letter, he generally finds that he can't possibly do it *today*. Having come to a pause in my work, I came back here yesterday afternoon — Mrs. Gibbens had been with Alice whilst I was away — and here I am at my writing table. We are on a quiet farm, with two good people and a good table, while the 2 children are going all day long, in the hay wagon, in the barn or in the berry pasture, and drop asleep like logs at night. Alice and I jog about after a slow old horse in the afternoons and evenings, and it is good all around. Alice is enduring her loss beautifully, without a word of murmur or a bit of morbidness. It makes the world seem smaller and deeper and more continuous with the next, and I have often felt in these last days how natural a thing *your* sense of that continuity was. We have got so many genuine letters of sympathy that it makes one feel also how, under superficial disguises, men feel close together in these old simple human griefs, and how they make the whole world kin. We shall stay here till Sept. 1, then to Cambridge. I will in Sept. pay you my little six dollar visit — the money burns in my pouch! I hope dear Kitty that your summer has been a tolerably good one, tho' in the absence of news I am always a little anxious about you. Pray send word shortly after receipt of this. Better always address simply " Cambridge " — letters are forwarded from there. Alice sends much love. So do I. Ever your

W. J.

The next three letters refer to losses sustained by Mrs. Prince:

CAMBR. *Mch* 4, '86

My dearest Kitty,

Just now comes your letter with its for you fateful news. So indissoluble is the tie of dependency on our parents that I suppose, notwithstanding your poor mother's inability to do anything for you during all these years, you now must have a feeling of unprotectedness greater than ever before. But you have the satisfaction of being assured that no clouds now veil the essence of her soul. . . .

JAFFREY, N. H.
July 11, '86

My dear Kitty,

Your letter of July 3d came duly, and rejoiced us by the good news it brought of you all. I meant to have written long since to acknowledge the receipt of the box-making materials for Billy — which certainly proved the *best* present for childhood I have ever seen. Billy, with some help from Harry at first, has succeeded in making a perfect box, and was delighted with his prowess. Our thanks are due to the painstaking benevolence of your young friend who sawed the wood and punched the nail holes. My not writing was due to the extreme multifariousness of my duties etc. You know how it was when you were there; well, it became tenfold worse afterwards. We then made a week's visit to the ———s. . . . Poor Aunt begins to feel her old age — loss of memory and so forth — in a rather sad and stoic fashion, and I was too fagged to carry on very vivacious conversation. The fall is the time for visiting, when one's youth is renewed like the eagle's by the vacation delights. In spring the cobwebs of the winter's work are spun too thickly over one's soul. One ought to be buried in the moist earth for three weeks to let that scuff all rot away, so that the soul may sprout again. Mine is just beginning to now, after a week at the sea-shore near Portsmouth, all alone with the waves and the pines and the bayberries, and half a week here on this peaceful and salubrious farm with Alice and the babes. I have read a lot of profane french novels — the first step towards cleansing my metaphysic-crammed brain, and am now advanced to biography. Chas. Kingsley's life, were it not so long, is a book I should strongly recommend, for its picture of a man of intense emotional susceptibility coupled with great generosity of disposition and the broadest sympathies. — Of course I agree about what you say of the battle-fields of each individual. There will be a strange transformation scene about the relative importance of various careers, on the day when the veil shall be lifted. Then indeed the last shall be first! — I must not forget to speak of the inscription. I cashed the order and have the money. But I actually have not had a moment of time to ascertain whether the work has yet been done. I shall await McNamee's bill, and visit the spot to see that all is right before paying it. That probably cannot be before September. Meanwhile if you would like the use of the money drop me a card and I will send it. Otherwise I shall not expect to hear from you till after the middle of August. You had better address "Cambridge." Please give my love to the Seelyes. Alice sends you hers.

Always your affectionate
W. J.

Cambr. Aug. 5, '86

Dearest Kitty,

I am home for a week or so of solitary work, and yesterday I paid the marble-cutter's bill, having walked the afternoon previous from the Newton car terminus to the cemetery to see whether the work had been well done. It was a splendid cool day, and I never knew that a place could be as beautiful as Newton was. It makes Cambridge look *scrubby* in the extreme. The inscription " A new song before the throne " looked beautiful, and just fitted rightly into its place. I hope the blessed Doctor in some way takes cognizance of its being there.

We have had a splendid month at Jaffrey and are all very

well. I have been writing since 8.30 A. M. till now, 5.45 in the afternoon — a good day's work for me. . . .

Is it not permissible, then, to question the statement that James had only a " comparatively slight interest in immortality? " Does it not seem rather that he had not only an interest but a fair share of belief? May we not ask, also, if such a belief is not an appropriate part of James's whole philosophic outlook? Immortality seems to be precisely the sort of subject with which the will to believe is fitted to deal. The issues here are living and forced and momentous. And it is an appropriate question for pragmatism to attack, for the latter is simply " a means of settling metaphysical disputes that otherwise would be interminable," an " attitude of orientation toward last things," a way toward " fruitful relations with reality," and so a justification of belief in whatever is truly significant for an optimistic and stimulating view of life. Similarly meliorism, with its faith in a better realm for which God and men labor together needs a belief in immortality for its completion. And the whole pragmatic emphasis on the capacity of the free creative human spirit to effect changes in its environment surely hints at the possibility of its being able to survive material changes in that environment. Pluralism gives no assurance of immortality but the very riskiness of a pluralistic universe makes faith in personal immortality almost essential. As James suggested in the letter to his father quoted above, if we could believe that the loose ends of this pluralistic life on earth were gathered together in a more abundant life hereafter, then indeed " all would be solved and justified." And it should be remarked that while pluralism brings the possibility of failure to achieve immortality it contains also the assurance that immortality if attained will be active and rich and creative and, most important of all, individual. Finally empiricism, taking its stand not upon *a priori* grounds but upon the yearnings of the human heart as they make themselves felt in daily experience postulates immortality for the satisfaction of an abiding human demand. It seems not too much to say that

James's philosophy furnished a congenial setting for his belief and formed an appropriate background for the remark which he frequently made in his last illness, as quoted in an unpublished letter from Mrs. James to Professor Mary W. Calkins of Wellesley: " Death has come to seem a very trifling incident."

IX

MYSTICISM

IN FREEDOM, God, and immortality we will to believe. To satisfy our moral and religious demands we postulate their existence. Any belief, in James's view, requires an act of attention and so of will, but in these beliefs based on moral postulates instead of sense experience the active element is especially prominent. The belief in God, however, has another side. We may approach God by an act of will, but God on his part stoops to our weakness. In the essays published with *The Will to Believe* James had said that our power of moral and volitional response is probably our deepest organ of communication with the nature of things.[1] But in the *Varieties* the deepest organ of communication is the passive experience,[2] the experience of reconciliation,[3] when man feels the touch of a Power greater than himself, and when instead of selecting and creating his own reality he is content to contemplate the Ideal as presented, finding in it a new authority and a new source of strength.

The mystical is such an experience, marked off from other phenomena, such as conversion, in which healing grace is seen at work, by the emphasis it places on the cognitive element. The mystical experience is primarily one of revelation. In religion it has been accepted as bringing an immediate communication from the Deity, while in philosophy it has been accorded a place among epistemological attempts to know the heart of reality.

In James's philosophy mysticism is of interest to us first of all as representing the passive tendency in what we have

[1] P. 141. [2] P. 381. [3] P. 388.

called his religious conflict, and as aiming to fill the need for assurance and for a final reconciliation which we saw was deep-seated in one type of religious mood. Where pragmatism stresses the active element, mysticism gives its attention to the contemplative. For pragmatism's interest in ideas and in truth as means, mysticism substitutes an experience of illumination which is an end in itself. And where the will to believe suggests tentative postulates, mysticism claims to have access to truths that are intuitively certain. The discussion of mysticism in this chapter will endeavor to do two things: first, to set forth the mystical experience as James described it, giving his own view of its value and cognitive content; and second, to point out the close contact which the philosophy of mysticism makes with James's thought as a whole by showing three places at which it offers a natural and legitimate supplement to his views.

First as to James's account of mysticism, — briefly the mystical experience may be described as an extension of the ordinary state of consciousness. As James shows so frequently, we have grown away from the Lockian notion that the unit of mental life is the " idea " or is any single isolated mental element. In his own psychology the mental unit is the entire psychic state. Consciousness is a succession of these, each of them a unity. This is true not only of the uncompounded mental states described in the *Principles* but also of the more complex, " many-in-one " states of consciousness hinted at in *A Pluralistic Universe*. In either case the state itself is experienced in its wholeness.

But although psychic states are like each other in their unity, they may differ greatly from each other in extent. Investigation has shown that the " margin " surrounding the field of consciousness may vary greatly from one moment to another. At certain times the margin is extended, and a vast amount of material, usually trans-marginal, is included in consciousness. Or to use Fechner's metaphor, at certain moments the " threshold " falls and material that is ordinarily below the threshold comes into view. Combining this with the results of Myers's researches we may say that this material which is ordinarily below the threshold is a part of the " subliminal self." The material is usually *sub*conscious, but with the lowering of the threshold it becomes conscious, — the conscious state is widened to include it.

This material in the subconscious self consists largely of memories, — thoughts and feelings which were explicitly noticed at one time or have slipped into the marginal region unnoticed by the conscious attention. But James, like Myers, does not limit subconscious material to memory. Unlike Myers, however, he does not definitely suggest its extension telepathically into the mind of another person. We do not know how far it extends, but we do know that at certain times its content comes within the focus of consciousness and goes to make up the unified conscious state.

Now the mystical, in James's theory, is just such a psychical state as this, when the field of consciousness has widened, and matters usually subliminal have come into view. As such it differs from the ordinary psychical state not so much in kind as in extent. It has nothing to do with sense-perception, for sense stimuli are absent, but its form is perceptual, just as any conscious state is perceptual in its immediacy, that is, before the concepts have had time to get in their work. It is a moment of perception of a great mass of memories, concepts, feelings, relations, all at once, a much larger mass than the ordinary " rational " consciousness reveals, but still an undifferentiated one. As soon as an object in it is singled out and recognized and classified, the experience becomes conceptual, but in its much-at-once character, as it is immediately presented and apprehended, it presents an undiscriminated perceptual field. But this is to say that it is a moment of *experience* in the fullest sense of the word. It is a moment of unlimited possibilities, of vaguely suggested wider relationships, of illumination and exhilaration and newness of life, in which the personal consciousness may feel itself profoundly though indescribably moved and even transformed, and in which wholly unsuspected sources of power may make themselves felt.

These states are to be distinguished from other psychical states, James tells us,[4] by their ineffability, noetic quality, transiency, and passivity. They are ineffable, for one must have direct experience of them one's self to know what they are like. Yet for the one who has them they seem to have noetic quality, indescribable though they are, and bringing insight as they do into a kind of truth of which the rational consciousness knows nothing. At the same time they are transient, for their intensity is so great that they cannot be lasting, and they are passive, for when they come the experient feels himself in the grip of a power not his own.

Mysticism thus fits naturally into an empirical philosophy, since its approach to truth is so thoroughly experiential. " Reason, operating on our other experiences, even our psychological experiences, would never have inferred these specifically religious experiences in advance of their actual coming." But now that they have come, empirically, " they suggest that our natural experience, our strictly moralistic and prudential experience, may be only a fragment of real human experience. They soften nature's outlines and open out the strangest possibilities and perspectives."[5] And mysticism is also *radically* empirical. For radical empiricism is a demand that the relations between terms, just as truly as the terms themselves, shall be matters of direct particular experience. And mysticism is the process of finding that the larger relations of life, one term of which is the individual self, are directly experienceable.

What then shall we say of its cognitive content? In the first and most important place, as a cognitive experience it is perceptual. Although in one context [6] James seems to ally himself with the intellectualistic tradition dating back to Plato, and to suggest that worship of the religious object is comparable to the contemplation of abstract ideas, in the main he takes a position similar to Bergson's intuitionism and brings out clearly mysticism's perceptual character. The knowledge it

---

[4] *Varieties*, p. 380.
[5] *A Pluralistic Universe*, p. 306.
[6] Chapter III of the *Varieties*.

brings is knowledge of acquaintance, not knowledge about. As such it has the advantage of being the kind of knowledge which gives *insight*, which goes to the heart of its object, and which is able to appreciate and enjoy all the color and life and richness which its object may have. As such also, however, it suffers from its lack of conceptual function by being individual and incommunicable. It brings insight, it is intuitively penetrating, it is illuminating, yet it hardly deserves the name of knowledge, since it is indefinable and limited to the individual experiencer.

It is not limited to the individual, however, in the sense that it reveals only the individual's own consciousness, his memory and past experience. James definitely states that it links the individual with a consciousness not his own. He says, for example, that as a result of his experience with nitrous oxide one conclusion forced itself upon him. " It is that our normal waking consciousness, rational consciousness as we call it, is but one special type of consciousness, whilst all about it, parted from it by the filmiest of screens, there lie potential forms of consciousness entirely different." [7] The mystical, waking contact with a part or parts of this surrounding consciousness is an experience of illumination,[8] of reconcilation,[9] of exhilaration,[10] and of power, " new ranges of life succeeding on our most despairing moments." [11] Such experiences " render the soul more energetic," [12] they " add a supersensuous meaning to the outward data of consciousness." [13] And the whole tendency of mysticism is to incline the experiencer toward optimism and pantheism, to an " anti-naturalistic " and " so-called other-worldly " state of mind.[14] James's final observation on the adequacy of mysticism as a means to truth is recorded as follows:

(1) Mystical states, when well developed, usually are, and
   have the right to be, absolutely authoritative over
   the individuals to whom they come.

[7] *Varieties*, p. 388.

[8] *Varieties*, p. 408.

[9] *Varieties*, p. 388.

[10] *Collected Essays, etc.*, p. 501. .

[11] *A Pluralistic Universe*, p. 305.

[12] *Varieties*, p. 415.

[13] *Varieties*, p. 427.

[14] *Varieties*, p. 422.

(2) No authority emanates from them which should make it a duty for those who stand outside of them to accept their revelations uncritically.

(3) They break down the authority of the non-mystical or rationalistic consciousness, based upon the understanding and the senses alone. They show it to be only one kind of consciousness. They open out the possibility of other orders of truth, in which, so far as anything in us vitally responds to them, we may freely continue to have faith.[15]

This third conclusion is the one which James emphasizes and from which he goes on to record his own " over-belief." There is always the *possibility* that new truth may come through the mystical experience. " It must always remain an open question whether mystical states may not possibly be such superior points of view, windows through which the mind looks out upon a more extensive and inclusive world." [16] This kind of utterance is indeed one of the most distinctive things about James's whole discussion. It marks him off for example from those psychologists who in their study of mysticism have made the physiological or even the pathological element the significant feature, from Leuba with his " Tendance à la jouissance organique " and " transe amoureuse," [17] from Coe and his notion of muscular relaxation,[18] from Murisier and his theory of monoideism, — even from Delacroix, considered a sympathetic student of the subject, who finds that St. Teresa's supposed communion with the Deity is really nothing but communion with her subconscious self.[19] For James such a position is much too dogmatic. " Just as our primary wide-awake consciousness throws open our senses to the touch of things material, so it is logically conceivable that *if there be* higher spiritual agencies that can directly touch us, the psy-

---

[15] *Varieties*, pp. 422–3.
[16] *Varieties*, p. 428.
[17] *Revue Philosophique*, 54: 483, 486.
[18] *The Psychology of Religion*, p. 276.
[19] Cf. Chapter on " St. Teresa," in Delacroix's *Études d'Histoire et de Psychologie du Mysticisme*.

chological condition of their doing so *might be* our possession
of a subconscious region which alone should yield access to
them." [20] " The whole drift of my education goes to persuade
me that the world of our present consciousness is only one out
of many worlds of consciousness that exist, and that those
other worlds must contain experiences which have a meaning
for our life also; and that although in the main their experiences and those of this world keep discrete, yet the two
become continuous at certain points, and higher energies
filter in." [21]

This willingness to follow the lead of mystical experiences
in the search for truth and eagerness to find in them evidence
of contact with a consciousness other than human is further
brought out in two hitherto unpublished letters to Miss Ethel
D. Puffer. In an article on " The Loss of Personality " printed
in the *Atlantic Monthly* for February 1900 and republished
with some changes as Chapter III of *The Psychology of
Beauty,* Miss Puffer, who is now Mrs. Benjamin Alfred Howes,
had argued that the mystical experience may be described
in terms of the loss of those bodily sensations on which
depends the sense of self. The feeling of selfhood and personality results from the feelings of transition which make
clear the distinction between objects attended to in the fore-
ground of consciousness and the less clearly noted but intimately felt organic sensations in the background of consciousness. In the mystical experience the distinction is lost sight
of and subject and object merge. Two of James's letters concerning the article, although containing some irrelevant material, are quoted here in unabridged form on account of the
characteristic and inimitable Jamesian quality which breathes
through them.

July 8, '99

Dear Miss Puffer

Münsterberg has just been telling me of your essay on Mysticism, etc. I am certain that the " perusal " of it will be of

20 *Varieties,* p. 242.   21 *Varieties,* p. 519.

the greatest advantage to my Gifford lectures — written as the latter are doomed to be in the greatest ignorance of the original sources of religious life. I am sure also that I " wisht to heaven " I had known of all this before — I should have tried to pump you ere you went away. Meanwhile can't you entrust the ms. to me for a few days? Whatever I filch from it won't be " published " in the proper sense of the word till yours is publisht, and then with full acknowledgment. I will give you a copy of the Gifford lectures in return, just think of that! — and I herewith send you an interesting document, which, however, you doubtless know already.

Pray mail the essay immediately, for I leave here on Friday and sail Saturday.

With cordial regards, and regrets at not having seen more of you (no one's fault but my own!) I am very truly yours,

WM. JAMES

CARQUEIRANNE, FRANCE, *March* 14, 1900

Dear Miss Puffer

I was most agreeably surprised a couple of weeks ago by the *Atlantic* and *Smith Monthly* from your hand. I had begun to wonder when that famous *Atlantic Monthly* article was ever going to appear. My first reaction must be to *praise* you tremendously for the *nervi-ness* of your thought and style. We have a new thorough-bred in American serious literature, and I for one can't tell how far she'll go. Candidly isn't that sort of reaction the thing for which you most genuinely hunger and thirst — to be called simply *great,* without hair-splitting distinctions, and such like foolishness? If you were a man, that would be the case; and I doubt whether your being a woman, however humble-minded, alters it much. Prof. Howison in California told the truth when he said to me a couple of years ago, in memorable words: " J., what we philosophers really need is *praise!* Harris calls it " recognition " — but what it is is really praise, just bald rank praise." Dear Howison! to tell the truth so simply! So I begin, my dear young lady, by acknowledging your simple greatness. You give the marks of great power, and I hope you will go indefinitely forward, writing articles as strongly reasoned and as gracefully turned as the one in the *Atlantic,* and raising the level of our literature in such subjects. As for the *Smith* article, it had the same qualities, and was moreover a *cri du cœur,* from the midst of life. But of course it was of slighter content, and doesn't exclude the simultaneous propriety of another cry from the heart, rending the sky from life's just opposite pole, from someone else.

I read the *Atlantic* article with the deepest attention, because a good deal of my poor scanty reading since I have been away (you have very likely heard that I have been very ill) has been of a mystical order, and I was curious to see how your formulation now appeared to fit the facts. I can't say that I am convinced that it is adequate, for it seems to me too ultra simple. There may be new *genera* of consciousness just yawning for us to tumble into; and your attempt is to apply to them only such structural laws as are found in the ordinary genus. That, of course, may be vicious from the start. Nevertheless since your formulation is a first attempt at making articulate tracks in a field hitherto untracked, it must remain an integral part of the literature of the subject, to be taken account of by all later students thereof. I rather feel, myself, like leaving it in that undecided position for a long time to come. I don't see why it mightn't be a satisfactory account of many forms of rapturous immersion in truth, yet not of all. In some a new kind of *object* may swim into the ken, and the peculiarity of the object may not consist in the *mere* fact that the subject has vanished, though that fact may be included, as it is in lower raptures. I wish I could see my way to being as confident as you are that the feelings of muscular adjustment are the all in all of the sense of self. Of course they have much to do therewith, but why can't there be substantive sensations as well? The muscular transitions and adaptations exist between the parts of every complex object, however aesthetically unified the latter may be, and however self-forgetful the observer. You say they don't connect the "background" in that case. But that suggests just the question: isn't there then something substantively of the *me* in that background already, and are then the feelings of adjustment all alone enough? My great doubt about the whole business is whether a merely negative formal condition like the dropping out of these muscular feelings can possibly account for the immense power and sense of new verity which the higher mystical experiences seem to bring to those who have them. They may be all folly — I certainly think they are for the uses of this world; but I don't feel like closing the door off-hand on the notion that there may be new materials of consciousness altogether, lying beyond our ordinary margin, for which our ordinary conceptual categories are insufficient, and of which our words can articulate no sufficient account.* Nevertheless, as aforesaid, there stands your little hypothesis, perfectly definite and precise, challenging the judgment of posterity, and there I leave it, for the present.

This letter of mine to you is a great intellectual and scriptorial achievement — I am still so weak. Münsterberg writes that psychology is at a low ebb this year in Radcliffe. I'm sorry, on every account. Does any better opening show itself for *you?* I wish I were at home with the leisure I now enjoy, to cultivate the philosophical-social relations that Cambridge affords. — But no more now, from yours most sincerely,

WM. JAMES

* It strikes me that I am probably away from the mark in this point — you are only trying to account for the loss of self; and not for everything in the mystical experiences by that loss.

It is clear therefore that James was inclined to regard the mystical experience as significant and helpful in the search for truth. It may and probably does put us in touch with other forms of consciousness with which our present categories are ill equipped to deal but which we have a right to call by the name of God. It is an experience of illumination, exhilaration, and power, perceptual in form, authoritative for the one who has it, but exerting no authority over anyone else, a legitimate basis, however, for an over-belief.

So much for the value that James himself definitely ascribes to the mystical experience. Now let us take up some of the points of contact which mysticism as worked out in the lives and the ideas of its greatest exponents makes with James's philosophy. Our argument is that in three ways mysticism offers a natural and legitimate solution for problems with which James was confronted. In the first place, it has a solution for the religious conflict; secondly, it supplements the phenomenalism of James's pragmatism; third, it relieves the individualism of his ethical theory.

First, then, as to the conflict. We have seen that James emphasizes the passive side of the mystical experience, yet historically mysticism has been more than passive. James's problem, we remember, was to know which is better, deeper and truer, an attitude which finds the last word in creative human achievement, or that which sees that " healthy-mindedness is not the whole of life " and reaches out for something which human effort cannot bring. We saw that James solved the difficulty in a manner only partially satisfactory even to himself by the paradoxical idea of a pluralistic universe. Since the world is a universe it is able to respond to our need for stability, but since it is pluralistic it affords scope for our creative activity as well. God is the author of saving experiences, and to that extent is dependable, yet he is limited, and needs man's aid in carrying his purposes to fruition. It is clear that a reconciliation of the two demands is difficult. If the universe is to be safe it cannot at the same time be risky. There cannot be a real possibility of loss and at the same time an assurance of final salvation.

We do seem, in other words, to reach a dilemma when we try to formulate a theory which will do justice to both the demands which James makes. But the mystic attacks the problem from the practical side. The great mystics have always been able to reconcile the experienced need for human effort with the also experienced dependence on a source higher than human by recognizing the supplementary parts played by the active and the contemplative moods. The mystic has always insisted on a strenuously moral preparation for the ecstatic experience. Thus an experience which in itself is passive is preceded by vigorous, active effort, and leads again to energetic effort in the "mystic life" of active well-doing which always follows. Each taken by itself is insufficient, but when the two supplement each other the mystic finds that the goal of life has been achieved. No writer on mysticism has brought this out more suggestively than Professor W. E. Hocking in his book on *The Meaning of God in Human Experience*. The principle of alternation, this author indicates, is normal not merely for the mystic, but for everyone. Alternation lies deep in the nature of things. The will to work and the will to worship reinforce each other. Attention must be directed at times to the particular things of daily experience and at other times to the source and background from which experience itself issues. Martha and Mary each play a desirable and necessary part. As Havelock Ellis expresses it, in *The Dance of Life*, rhythm marks all of life's physical and spiritual manifestations. Longfellow's "Legend Beautiful" in *Tales of a Wayside Inn* symbolizes this truth with sympathy and skill in its story of the monk who left a vision of the Master at the call of the bell to distribute alms, and who returning, disconsolate, to what he supposed was his deserted room was greeted, to his immeasurable surprise and joy, by his Master with the words: "Hadst thou stayed, I must have fled."

It is interesting to find that James himself discovered in the mystical experience a hint as to the need for satisfying both the active and the passive moods. In the chapter on Mysticism in the *Varieties* he stresses *passivity* as a characteristic of the mystical state,[22] emphasizes its monistic background,[23] and brings out its message of comfort and assurance.[24] But in his article on Benjamin Paul Blood, now reprinted in *Memories and Studies* he calls that writer a pluralistic mystic, stressing the independence which the mystical experience

[22] P. 381.　　　[23] P. 419.　　　[24] P. 428.

brings. And in a little known because unsigned review of
Blood's *The Anaesthetic Revelation and the Gist of Philosophy* printed in the *Atlantic Monthly* [25] he emphasizes the
part that volition must play in any religious experience worthy
of the name. " Interpretation of the phenomenon which Mr.
Blood describes," he here says, " is yet deficient. But we may
be sure of one thing now: that even on the hypothesis of its
containing all the ' revelation ' he asserts, laughing-gas intoxication would not be a final way of getting at that revelation.
What blunts the mind and weakens the will is no full channel
for truth, even if it assist us to a view of a certain aspect of it,
and mysticism *versus* mysticism, the faith that comes of willing,
the intoxication of moral volition, has a million times better
credentials."

Mysticism, then, even on James's own statement, offers a
fruitful suggestion toward a solution of the conflict by which
he was troubled. The second connection which it makes with
his religious philosophy is its suggestion as to a release from
the phenomenalism of his religious pragmatism. Pragmatism,
as James describes it, is avowedly positivistic. Truth is a
matter of definitely experienceable workings; it is determined
by its empirical consequences; at times James even says it is
the consequences themselves. Men live by postulates rather
than by certainties. Even when they have hold of a certainty
they do not know it to be such. The case against pragmatism
in this regard as a philosophy of religion has been put by
Professor James B. Pratt in his book *What is Pragmatism?*
when he argues that the " logical outcome of pragmatism
when applied to religion is not salvation from philosophic
doubt, but a necessary and ineradicable skepticism." [26] For
" since the truth of an idea means merely the fact that the
idea works, that fact is all you mean when you say the idea
is true, nothing more, nothing ' transcendent ' or ' cosmic '
must be sought for it." [27] And " 'tis idle for us creatures of a
day who cannot even *mean* anything beyond our own experience, to spend time on questions necessarily so remote and in-

---

[25] Vol. 34, p. 628.   [26] P. 205.   [27] P. 206.

accessible as are those which religious people *think* they are discussing and about which they *think* they care." [28]

With all the truth which this statement of the limitations of pragmatism as a philosophy of religion contains, it appears also to be true that mysticism as James treats it affords a way out of pragmatic phenomenalism, and a way which is justified by pragmatism itself. For pragmatism relies for the completion of its process of verification on a perceptual experience, an experience of immediacy, a face-to-face presentation. [29]

Now this immediate, perceptual experience may be a sense-experience, but it need not be. It seems entirely fair to James's thought to claim that it may be a mystical experience. To be sure, the mystical experience has nothing to do with sense-perception, for sense stimuli are absent. But its form is perceptual, just as any mental state is perceptual in its immediacy before the discriminating and classifying processes have had time to begin. That James regarded it so and that he considered it as legitimate a perceptual experience for the individual as a sense experience seems to be clear from the chapter on Mysticism in the *Varieties* and from the article "A Suggestion About Mysticism." And his way of treating the whole subject of perception is at times strikingly similar to the treatment of the mystical experience by the mystics themselves. Like a religious man speaking of the Deity, James says of perceptual objects of acquaintance, "At most I can say to my friends, Go to certain places and act in certain ways, and these objects will probably come." [30] And again he talks as though in a mystical strain when he says: "The maximal conceivable truth in an idea would seem to be that it should lead to an actual merging of ourselves with the object, to an utter mutual confluence and identification." [31]

Yet when all is said the feeling persists that there is a discrepancy between the perceptions of the mystic and the kind of perceptual verification for which pragmatism is looking, a

[28] P. 208.
[29] Cf. esp. the first two essays in *The Meaning of Truth.*
[30] *Principles of Psychology* 1: 221.
[31] *The Meaning of Truth,* p. 156.

discrepancy which mystics and pragmatists have vied with each other to point out. One chief reason for this seems to be the contrast between pragmatism's social point of view, and mysticism's individualism. Mysticism does indeed reach out beyond the phenomenal world, but the mystic himself is the only one who feels the direct touch with the noumenal Object. Ethically pragmatism is a philosophy of social amelioration; epistemologically it requires social verification. But the mystic's truth exists for him alone. The mystic is indeed invulnerable, but it is a lonely kind of invulnerability.

This brings us face to face with one of the central questions of James's theory of knowledge. On the one hand we have the will to believe with its hypotheses about life and destiny, making postulates which are tentative, offering something to live by, but adopting an agnostic attitude toward ultimate certainty. Allied to this is the pragmatic tendency to think of truth as known and even conditioned by its value, dependent for whatever being it may have on the "working" of particular experiences. On the other hand we have James's description of the thorough-going, though lonely, certainty of the mystic, and his obvious sympathy with the whole mystical-perceptual procedure. And in *A Pluralistic Universe* we find him accepting Bergson as an ally, and adopting with enthusiasm Bergson's notion of a perceptual intuition by which reality, even ultimate cosmic reality, is grasped by a stroke of intuitive sympathy.

Is it possible to bridge this chasm, and to have certainty which is yet socially available? It seems to be possible, even on James's own statement of the case. One of his earlier works, the essay on "The Sentiment of Rationality" contains this passage: ". . . however vaguely a philosopher may define the ultimate universal datum, he cannot be said to leave it unknown to us so long as he in the slightest degree pretends that our emotional or active attitude toward it should be of one sort rather than another. He who says 'life is real, life is earnest,' however much he may speak of the fundamental mysteriousness of things, gives a distinct definition to that mysteriousness by ascribing to it the right to claim from us the particular mood called seriousness, — which means the willingness to live with energy, though energy bring pain. The same is true of him who says that all is vanity. For indefinable as the predicate ' vanity ' may be *in se,* it is clearly something that permits anaesthesia, mere escape from suffering, to be our rule of life. There can be no greater incongruity than for a disciple of Spencer to proclaim with one breath that the substance of things is unknowable, and with the next that the thought of it should inspire us with awe, reverence, and a willingness to add our co-operative push in the direction toward which its manifestations seem to be drifting. The unknowable may be unfathomed, but if it make such distinct demands upon our activity we surely are not ignorant of its essential quality." [32]

When it is a question of the ultimate datum, then, a definition is possible. A reaction which calls for a certain emotional or active attitude toward life is itself a definition and communicable. But the mystic reaches just such an ultimate datum, on James's own showing in another part of the same essay.[33] And the history of mysticism bears out the fact that the mystic does not rest content with his intuition, but spends his life trying to translate it into an " emotional or active attitude." He defines the Object of his vision by the attitude toward life which he takes. By so doing he communicates and socializes his experience. And the active attitude in its turn influences the vision itself.[34]

As a matter of common observation, the truly religious man is always translating his vision into action and the true mystic has always transmitted to others the content of his experience in terms of conduct. Indeed it was James himself who argued in the *Varieties* that most men get their religious experience at second hand, and that the deities whom they worship " are known to them only in idea," that many men

---

[32] *The Will to Believe and Other Essays,* p. 86.
[33] *The Will to Believe, etc.,* p. 74.
[34] Cf. *The Will to Believe, etc.,* bottom p. 60.

are Christians, though few have had an immediate vision of the Savior. The common experience of mankind bears out the theory of the social quality of mysticism and supports the claim that mysticism furnishes a legitimate means of escape from the positivistic side of pragmatism.

The final contribution offered by mysticism is to James's ethical theory. As we saw above, in the essay on " The Moral Philosopher and the Moral Life " James makes the point that obligation must be understood in terms of desire and that the essence of good is to ratify demand. But since all demands cannot be satisfied at once our practical aim can only be to fill as many as possible of the more permanent ones. And we can best accomplish this by taking experience as it comes instead of relying on *a priori* rules. In his enthusiasm for the empirical attitude in ethics James makes one of the strongest defenses of the radical ever penned. " In point of fact," he argues, " there are no absolute evils, and there are no non-moral goods; and the *highest* ethical life — however few may be called to bear its burdens — consists at all times in the breaking of rules which have grown too narrow for the actual case. There is but one unconditional commandment, which is that we should seek incessantly, with fear and trembling, so to vote and to act as to bring about the very largest total universe of good which we can see. Abstract rules indeed can help; but they help the less in proportion as our intuitions are more piercing, and our vocation is the stronger for the moral life. For every real dilemma is in literal strictness a unique situation; and the exact combination of ideals realized and ideals disappointed which each decision creates is always a universe without a precedent, and for which no adequate previous rule exists." [35]

But how and when are we to know whether our piercing intuitions really pierce? Do they bring with them anything by which we may know their authority? Here once more the mystic offers his aid. Just as James's empirical philosophy attains greater sureness by following its empiricism through, and

[35] *The Will to Believe, etc.,* p. 209.

finding a noumenal realm which is at the same time an object of direct experience, so the cure for an individualistic and pluralistic ethics seems to be more pluralism of a religious sort. For pluralistic mysticism, in its own paradoxical way, gives the individual an independence which brings its own authority. This seems to be the message of that arresting writer, B. P. Blood, mentioned above.

And even if he reject the title " pluralistic " the mystic is still of service here. For the mystic has his own intimate touch with reality, bringing, as he believes, a higher than human authority. He has his own " piercing intuitions " which he has always trusted as against the authority of tradition. He is a " radical who confronts the existing order not with the intent of pure destruction but with a new standard of what human nature really needs." [36] The mystic can break with custom because he is a man who knows what he is about. His is " a deliberate undertaking to recover the principle of value self-consciously." [37] As Jesus observed in the story reported in Codex Bezae of the conversation with the man working on the Sabbath: " If thou knowest what thou art doing, blessed art thou; but if thou knowest not, thou art accursed and a transgressor of the law." This is just the issue which the mystic feels equipped to meet. He does know what he is doing, and he knows that his authority is greater than that of any external law. The mystic, in a word, transcends the average. Out of the riches of his abundant life he creates new truth and new value. His prophetic insight is greater in degree but similar in kind to that of James's empirical, creative individual who is able to envisage the highest values in any given human situation. And the activity to which he is led by his confidence in his own inner authority has ever served to demonstrate to his fellows the practicability of the new truth he has discovered. His basis for judgment between conflicting desires has proved acceptable. He knows whereof he speaks.

In these three ways, then, do we find mysticism making a

[36] C. A. Bennett, "*A Philosophical Study of Mysticism*," p. 174.
[37] *Ibid.*, p. 40.

connection with James's thought. The connection is illuminating in both directions. Mysticism, it would seem, cannot be, as some regard it, merely a philosophy of the abnormal if its relation is so close to the thought of a healthy humanist like James. And correspondingly the religious element in James's thought must be fundamental if the points of contact are so many. Yet is this not what one would expect, if religion be a natural human attitude and activity?

X

FURTHER CHARACTERISTICS

OUR study of James's religious philosophy in its attempt to throw new light on his religious conflict,
his developing conception of God, his belief in immortality, the relation of his mystical bent to his pragmatism
and to his philosophy in general, has necessarily devoted itself
to some parts of his religious *Weltanschauung* to the exclusion
of others. For a well rounded view these other elements must
at least receive mention. This chapter will accordingly take
up: first, some of James's general definitions of religion; second, some of his more specific religious interests; and third,
a few characteristics of his personal religious belief.

In the second chapter of the *Varieties* (which we know,
from the *Letters*,[1] caused him a good deal of trouble to com-
pose) James addressed himself to the task of defining religion.
His very first statement is rather discouragingly negative.
" The word ' religion,' " he says, " cannot stand for any single
principle or essence, but is rather a collective name."[2] This
remark has frequently been quoted as the wild and destruc-
tive vagary of an ultra-pluralist. Religion has no essence, religious phenomena have nothing in common, therefore religion,
having no distinctive qualities, cannot itself be anything — so
the critics have argued. Yet it is easy to see that by this statement James simply meant to prepare the way for an empirical
investigation. Indeed he goes on to say, " Let us not fall immediately into a one-sided view of our subject, but let us
rather admit freely at the outset that we *may very likely* find

---

[1] 2: 127. [2] P. 26.

no one essence, but many characters which may alternately be equally important in religion." [3] We *may* find no common essence, that is, in the sense that we may find varying features of religion alternating in importance. That James did find such an alternation himself our study of the conflict has suggested. Especially unwarranted does the fear of the critics seem when in the next to the last chapter of the book we find the question: "Is there, under all the discrepancies of the creeds, a common nucleus to which they bear their testimony unanimously?" And the answer is affirmative: "The warring gods and formulas of the various religions do indeed cancel each other, but there is a certain uniform deliverance in which religions all appear to meet." [4] But this common experience of deliverance need not come to all persons in the same way at the same time. "No two of us have identical difficulties, nor should we be expected to work out identical solutions. . . . So a 'god of battles' must be allowed to be a god for one kind of person, a god of peace and heaven and home the god for another." [5]

After this relativistic insistence a definition will be difficult. Affirming that for his purposes religion must have to do with " the inner dispositions of man himself " rather than with institutions, James formulates the following: " Religion, therefore, as I now ask you arbitrarily to take it, shall mean for us *the feelings, acts, and experiences of individual men in their solitude, so far as they apprehend themselves to stand in relation to whatever they may consider the divine.*" [6] The individualism of this definition has received unfavorable comment. Yet religion is a matter of individual experience just as truly as it is a social institution. So far has the pendulum swung toward the socialized view among students of religion that James's insistence on the reality of religious values in the life of the individual seems like a return to the point of view of common sense. The social aspect of religious practises must be studied, by all means, but it should be combined

---

[3] *Letters*, italics ours.
[4] Pp. 507–8.

[5] *Varieties*, p. 487, cf. pp. 75, 133, 135.
[6] P. 31.

with an analysis of what religion means to the individual, aspiring human spirit — the analysis that James has so competently given us.[7]

The word "divine" needs further explanation. James's comment here is "Whatever . . . were most primal and enveloping and deeply true might at this rate be treated as godlike, and a man's religion might thus be identified with his attitude, whatever it might be, towards what he felt to be the primal truth."[8] But this requires still further qualification. Religion is a man's total reaction upon life. May we, then, call any total reaction a religion? James thinks not, for to do so would offend our sense of the fitness of things. Voltaire's sneering attitude toward life has a certain robustness, but we should hardly call it religious. Similarly we should hesitate to apply the term to the "dandified despair" of Renan's later years.[9] Again, James has often used the expression "religious melancholy," but melancholy, as he goes on to show, "forfeits all title to be called religious when, in Marcus Aurelius's racy words, the sufferer simply lies kicking and screaming after the fashion of a sacrificed pig."[10] "There must be something solemn, serious, and tender about any attitude which we denominate as religious. . . . The divine shall mean for us only such a primal reality as the individual feels impelled to respond to solemnly and gravely, and neither by a curse nor a jest."[11] And to distinguish the religious from the moral attitude we must add the sense of victory and consciousness of new resources of power. "If religion is to mean anything definite for us . . . we ought to take it as meaning this added dimension of emotion, this enthusiastic temper of espousal, in regions where morality strictly so-called can at best but bow its head and acquiesce."[12] "*Religion thus makes easy and felicitous what in any case is necessary.*"[13] So, including both volitional and intellectual elements specifically, and the emotional implicitly, James sums up his discussion by saying:

[7] Cf. Hopkins, *The Origin and Evolution of Religion*, pp. 6 ff.
[8] P. 34.
[9] Cf. *Collected Essays, etc.*, pp. 36–39.
[10] *Varieties*, p. 38.
[11] *Ibid.*, p. 38.
[12] P. 48.
[13] P. 51.

"Were one asked to characterize the life of religion in the broadest and most general terms possible, one might say that it consists of the belief that there is an unseen order, and that our supreme good lies in harmoniously adjusting ourselves thereto. This belief and this adjustment are the religious attitude in the soul." [14]

The emotional attitude of passive dependence which is so prominent throughout the *Varieties* receives more explicit notice in the characterizations of religious beliefs given in the chapter on " Conclusions."

" Summing up in the broadest possible way the characteristics of the religious life, as we have found them, it includes the following beliefs: —

1. That the visible world is part of a more spiritual universe from which it draws its chief significance.

2. That union or harmonious relation with that higher universe is our true end;

3. That prayer or inner communion with the spirit thereof — be that spirit ' God ' or ' law ' — is a process wherein work is really done, and spiritual energy flows in and produces effects, psychological or material, within the phenomenal world.

Religion includes also the following psychological characteristics:

4. A new zest which adds itself like a gift to life, and takes the form either of lyrical enchantment or of appeal to earnestness and heroism.

5. An assurance of safety and a temper of peace, and, in relation to others, a preponderance of loving affections." [15]

From general definitions we turn to specific qualities which James looked for in religion. Among the most important of these would seem to be " richness." " Although some persons

[14] P. 53   [15] Pp. 485-6.

aim most at intellectual purity and simplification," he tells us in the *Varieties*, "for others *richness* is the supreme imaginative requirement." [16] Some minds, as he goes on to say, need "something institutional and complex, majestic in the hierarchic interrelatedness of its parts, with authority descending from stage to stage, and at every stage objects for adjectives of mystery and splendor, derived in the last resort from the Godhead who is the fountain and culmination of the system. One feels then as if in presence of some vast incrusted work of jewelry or architecture; one hears the multitudinous liturgical appeal; one gets the honorific vibration coming from every quarter." [17]

Much in James points to a sympathy with the general position of Protestantism. His attitude of reliance on individual authority, distaste for institutionalism, and belief in the possibility of loss which should be eternal is indeed just what Professor George Cross of Rochester Theological Seminary has called the characteristically Protestant position. But passages like the above indicate how strongly he was attracted to the liturgical in worship. This attraction was undoubtedly closely linked with his aesthetic interest. As is well known, he tried his hand at painting when a young man. Henry James has given us this picture of his youthful habit. "As I catch W. J.'s image, from far back, at its most characteristic, he sits drawing and drawing, always drawing, especially under the lamplight of the Fourteenth Street back parlor; and not as with a plodding patience which I think would less have affected me, but easily, freely, and, as who should say, infallibly. . . ." [18] The attempt has frequently been made to relate James's aesthetic to his philosophic insight.[19] The argument seems always to have run along the following lines. James

[16] P. 459.
[17] P. 460.
[18] *A Small Boy and Others*, p. 207.
[19] E.g. by Flournoy, Chap. 1 of *The Philosophy of William James*, Lovejoy, "William James as Philosopher," *International Journal of Ethics*, Jan. 29, 1911; D. S. Miller, "Some Aspects of William James's Philosophy," *Journal of Philosophy etc.*, Nov. 24, 1910; G. Vorbrodt, "William James's Philosophie," *Zeitschrift für Philosophie und Philosophische Kritik* (Leipzig), 157: 1.

was a pluralist and individualist, also an artist. His artistic insight must, then, have displayed itself in his sense for significant detail. As Professor Lovejoy has especially well expressed it, " James had the artist's ' purity of eye ' applied to human nature, he could see distinctions and differences. . . . James's genius lay chiefly in this — that he retained an extraordinary immunity to the deadening influences of the intellectual process of classification and generalization. . . . Each separate fact was unique."

The only fault that can be found with this statement is that it does not go far enough. James surely did have the artist's sense for significant detail. But the artist notices more than details. He sees details in their larger relationships. And James had an interest in wholes as well as in parts. Empiricism, as he claimed, does begin with the parts, but it leads toward wholes, especially radical empiricism with the larger relationships of which it brings a view. We have already seen James's aesthetic and religious interest in larger entities. We have observed that with true artistic insight he envisaged the universal in and through the individual, he understood man because he knew men, in the individual religious experience he found the common essence of religion. And have we not seen as well that the Whole made its own appeal to James apart from any reference to its details? For him the absolute had its own " majesty " and " nobility " and " formal grandeur," its " sweep and dash " attracted him. Its deficiency lay in the fact that it was *only* a setting. It furnished but a "pallid outline for the real world's richness."

To return to our quotation about the liturgy — " Compared with such a noble complexity," James goes on to say, " in which ascending and descending movements seem in no way to jar upon stability, in which no single item, however humble, is insignificant, because so many august institutions hold it in place, how flat does evangelical Protestantism appear, how bare the atmosphere of those isolated religious lives whose boast it is that ' man in the bush with God may meet.' What a pulverization and levelling of what a gloriously piled-up structure." [20] Clearly in this instance James's "aesthetic sentiment" is a sense for details *en masse* rather than singly. In the aesthetic and religious realms as elsewhere pluralism is not a plea for disconnectedness, but rather a protest against a too rigid and regular conformity.

This leads to a further observation on James's interest in details and its relation to his religious interest. We have just seen that the *significance* of details, both aesthetically and religiously, seems for James to have lain as much in their setting, their larger relationships, as in themselves. But James had a different kind of interest in particular, individual things. A belief to interest him had to give him immediate touch with particular phenomena, or perhaps one should say had to give him practical contact with tangible objects. Something concrete which he could, so to speak, handle, and deal with objectively, and react to with definiteness had to form a part of any view or theory which was to hold his attention. In the passage quoted above we observed his interest in the richness of the Catholic ritual. But he was attracted by its concreteness as well as its richness. A letter to Thomas Davidson, dated March 30, 1884, brings this out in interesting fashion: " . . . I confess the idea of engrafting the bloodless pallor of Boston Unitarianism on the Roman temperament strikes one at first sight as rather queer. Unitarianism seems to have a sort of moribund vitality here, because it is a branch of Protestantism and the tree keeps the branch sticking out. But whether it could be grafted on a catholic trunk seems to me problematic. I confess I rather despair of any popular religion of a philosophic character; and I sometimes find myself wondering whether there can be any popular religion raised on the ruins of the old Christianity without the presence of that element which in the past has presided over the origin of all religions, namely, a belief in new *physical* facts and possibilities. Abstract considerations about the soul and the reality of a moral order will not do in a year what the glimpse into a world of new phenomenal possibilities enveloping those

[20] *Varieties,* p. 460.

of the present life, afforded by an extension of our insight into the order of nature, would do in an instant." [21]

With this interest prominent it is not surprising that the religion of the *Varieties* is primarily the religion that does particular things. When it is healthy-minded it achieves salvation by relaxation,[22] using as its methods suggestions,[23] meditation,[24] " recollection." [25] The " sick soul " needs deliverance perhaps in the " coarser " revivalistic, orgiastic ways with blood and miracles.[26] The " divided self " is unified through religion either gradually or suddenly.[27] Conversions may be with or without volition [28] accompanied by sensory and motor automatisms,[29] and are interesting both in themselves and on account of their fruits for life. " Saintliness " and its values leads to a discussion of various kinds of excitements,[30] subconscious influences,[31] peace of mind, charity, equanimity, purity, asceticism, obedience, democracy, poverty, etc.[32]

From these two specific interests, the aesthetic and the particularistic, we turn to a comment on James's personal religion. In the first place, the interest in particular, concrete, and tangible things which we have just remarked as characteristic of his *study* of religion was also characteristic of his personal *belief*. Throughout his life his interest consistently centered in the things that are accomplished by religion, the lives that are touched, the healthiness of mind which is brought, the " last things, fruits, consequences, facts " of religion. The following unpublished letter to Mrs. Prince gives evidence of this kind of interest. And the date (indicated by the postmark on the envelope) shows that James had it long before either the *Varieties* or *Pragmatism* was written.

[21] *Letters*, 1: 236–7.
[22] Pp. 109 ff.
[23] P. 112.
[24] P. 151.
[25] P. 116.
[26] P. 162.

[27] P. 183.
[28] P. 206.
[29] P. 250.
[30] Pp. 262 ff.
[31] P. 271.
[32] Pp. 278 ff.

CAMBRIDGE, *April* 30 (1886)

My dear Kitty,

Your card and letter about Miss Robbins and her possible cook maid have duly arrived, and I will leave Alice whom they most concern, to answer them. Altho slow she is sure.

I mail you, with this, a very beautiful little book which it is possible you may know — *The Christian's Secret of a Happy Life*. It was given to me last winter by the author, Mrs. Pearsall Smith of Philadelphia, a Quakeress, who had a daughter in the Annex and a son in College. As you know, I am not a child of God after the fashion inculcated in this book, nor has the book given me any *active* impulse to become one. Yet strange to say it moves me, and makes me approve of it in the highest degree. I think that what I most feel is perhaps the firm consistent and unsentimental way in which the practical consequences of giving one's will to God are traced out which I like so. One can enjoy so healthy a tracing out of consequences even if one will not make the assumption that starts the whole. If you are able to read a little in it, I cannot but think you will like it. If you don't, that will interest me, possibly even more. Keep it until I ask for it again — many months hence.

Alice has found Kingsley's *Greek Heroes,* and sent it to the Warners.

I have been excessively busy. Too many irons! I am now, among other things, visiting materializing mediums! A strange and in many ways disgusting experience, which I have conscientiously undertaken to sit out. But next year I shall settle down to a narrower line of work. We are all well. Isn't the growth of spring delicious? Alice will write to you soon — but asks now for Miss Robbins's address. Won't you please send it on a post-card? I do hope you are pretty well.

Ever affectionately,

W. J.

Another letter, written apparently a few weeks before this one, concludes with these lines:

You cannot tell, my dearest Kitty, how the sight of your —what shall I say? — *soundness, robustness* of soul, under all you have to bear, refreshes and fortifies me. Your example has been the best religious lesson I have ever had in my life — yours and your doctor's.

Always yours,
WM. JAMES

("Your doctor" refers of course to Dr. William H. Prince.)

After this evidence of personal interest in the particular pragmatic and tangible consequences of religious belief, evidence which is borne out by our whole discussion of James's individualistic interest, let us take up the "mystical germ" to which allusion has been made before. Just what did James mean by saying that he had a "mystical germ"? The largest number of recorded references to it occur in letters written during the year 1904. Writing to E. D. Starbuck with regard to a review of the *Varieties* by the latter he says: "I have no mystical experience of my own, but just enough of the germ of mysticism in me to recognize the region from which their voice comes when I heard it." [33] To J. H. Leuba who had reviewed the *Varieties* he wrote in a similar vein: "Your only consistent position, it strikes me, would be a dogmatic atheistic naturalism; and, without any mystical germ in us, that, I believe, is where we all should *unhesitatingly* be today." [34] His reply in the same year to Professor Pratt's questionnaire carries out this thought.

Q. Why do you believe in God? Is it from some argument?

    A. Emphatically, no.

Q. Or because you have experienced his presence?

    A. No, but rather because I need it, so that it "must" be true.

[33] *Letters*, 2: 210.
[34] *Letters*, 2: 212.

Q. Or from authority, such as that of the Bible or of some prophetic person?

    A. Only the whole tradition of religious people, to which something in me makes admiring response.

Q. Or from any other reason?

    A. Only from the social reasons.

Q. Is God very real to you, as real as an earthly friend?

    A. Dimly (real) not (as an earthly friend).

Q. Do you feel that you have experienced his presence?

    A. Never.

Q. If you have had no such experience, do you accept the testimony of others who claim to have felt God's presence directly?

    A. Yes! The whole line of testimony on this point is so strong that I am unable to pooh-pooh it away! No doubt there is a germ in me of something similar that makes admiring response.[35]

The " mystical germ " then seems to have meant an intense interest in religious experience and a willingness to regard its data as fruitful in the search for truth, but an interest which at the same time was vicarious. The nearest to an account of a religious mystical experience of his own in all James's works is a beautifully suggestive description of a night in the Adirondacks spent under the open sky.[36] But James will not allow us to call that or any other of his experiences mystical in a religious sense. His own religious life was chiefly quickened, if we follow his word, by his imaginative interest in the experiences of others. This interest seems to have come to the fore in James's mind whenever his attention was focused on religion as expressed in the life of some individual or individuals. In the unsigned review of Blood's *The Anaesthetic Revelation, etc.* in the *Atlantic Monthly* for 1874 we find

[35] *Letters,* 2: 213–4.   [36] *Letters,* 2: 75 ff.

his sympathetic interest in Blood's experience clearly indicated. And is it not suggestive that the utterances on the subject of the "mystical germ" come from the period immediately following the publication of the *Varieties?* It seems reasonable to believe that the religious testimony which he had read in preparation for his Gifford lectures awoke his own mystical germ to activity. As he expressed it in the letter to Mrs. Prince, it was the "robustness" of this kind of faith that kindled a sympathetic interest within himself.

Here do we find, incidentally, a rejoinder to the remark of the commentator that "the union of religious mysticism with biological and psychological empiricism is characteristic of James's work from the beginning." For James seems to have had no mysticism in him except this "germ" and that developed late instead of early. In fact, instead of having to be "weaned from his father's monism" as this writer goes on to say, and influenced away from the "mystical Swedenborgian piety" which characterized the home in which he grew up, it appears to be true that he came to have more rather than less sympathy for his father's views as he grew older. For example, he wrote from Berlin in 1867 in a letter to his father, "I have read your article, which I got in Teplitz, several times carefully. I must confess that the darkness which to me has always hung over what you have written on these subjects is hardly at all cleared up. Every sentence seems written from a point of view which I nowhere get within range of, and on the other hand ignores all sorts of questions which are visible from my present view," [37] and more to the same effect. But twenty-four years later, in the letter to his sister from which quotation has already been made, he wrote: "Father would find in me today a much more receptive listener — all *that* philosophy has got to be brought in." [38] And the unpublished letter to Mrs. Prince quoted above in the chapter on "Immortality" told of how in the editing of his father's *Literary Remains* he had seemed to sink into an intimacy with his father which he had never before enjoyed. The "mystical germ"

[37] *Letters*, 1: 96.   [38] *Letters*, 1: 310.

appears to have grown greater rather than less as life advanced. This conclusion is supported by James's intention in the latter part of his life, reported to the present writer by Professor G. H. Palmer, to write a book on Swedenborg. And that the interest continued to be vicarious rather than direct is also suggested by James's reputed remark in connection with this intended work, that there must be truth in the matters which claimed Swedenborg's attention because so many good men had been interested in them.

Of the early household described by one writer as a place of "liberal culture" and "mystical Swedenborgian piety," Henry James has left us an intimate account in his *Notes of a Son and Brother*. Of his father he writes: " It was a luxury, I today see, to have all the benefit of his intellectual and spiritual, his religious, his philosophic and his social passion, without ever feeling the pressure of it to our direct irritation or discomfort. It would perhaps more truly figure the relation in which he left us to these things to have likened our opportunities rather to so many scattered glasses of the liquor of faith, poured-out cups stood about for our either sipping or draining down or leaving alone, in the measure of our thirst, our curiosity or our strength of head and heart." [39] " It is not too much to say, I think, that our religious education, so far as we had any, consisted wholly in that loose yet enlightening impression: I say so far as we had any in spite of my very definitely holding that it would absolutely not have been possible to us, in the measure of our sensibility, to breathe more the air of that reference to an order of goodness and power greater than any this world by itself can show which we understand as the religious spirit. Wondrous to me, as I consider again, that my father's possession of this spirit, in a degree that made it more deeply one with life than I can conceive another or a different case of its being, should have been unaccompanied with a single one of the outward or formal, the theological, devotional, ritual, or even implicitly pietistic signs by which we usually know it." [40]

[39] P. 157.   [40] Pp. 163–4.

Yet although he had none of the pietistic signs, the elder James liked to read chapters from the Bible to his family,[41] a custom which William James continued in his own household. William James during his professional life was also a regular attendant at the college chapel exercises although not a communicant of any church. " I am rather hopelessly non-evangelical," he once said. His indifference to church affiliations is not surprising in one whose interests were so catholic. " I mean by religion for a man *anything* that for *him* is a live hypothesis," he wrote.[42] And again he defined religious experience as " Any moment of life that brings the reality of spiritual things more ' home ' to one."

As his son, Mr. William James, has pointed out to the present writer, his religious interest after all is to be judged not by any outward observance but by the persistent recurrence of the religious question in his mind. Indeed James himself wrote, " Religion is the great interest of my life," and again " the life of it as a whole is mankind's most important function." In commenting on this interest his son has said that James's mind was continually playing with religious problems and seeking an answer to religious questions. Religion was a topic to which his mind kept returning. Professor Palmer has also said that this interest was a culminating one. James began his professional life as a physiologist, then turned to psychology asking what possible use there could be in spending all one's time over " bones." Later he dropped psychology as decisively as physiology, its interest for him having been superseded by that of philosophy. And the culmination of philosophy for him lay, according to his colleague, in the philosophy of religion.

[41] P. 166.   [42] *Letters*, 2: 64.

XI

JAMES AND THE RELIGIOUS THOUGHT
OF TODAY

W E HAVE now come to the end of our survey of
James's religious thought and it is time to take stock
of our findings. It has been our purpose to set
forth James's religious philosophy in terms of a conflict. James
was attracted by two different kinds of religious value whose
claims were at variance with each other. When his powers
were at their height and the active impulses were dominant,
he believed that the only religion worth having was that which
encouraged human achievement. When, on the other hand, he
felt the need of outward support and assurance, the religion
which appealed to him was that which brought comfort. We
have seen in detail that in his writings now one mood and
now the other gives evidence of being dominant. His final
decision was in favor of the more aggressive attitude toward
life, and the pluralistic religion which he thought it implied.
Yet the kind of religious view described in his last books is
such as to conserve some of the values of monism. The assurance of complete final salvation pluralism cannot bring, and
this lack will always be a point against it and in monism's
favor. But the complete certainty of monism is purchased at
too high a price. Better some risk and some chance of failure
than an absolute guaranty. And the pluralism of James's final
view conserves not only the possibility of real achievement
but also the peculiarly religious value of intimacy. From the
God of a pluralistic universe both comfort and " saving
experiences " can flow.

As our discussion of the conflict proceeded, several related features were noticed. The will to believe, representing the active and aggressive interests, was found to mark the intermediate point between James's psychological theory of the teleological character of human activity and his later pragmatic theory of the nature of truth. In discussing the objects of the will to believe we found a development in James's conception of God which reflected the phases of the conflict, the first stage representing the active interest, the second the passive, and the final stage a synthesis of the two. In our discussion of immortality evidence was adduced which suggested a strong personal faith in survival.

Through it all we have been interested in protesting against the notion that James's religious philosophy is not to be judged on the same terms as his metaphysics and epistemology. As a way of making this protest the attempt has been made to show the incidence of his religious thought upon his secular philosophy in varying ways. The very fact that the philosophical antithesis which he so often described became, in its religious implications, an actual conflict suggested that philosophical issues took on liveliness and importance for him when thought of in terms of religious value. We saw that because of its religious appeal James was actually attracted to the absolute. But because of its denial of other more important religious values he decided against it. The influence of his religious views was seen again in the fact that " The Will to Believe," an essay written in defense of religious faith, showed James's theory of the selective function of consciousness developing into a conception of the nature of truth. Then again his attitude toward freedom brought out the fact that the pivotal problem of his psychology and metaphysics was capable only of an ethical solution. And the most stable system of ethics was found on James's own statement to be that built on a religious foundation. We noticed in passing that James's pragmatic theory developed along lines which paralleled the development of his conception of God. Mysticism was seen to make three important connections with James's thought —

offering a solution of the conflict, a relief from phenomenalism, and a more authoritative criterion in ethics. Finally we saw that James's personal interest in religion while non-mystical was not of a merely academic order but was direct and vital. And the whole burden of the testimony pointed to a relation between his religion and his philosophy of such a sort as to make it impossible to cut one off from the other and to say as some have tried to say: " Here the rational element stops and here the vagaries begin."

The more one studies James the more he realizes how completely as well as how accurately James has interpreted the religious aspirations of humankind and how effectively he acts as spokesman for them. The yearning after a saving power has always been fundamental in religion. Schleiermacher was true to a basic human tradition when he framed his definition. Religion has meant a feeling of dependence more than it has meant anything else. The history of religion is the account of the progressive refinement of that feeling. But it is doubtful if it will ever be completely refined away. As James remarked in the passage quoted before: " . . . very little is said of the reason why we *do* pray, which is simply that we cannot *help* praying. It seems probable that in spite of all that ' science ' may do to the contrary, men will continue to pray to the end of time."

And when a reaction has taken place against this attitude of dependence as savoring of weakness the reaction itself in many cases has worked along the lines which James followed in his contrasting mood. Men have taken the common human virtues — courage, energy, honesty, charity, and claimed that they were godlike. Humanity is divine and worthy to be worshipped, they have said. These higher reaches of the human spirit are the surest clues we have to whatever spiritual reality there may be. And James's comment on a view like this seems to be simply that it must be pushed one step farther. We do not simply find in passive fashion that life is worth living, — we must make it worth living by putting ourselves into it. We are not merely to accept our constitutional desire that ideals may prevail but we are to transform it into a demand that ideals shall prevail.

Do men grope, then, in their finitude for a Power higher than human which shall complete their incompleteness, or do they in the flush of strength assert the force of the invincible human will, in either case James expresses their mood with a sympathy which is both sensitive and revealing. It is this intense humanness in his philosophy which has given it such an influence over the thought of the common man. To this day one can hardly enter into a conversation on religious matters with a reflective person without hearing a reference to James before the talk has gone far. This is partly because James furnished an apologetic which was easily grasped. As Professor Pratt has expressed it, many persons eagerly took up the cry: " The sword of the Lord and Pragmatism! " Or, in the words of Royce: " The glad tidings of the subconscious began to be preached in many lands."

But it is also because James's philosophy kept such intimate touch with the problems of conduct and belief with which the average man is confronted. The position maintained in this study of James has been that it is his reflective thought on the problems of man's duty and destiny — his philosophy of religion, that is to say — which is of permanent interest rather than his psychology of religion with its hypotheses as to how religious experience occurs at all — suggestive as the latter are. The hypothesis of the subconscious self as an intermediary between man and the Deity, a sort of " apex mentis," to use the phrase of mediaeval mysticism, has probably today outlived the major portion of its usefulness. We now know that intimations diabolical as well as divine come over the threshold. It is not merely our religious life that the subconscious region influences.

But this is not to say, as some critics have said, that James was mistaken in his emphasis on the rôle of experience in religion. Religion is indissolubly linked to experience. To mention only comparatively recent religious history, the mediaeval mystics regarded experience as authoritative, the Protestant reformers stressed its importance, the Pietistic movement emphasized it anew, Schleiermacher made it the basis of his influential theory of theology, and the Ritschlians among others have kept its importance alive to our own day.

James has been severely criticized on this point however, particularly by Professor George A. Coe in his article on " Sources of the Mystical Revelation "[1] and by Professor James H. Leuba in several books and articles, most recently in his *The Psychology of Religious Mysticism.*[2] The argument of both critics is that James takes as " pure experience " or a " datum " what is really an interpretation of the experience. " He has confused pure experience with elaborations of it," says Professor Leuba. James has, that is, taken as contact with some objective Presence or some " higher range of consciousness," an experience of which we can only say that the mystic interprets it as such a contact. As Professor Coe puts it, in words which have often been quoted, " The mystic brings his theological beliefs to the mystical experience, he does not derive them from it."

Of course it is true that the mystic brings his theological *framework* to his experience, though one would hesitate to assert dogmatically that the experience itself which the mystic fits into his own pre-arranged frame contains nothing new. And one may also admit the force of the claim which Professor Leuba urges with especial insistence, that religious, like all other experience, must be subjected to painstaking psychological analysis. Religious men today are willing to put their experience on the same level with all other experience as far as psychological description is concerned, because religion is no longer interested in the miraculous. We do not in this age look to religion to fill in the gaps left by science. The religious quality of an experience is seen not in its inaccessibility to scientific investigation but in its susceptibility to a certain kind of interpretation — an interpretation which involves relation to ethical values and to cosmic purposes so far as these can be discerned.

---

[1] *Hibbert Journal*, 6: 359.   [2] Pp. 307 ff.

If the question be raised as to whether cosmic purposes can be discerned at all, the answer would be offered that aside from any other method of approach — inference from the world of nature or postulation on the basis of the ethical consciousness — it still would seem that the mystical experience may help to reveal the nature of the highest knowable reality. The whole question of the objective validity of religious and mystical experience is indeed one which is as baffling as it is fascinating. But it is decidedly a live issue in the thought of our day and in the last five years (*i.e.* since 1920) some highly illuminating suggestions have been made concerning it. Professor Albert C. Knudson, for example, in Chapter III of his *Present Tendencies in Religious Thought* argues that the mystical experience does not suffer by being called an interpretation. All experiences are interpretations and the only important question is whether or not the interpretation be correct. " The Christian's conviction of the Divine Presence rests upon the quality of his experience and not upon its want of harmony with natural law." [3] Professor Douglas C. Macintosh throughout his *Theology as an Empirical Science* claims that the Object of religious experience is as knowable as the objects of sense experience and that religious experience follows regular laws. It is predictable, being dependent only on the individual's having the " right religious adjustment." Professor James B. Pratt while unwilling to admit that the object of religious experience is verifiable as are the objects of sense experience [4] nevertheless believes that the sense of Presence in religious experience is not to be explained by suggestion, and thinks that the mystic's experience may be " significant of something beyond itself." [5] For while the explanation of religious experience will have to be made by psychology if at all, Professor Pratt would have us remember the limits within which a psychological explanation operates. Psychology, he thinks, has never been able to give a completely satisfactory explanation

[3] P. 178.
[4] " Can Theology Be an Empirical Science? " *American Journal of Theology* 1920, p. 190.
[5] *The Religious Consciousness*, p. 453.

even of how persons think and act in ordinary life. And the influence of the spiritual world from which, in James's phrase, " saving experiences come " Professor Pratt believes is " in no wise incompatible with any descriptions of human experience which psychology has as yet given us or seems likely to give." [6] For illustration he uses a parable — already on the way to become famous — of blind men trying to account for the experiences of seeing men when the latter see the sun. The blind men describe in terms of raised eyelids, stimulated retinas, etc., the seers claim that they see the sun itself. Similarly our account of the mystics' experiences in terms of psychological laws may be true within its own self-imposed limits yet inadequate to deal with the actual significance of the experience to the mystic himself.

Professor R. H. Thouless in Chapter XVII of his *Introduction to the Psychology of Religion* finds evidence of the truth of the religious hypothesis in its capacity to rationalize experience, especially the experience of the particular type of mystic which his book is largely taken up with describing. That is, the power of religion to make ordered and harmonious the lives of neurotic patients where the creation of phantasies palpably failed to do so furnishes, he believes, a strong presumption as to the objective truth of the religious hypothesis itself. In *A Philosophical Study of Mysticism* Professor C. A. Bennett claims that the mystical intuition in which " the solving idea ' dawns on ' one, in which one discovers a clue, in which one recovers the forgotten subject of one's predicates " has a distinct noetic element and makes mysticism " not the enemy but the inevitable ally of philosophy." [7] And Professor Eugene W. Lyman in an article on " The Place of Intuition in Religious Experience " [8] argues that intuition reveals the reality of the self, relates religious judgments of value to judgments of existence, and that religious intuitions and religious beliefs help to validate each other. In a most discriminating article " Is Theism Essential to Religion? " [9] Professor Gerald

[6] P. 457.
[7] Pp. 101–2.
[8] *The Journal of Religion*, March, 1924.
[9] *The Journal of Religion*, July, 1925.

B. Smith maintains that the religion of the future will consist of a great mystical experiment rather than the acceptance of a theological system. The experience of God, he thinks, will take the form of communion with the spiritual quality in the cosmos, comradeship with that part of it which is found to enrich our life. Finally Professor Rudolf Otto in his strikingly suggestive book *Das Heilige* sets up a claim for the autonomy of the distinctively religious way of knowing.

Now has not each of these writers taken, and must not anyone who attacks the subject follow them in taking as his starting point the facts about religious experience which James brings out so clearly? In this experience something is done, power is felt, the individual after the experience feels himself to be different from what he was before. And it comes with a sense of significance difficult to define but impossible to ignore. And if we reduce the experience to its very lowest terms, suggesting nothing which is not psychologically describable and indulging in no over-belief, is it not still possible to consider the type of experience with which we are familiar from the mystical literature one which can legitimately be called revealing of the highest reality? At the very least it is a period of meditation upon that which is ultimately and socially desirable, an experience which brings with it a sense of the significance of the desirable ideal and an urge to go out and work for it. Furthermore, if there be a spirit or power higher than human which desires the ultimate well-being of humanity, why should not the believer come into touch with that spirit, by whatever psychological means, more intimately and directly at such moments than at other times? And if there be no such spirit, is not the religiously inclined individual at least putting himself at such moments in line with the most godlike thing the universe contains — the moral purposefulness of mankind?

In any attempt at evaluating the mystical experience we find ourselves back once more in the situation which James describes as confronting the " will to believe." Shall we take these moments of heightened significance at their face value, pragmatically justified as they are by their moral effect? We do not *know*, in any *provable* way, that they are any more indicative as to what is true of the universe and its relation to us than are any other moments in life. But he who has felt

A sense sublime
Of something far more deeply interfused
Whose dwelling is the light of setting suns

is loath to give up the idea that new sources of insight have been opened up to him. And the will to believe comes to his aid at this juncture by giving him the *right to interpret* such experiences as revealing in the highest sense.

What the religious man wants more than anything else, as modern philosophers of religion from Höffding to W. K. Wright have pointed out, is to feel that value and existence in some merge, that human efforts have a real outward significance, as James once put it, and that human purposes have some kind of ultimate validity. Why may not religious experience justifiably bring us the sense that there is such validity? The aesthetic moment gives us a vision of harmony. It " brings home " to us, as we say, the reality of much that we forget in the workaday world. Similarly religion at the very least keeps before us the moral value which we will to make real. And if we can trust our " reasons of the heart " it brings assurance that another power than ours is working for the same end. In either case it operates to bring harmony out of chaos, purpose out of disorder, durable satisfaction out of despair.

Whatever attitude we finally assume toward the question of religious experience and its authority for us it is well for us to remember the insistence of the true mystic and the emphasis which James himself puts on the volitional preparation. We must will to have righteousness operative in the world before the sense that it is operative will come to us. The active belief and effort is one part of the process, and the sense of significance is the counterpart. And our immediate concern, as James so often urges, is to play the game like men, *making* values valid, insisting that the moral ideals of our everyday life *shall* have eternal significance, demanding recognition from the cosmos for the victories won daily by the human spirit, in Donald Hankey's phrase, betting our lives that there is a God.

So the main currents of the religious thought of our day have met in James to emerge in clarified form. Religion by its nature will always depend on "inner experience." Men will be religious because "they have to be," because their experience makes them so. And until human nature changes they will respond to the challenging summons which pragmatism issues to a life of free creative achievement. For James strikes as fundamentally human a chord in his eagerness to set men tasks that will call forth their highest energies as he does when preaching the gospel of comfort. Pragmatism, pluralism, and the active aspect of empiricism are worthy vehicles for the expression of the conquering human will.

Pragmatism, as we have seen, is first of all a protest against narrowness in thinking. With its theory of truth as conditioned by particular experienced human values it is a claim that philosophy must widen its range to meet as many human needs as exist. As such it is a stimulating theory for human beings living in a temporal world, in daily contact with evil, cherishing hopes, subduing fears, and struggling onward toward achievement. In its endeavor to help men live more abundantly pragmatism offers a God who is a personal friend and ally instead of a formalistic conception. On the dangers of abstractionism in religion Professor A. K. Rogers has written: "Consistency is a jewel which may be purchased at too dear a rate." And "if it is a question of giving up a good share of the content of life in the interests of a formal consistency, it may be the part of wisdom to take the former. Better a fulness of life which outstrips the logical insight than an intellectual satisfaction won by reducing life to Procrustean limits." Better especially where religion is concerned, for "We never should take the trouble to recognize, much less worship that which had no possible bearing on the demands of our own lives." [10] And Professor Lyman adds: "If we are to gain

[10] *The Religious Conception of the World,* pp. 73, 81.

a genuinely spiritual interpretation of the universe we must draw upon the entire spiritual experience of man." [11]

Secondly, pragmatism not only requires that a religious view of the world shall show a sensitiveness to the demands of the whole being, it also emphasizes the *moral* element as religiously essential. Here as in the former case it attacks absolute idealism with especial vigor. The attempt of the latter to find an ultimate synthesis in which the distinctive quality of evil is transcended is for pragmatism the unpardonable sin. We must not eliminate the actively and combatively moral element from religion, and we do eliminate it if we refuse to recognize evil's realness. And, further, the claims of morality must be taken into account in any determination of truth. The issue between theism and materialism, like any ultimate issue, may have meaning only as its implications for morality are made explicit. Not only religion, but truth itself must take account of the claims of the moral consciousness. God cannot be beyond good and evil, and truth itself is no more final than the moral law.

Third, allied to pragmatism's stress on the moral is its stress on the need for courage, especially the need for a courageous selective faith which will fix its attention on the desirable things in life and refuse to let them be overwhelmed by the things that are less desirable. Pragmatism raises to the status of a philosophy of life the implicit attitude of the man who keeps his gaze fixed on the things that are of good report and by a sheer act of will refuses to allow them to become obscured. It looks on the life of the universe itself as an adventure and on God as risking as much or more than we. Rather paradoxically it combines moral seriousness with an optimistic faith that life's fight can be won if we will to win it. "Why is not the realist, with all his sad heroism and resigned courage, the noblest and best that man has imagined?" asks Professor E. A. Singer.[12] "Because realism is a philosophy of little faith! Faith it is that makes worlds, realistic

[11] *Theology and Human Problems*, chap. i.
[12] Chapter on "Pragmatism" in *Modern Thinkers and Present Problems*.

science has only the wit to acknowledge and the strength to suffer what faith has wrought. Bold to endure, it is timid to change, and a world in the making needs its makers, needs its poets and actors more than it needs audience or spectator. At the bottom of the realist's brave heart lurks an abiding fear — the fear of making a fool of himself. But a world in the making like a battle in the fighting cries out for fools and the foolhardy. Faith risks to the point of folly, and because all making anew is a colossal risk, let us have colossal faith." [13]

Along with its courageous faith pragmatism offers, fourth, a freshness of outlook which only a dynamic creative view can bring. Reality itself awaits the imprint of our will. Novelty does enter the world, especially where we will to have it. " All James's cherished theories," says Professor D. S. Miller, " ' free will,' ' will to believe,' ' pluralism,' ' pragmatism,' ' radical empiricism ' meant for him what the Church calls ' newness of life.' They meant a possible emancipation from what he conceived as the cramping clutch of the past — though he also emphasized the treasure of the past. They meant the possibility of ' genuine novelty ' in our experience, the blowing of a fresh wind, the breathing of an indescribably new atmosphere." [14]

With all these qualities which make it well fitted to deal with religious problems go some disadvantages, which its critics have not been slow to point out. It has been argued, in the first place, that pragmatism is contaminated by its affinities with materialism. It defines truth as that which aids survival, and its interests, claim its opponents, actually do not extend beyond man's physical well-being. But this criticism can hardly be expected to touch James, for in his advocacy of the will to believe he has suggested that we treat not only our notions of the physical world, but our moral and spiritual aspirations as hypotheses by which future experience can be molded. The higher needs of man are factors in the determin-

---

[13] P. 232.

[14] Art. "Mr. Santayana and William James," *Harvard Graduates Magazine,* March, 1921, p. 363.

ing of belief and conduct and are to be regarded as such. Truth must take these needs into account as well as those of the physical organism.

If the objection be raised further that even this makes pragmatism apply only to the needs of the individual, we would point out as before that the social requirements are provided for implicitly in James's individualistic philosophy. In any individual scheme of abundant living social values take their place as a matter of course.

If we transfer the discussion to the realm of epistemology, the objection may be raised that pragmatism, with its essentially phenomenalistic view, making truth a matter of particular experiences, can have no access to religious truth which must by its nature be transcendent. But it seems perfectly clear that pragmatism does not affirm that the truth of the belief of the religious man has no connection with the reality of the object of his belief. A necessary requirement for the " working " which for pragmatism constitutes the truth of a religious belief is a transcendent *reference,* a pointing to a transcendent realm on the part of the belief itself. No consequences will flow from the belief unless the believer himself is convinced of the reality of its object. As Professor G. B. Foster once wrote, if one " try to act upon the idea of God, no matter how it arose, and at the same time disbelieve in his existence; he will find that no action will follow, if *ontological* reference be denied to the idea." [15] Religious pragmatism cannot deny the ontological reference, and indeed it seems to point to the probable validity of such a reference. May it not even point with more assurance than is possible for other systems of truth when dealing with such subjects? " If there is to be any thinking beyond phenomena, it must imitate science, it must refer to experience whenever it is able to do so and find truth only through some kind of verification of working hypotheses." [16] James has offered

[15] " Pragmatism and Knowledge," *American Journal of Theology,* 11: 591.
[16] D. C. Macintosh, " Can Pragmatism Furnish a Basis for Theology? " *Harvard Theological Review,* 3: 125.

an especially clear path to the transcendent realm through the perceptual experience of the mystic, as we have seen.

Finally, if the right of pragmatism to contribute to a philosophy of religion be opposed on the ground that it has not vindicated itself as a theory of truth in general, the comment may be offered that while pragmatism has indeed been variously interpreted, its distinctive contribution is conserved in what Professor Macintosh has called " essential pragmatism." " The necessary — that is, what man really needs to believe in order to live as he ought — is true."

It seems very significant, we may remark in concluding this discussion of pragmatism, that the two methods of discovering truth which James suggests are the two which have always been recognized by religion — direct acquaintance with the object under discussion, or " working " interpreted in terms of fruits for life. If an idea is valuable, that for pragmatism constitutes a presumption as to its truth. If it leads to direct acquaintance with its object it is surely true. Religion similarly has judged the genuineness of divine intimations by their fruits for life and by their relation to a peculiarly intimate intuitional experience. The parallel path along which pragmatism and religion work is shown in other ways as well. Pragmatism makes postulates where direct evidence is lacking, and religion will always have to depend much on postulates. Pragmatism is interested in truth's ability to fill the needs of the emotional nature, as contrasted with its ability to reproduce copy already existing, — it is interested, that is to say, in filling a distinctively religious rather than a distinctively scientific need. It is not without significance that James in his first paper on pragmatism, the address at Berkeley, drew his illustrations of the working of the pragmatic method almost exclusively from the field of religion. And just as pragmatism is especially well fitted to deal with religious problems, so religion in its turn would seem to offer material which must be taken into account by pragmatism. We may not claim that every religious man should be a pragmatist, for many men have found that the needs of the religious life as of all life were better served by other philosophies. But it seems as though every pragmatist should be a religious believer in some significant sense. As Professor Macintosh has expressed it: " Any pragmatic philosophy which is to satisfy the whole man at his highest and best, and the race at its highest and best, cannot afford to ignore a religion which meets fundamental spiritual need with abiding satisfaction, and which necessarily expresses itself in a theology for which it just as necessarily claims objective validity." [17]

Pragmatism thus offers a religion worth having, worth believing in and worth fighting for. It may lack the note of assurance, but it sounds the note of creative achievement. It suggests the idea of a Power which with ourselves makes for righteousness. Some of its interpretations of the nature of truth may be open to question, but its essential office, that of making truth relevant and applicable to human situations, finding truth in and through particular human experiences, and making it conform to the needs of the whole man, is one which is certain to facilitate the religious task of interpreting ultimate realities in humanly intelligible terms.

Ultimate *realities,* be it said emphatically, because pragmatism brings us to a pluralistic interpretation of reality. For what is pluralism but a description of the world as we find it when we examine it open-eyed and unafraid? The charge is often brought against pragmatism that it is unwilling to look objective fact in the face, that it caters in weak-kneed fashion to human desire. But what can be more unflinching than the way in which a pragmatic pluralistic philosophy faces the fact of evil?

For we do live in a world parts of which are unalterably opposed to other parts — how can anyone doubt it? The great cosmic unity which the monists envisage as running through all things and regulating the conditions of each individual life would be indeed a beautiful thing if we could find it in experience. But life as one views it sweating in the stoke-hole or entangled in the barbed wire of no-man's land or confined

[17] *Op. cit.*

in the psychopathic ward of the municipal hospital not only suggests incompleteness but brings out the *ultimate* nature of its fragmentary quality for many, many individuals. And even if we disregard those lives which are prevented from becoming complete by outward circumstances, what can one say of the lives spent in more favorable surroundings? How many of those upon whom opportunity smiles achieve anything like a unified plan? Life is like a hockey game, one monistic philosopher tells his class, with its unified basis implicit throughout the game and coming to consciousness at special moments. But while the players are few the spectators are many, and of most lives it would seem to be more nearly true that theirs was the rôle of experiencing many different situations with varying degrees of unity, watching a hockey game at one moment and seeking an escape from the cold at the next.

This is not to say that a unified life is undesirable. It is merely to assert that in most cases it is unattainable. Unity must be fought for, we must will into our lives what unity we can. And we are better equipped for the strife if we realize at the start that unity is a goal and not a pre-condition. Furthermore, whatever unity is gained is susceptible to many interpretations. As James wrote to Mrs. Ethel Puffer Howes (in an unpublished letter): " There is always more than one formula of the unity to be found in the variety of a human being."

So pluralism gives us a more accurate and helpful account than does monism of the conditions with which we are confronted. In addition it gives us more scope for that essentially religious quality, the imagination. The " unclassified residuum " of which James talks suggests both undetermined possibility in the individual life and ultimate mystery in the cosmos. The one, as James has told us, is not only too big to be worshipped, it is too small to represent the unlimited. As Francis Bacon has said, " Nature is too subtle for any argument." A worshipper in that triumph of Byzantine skill, St. Sophia at Constantinople, has the feeling of infinity rather

than of unity. The Gothic cathedrals of France suggest unlimited possibility rather than an unimaginative definiteness.
It is not difficult to agree with Renouvier that the type of
mind which produces the conceptions "I am that I am"
and "There is no God but God" is the type which becomes
most narrowly and arrogantly fanatical.

Finally, as we have seen in detail, in James's view pluralism both provides for religious intimacy and suggests the only
possible scheme wherein the pragmatic life of freedom and
moral creative activity can be carried on. And is it said that
in spite of these virtues pluralism never can become a philosophy of religion on account of its denial of the One whom
the mystics commonly proclaim as the Object of their vision?
Let us hear the comment of one of the greatest of our modern
mystics on this. "It is only partially true," he says, "to
assert that the mystic experiences the unity of divinity; his
experience lies beyond all enumeration. When he speaks of
unity, he refers to something which has neither unity nor multiplicity, and simultaneously possesses both. . . . Such a man
cannot deny any expression of life." [18]

And just as we found that pragmatism and religion supple-
mented each other so here again we find religious experience
offering data which point toward a pluralistic theory. The
"saving experiences" of religion, as James interprets them,
are a clear case of the coming of genuine novelty. They could
not have been predicted by rationalism.

So pluralism brings us to empiricism. And empiricism con-
tributes to religious philosophy not merely by passively accepting these saving experiences but by actively asserting the
power of faith. With rationalism faith has little in common.
As Sabatier expresses it, rationalism "in giving to religion a
rational or doctrinal content . . . empties it of its real content, of specific religious experience; it kills faith, which no
longer having an object of its own has no *raison d'être*." [19]
Radical empiricism in its turn finds a place in a philosophy

[18] Count Hermann Keyserling, "*The Travel Diary of a Philosopher*,"
Eng. tr. 1: 104.
[19] *Outlines of a Philosophy of Religion*, p. 339.

of religion through its requirement that good and evil be clearly distinguished, that the relations between the two be external; and in the second place by requiring that relations shall be empirically known, a requirement which as we have seen is fulfilled in religion by the mystic.

Pragmatism as an attitude, pluralism as a description of reality, empiricism as a method. All are open to abuse, empiricism probably more than the others. If it be taken as justifying the accepting of all unusual experiences as revelations of the will of the Deity, the result will of course be chaos. And the difficulty of knowing how to distinguish false from true revelation is increased since the mere fact of givenness is no necessary sign of objectivity. An " uprush from the subliminal " brings with it a wholly convincing sense of externality. But if the empirical method is employed in the larger sense of making discriminating use of data other than those which enter into an exclusively logical process, subjecting them to experiment and verifying them by as many tests as possible, it furnishes a legitimate method to use in the quest for religious truth. In the field of religion apodictic certainty seems to be out of the question. The logical proofs of God of one generation have rarely proved acceptable to the next. For one thing, the God which they demonstrate is a God of the rational consciousness, an " Inevitable Inference " as James says. For another thing, we feel that the final truth about ultimate reality is too great to be demonstrated as completely as logic attempts to do it. Empiricism, with its more modest method, claiming inductive probability instead of rational certainty, seems better qualified than rationalism to deal with the Great Unknown.

And when empiricism is supported by the use of the pragmatic test the combination is formidable. As a matter of history religion has been taught experimentally. Men have been told to taste and see that the Lord is good. The voluntaristic element has also been stressed. It is he who has willed to do God's will that has known of the doctrine. And the test of moral working has been freely applied. The author of the epistle of St. James wrote that faith without works was dead. St. Teresa judged which of her experiences were of God by their moral results. Jonathan Edwards applied the same test to discover the genuineness of conversions in times of revival.

So if we grant that religious belief must deal with probabilities rather than certainties, it would follow that once we are armed with the empirical method, the pragmatic test, and the will to believe, we are as well equipped to find religious truth as it is possible for us to be. James's statement of the case for the will to believe still holds. It is true that life demands a decision from us, and that to doubt is to decide in the negative. And James's qualification that the issues must be " live " removes any possible interpretation of his thought as justifying belief in " whatever we like to believe." An active life attitude must be assumed, and whichever way we decide we act on probabilities and make postulates. And, remembering that we are still in the realm of probabilities only, is it not true that the testimony of religious experience tends to verify the postulates made by the will to believe? When a religious experience bears moral fruits for life pragmatic empiricism seems justified in claiming that it may be of God. What experience can be said to come from God and to be a revelation of primal reality if not one that suggests the ultimate significance of everyday moral activity? What kind of experience can be either more " saving " or " revealing " than that which suggests, as James would put it, that " the ideal and the real are dynamically continuous " ? We all have enough of what James called the " mystical germ " in us to feel the glow that comes in moments when life takes on a larger significance, to understand what Schleiermacher meant by his beautiful phrase " sense and taste for the Infinite," and to respond when the larger relationships of living seem in a measure to be revealed, all ineffable though the experience must be.

One thing is certain. Whatever be the verdict of posterity as to James's contribution, whatever criticism be made, as has been made already by so many, of his " over-beliefs," the religious attitude that he describes is sure to appeal and is already appealing to the members of the generation just coming to maturity. The empirical element appeals to them because they have grown up in an age dominated by scientific activity. They have been fed on facts and imbued with the method of experiment. And the discoveries made in their own day have shown so many things in heaven and earth that were not dreamed of in the science or the philosophy of their fathers, that the whole trend of their thinking will be tentative rather than dogmatic. Secondly, the pluralistic element will appeal to them because they have seen the war. And while the war furnishes no more coercive argument for the presence of evil in the world and its distinctive irreducible qualities than a smaller catastrophe or than the facts of everyday life might have furnished, still it has impressed its own enormity and colossal insanity upon men's minds and especially upon their subconscious minds in a way that will make its influence hard to escape.

Finally, pragmatism will appeal to the coming generation because of its creative faith. The present is an age of vision. Our horizons have been tremendously enlarged. In all lines of research the possibilities disclosed are fairly staggering. And with it all the melioristic note is prominent. Never before were the problems of " The Moral Philosopher " so comprehensively and so intelligently treated. And James's believing, achieving, creative individual will find a scope for his powers and an application for his ideals unparalleled in history. The religion of the immediate future will be an imaginative realism, a Romanticism which has not lost touch with the concrete realities of every-day living. And the God James proclaimed whose vision is of the empyrean, but whose energies are " so sorely needed in the sweat and dirt of our daily life," will summon the coming generation to belief and to action with the message which James loved to repeat: " Son of Man *stand upon thy feet,* and I will speak to thee."

INDEX

Absolute, the, of absolute idealism, 11, 20, *21* ff, 139

Absolutism, 45, 47

Achilles and the tortoise, 34

Active attitude defines the ultimate datum, 181

Active element in the truth-attaining process, 88 ff, 119

Additive knowledge, 50

Aesthetic interest of Wm. James, 189 ff

Alien lives, their importance, 56

Alternating moods of James, 6, 7, *et passim*

Alternation in the mystical experience, 176, 177

Ames, E. S., 137

Anselm, 23, 140

Anti-intellectualistic movement in England, 84

Aristotle, 140

Associationism in psychology, 72, 73, 75, 110

Attention, 70, 72, 74; as moral activity, 75

Authority, religious need for, 114; of mysticism, 170

Automaton theory, 72

Auto-soterism, 16

Bacon, Francis, 214

Baillie, J. B., 21

Bakewell, C. M., xii

Baldwin's *Dictionary of Philosophy,* 46

Balfour, A. J., 85, 86, 141

Belief, influenced by volition as opposed to reason, 84

Beliefs, religious, and their formation, *82* ff; their practical, subjective, and creative aspects, 90 ff

Benevolence of the universe, 22

Bennett, C. A., 183, 205

Bergson, Henri, 33, 115, 180

Block universe, 33

Blood, B. P., 44, 177, 196

Boott, Francis, James's memorial address on, 157

Bush, W. T., 143

Butler, Samuel, 141

Calkins, Miss Mary W., xi, 23, 46, 47, 165

Carlyle, Thomas, 56

Causality, altar to an unknown god, 78

Chance, 76

Characteristics of the religious life, 188

Chess-player, illustration of freedom, 80

Child, Francis J., 155

Circumscribed field for operation of freedom, 71 ff; will to believe, 92

Classifiability of experiences, 64

Coalescence of bits of experience, 53

Coe, G. A., 171, 203

College education, its aim, 108

Common virtues, 106

Concatenated relationships, 52

Conflict, the, in James's mind, *1* ff, 113, 166, 176 ff, 186

Confluent consciousnesses, 26, 48, 150 ff

Conjunctive relations, 69

Connections in pluralism, 48, 50

Consciousness, does it exist? 63

Consciousness of responsibility, 76

Consistency not the only concern for religion, 208; in philosophy, 23, 144

Constraint in the truth-attaining process, 95 ff

Unpredictability of human experience, 76
Utility of the categories, 65; of the God idea, 137

Vaihinger, 138
Value, of pluralism, 66 ff
Values, 66, *104* ff; contrasted with logic, 82, 85, 88 ff; James's sense for, 118; origin of, 110
Value-judgments, 105
Varieties of Religious Experience, The, viii, 6, 12, 13, 24, 36, 40, 55, 57, 62, 107, 109, 111, 123, 128 ff, 144 ff, 166 ff, 177, 181, 186 ff, 191, 192; James's comment on the chapter on "Mysticism," 173
Verification more important for empiricism than for absolutism, 98
Verity of religious experience, 174
Vicarious interest, James's, in the experiences of others, 196
Vicious intellectualism, 51
Vision, the, and its claim, 100
Volition, contrasted with intellection, 82; its importance in religion, 208; in mysticism, 178
Voluntarism in religion, 216
Vorbrodt, G., 189

Wager, as illustration of religious belief, 83, 84
War and religion, viii, 218
Ward, James, 44, 142
Wells, H. G., 142
"What Makes a Life Significant," 106
Whitman, Walt, 109
Will, *67* ff, 88
Will to Believe, and Other Essays, The, xiii, 8, 13, 25, 59, 60, 63, 76, 80, *82* ff, 111, 123, 124, 148, 164, 166, 181, 200, 206
Wisdom and virtue, 74
Woodbridge, F. J. E., 46
World of independent personalities, 54, 55
Worship, 62, 206
Wright, Chauncey, 2
Wright, W. K., 76, 105, 207
Wundt, W. M., 44